Adele Marion Field

Adele Marion Fielde, born in 1839, was a teacher, an evangelist, a social activist, scientist, lexicographer, writer and lecturer. As an American missionary in China she became an advocate for public health, staunchly committed to the improvement of women's lives. Struggling to reconcile her Baptist upbringing with her restless intellect she returned to America and left the Church to become an important figure in the suffragist movement and in the political education of women. As a scientist, she conducted seminal research on the behavior of ants.

This book provides an in-depth biographical study of the life of this remarkable woman, who, despite social and religious constraints on her life and work, transcended them through her belief in service to others. The author demonstrates how, as a woman of immense energy and intellectual ability, Fielde was able to influence religious, scientific and political communities despite their prevailing negative attitude towards women.

Adele Marion Fielde will be of vital interest to scholars concerned with the study of gender and the history of science.

Leonard Warren was born in Toronto, and received his BA and MD degrees at the University of Toronto, and a PhD in biochemistry at MIT in Cambridge, MA. He did research at the National Institute of Health, and the Wistar Institute as Institute Professor, and the University of Pennsylvania as American Cancer Society Research Professor (emeritus). He spent sabbatical years at the Pasteur Institute (Paris), and the Imperial Cancer Research Fund (London). Recently, he had published a biography *Joseph Leidy, the Last Man Who Knew Everything*. He has completed a biography of Constantine Samuel Rafinesque, and is presently writing the life of William Maclure, philanthropist, educator, and 'father of American Geology'.

Women in Science

Series Editor: Marilyn Bailey Ogilvie

History of Science Collections, University of Oklahoma, USA

1 **A Dame Full of Vim and Vigour**
A biography of Alice Middleton Boring: biologist in China
Marilyn Bailey Ogilvie and Clifford J. Choquette

2 **Science, Women and Revolution in Russia**
Ann Hibner Koblitz

3 **Revealing New Worlds**
Three Victorian women naturalists
Suzanne Le-May Sheffield

4 **Adele Marion Fielde**
Feminist, social activist, scientist
Leonard Warren

Frontispiece A late photographic portrait of Adele M. Fielde

Adele Marion Fielde

Feminist, social activist, scientist

Leonard Warren

LONDON AND NEW YORK

For Noah, Will, and Naomi

First published 2002 by Routledge
2 Park Square, Milton Park, Abingdon, Oxfordshire OX14 4RN

Simultaneously published in the USA and Canada
by Routledge
711 Third Avenue, New York, NY 10017

First issued in paperback 2014

Routledge is an imprint of the Taylor and Francis Group, an informa business

Typeset in 11/12pt Garamond 3 by Graphicraft Limited,
Hong Kong

British Library Cataloguing in Publication Data
A catalogue record for this book is available from the British Library

Library of Congress Cataloging in Publication Data
Warren, Leonard, 1924–
Adele Marion Fielde: feminist, social activist, scientist / by Leonard Warren.
p. cm.
Includes bibliographical references and index.
ISBN 0-415-27121-5
1. Fielde, Adele M., 1839–1916. 2. Feminists–United States–Biography. 3. Suffragists–United States–Biography. 4. Women missionaries–China–Biography. 5. Women scientists–United States–Biography. I. Title.

HQ1413.F5 W37 2002
305.42′092–dc21
[B] 2001045705

ISBN 13: 978-1-138-86792-5 (pbk)
ISBN 13: 978-0-415-27121-9 (hbk)

Contents

Illustrations and abbreviations

The Frontispiece, figures 1.1, 2.1, 2.2, 5.1, and 12.1 are reproduced from Steven's 1918 biography of Fielde. Figure 11.1 is from the Archives of the Marine Biological Laboratory, Woods Hole, MA.

Abbreviations

ABC American Baptist Center
ABMU American Baptist Missionary Union
ANS Academy of Natural Sciences of Philadelphia
APS American Philosophic Society
BMM *Baptist Missionary Magazine*
DAB *Dictionary of American Biography*
DSB *Dictionary of Scientific Biography*
HUA Harvard University Archives

Preface

I first came across the name *Adele Fielde* while writing a biography of Joseph Leidy, a gifted, but now a little-known American scientist of the nineteenth century who was head of the Academy of Natural Sciences of Philadelphia. Adele Fielde, an American missionary in China, wanted to study science and carry out research, and had been told by David Starr Jordan, another scientist of interest to me, to apply to Leidy. Intrigued that a Baptist missionary in China would want to devote herself to science, I read on. Following one lead after another I found that, indeed, the Academy had turned her into an active, productive scientist, whose scientific papers are still quoted today. Her life as a scientist, which was the magnet that drew me to her, turned out to be only a small part of the grand mosaic. I discovered that she was also a powerful evangelist, political activist, suffragist, advocate of temperance, author and lecturer of considerable stature. She was uncommonly fluent in Chinese (Swatow dialect), and had written a large Chinese–English dictionary. When I beheld the dictionary, I realized that I was not dealing with some ordinary mortal. I was captivated, and this book is testimony of my devotion to this brilliant, admirable person.

Very little has been written about Fielde. In 1918, Helen Norton Stevens, her friend and companion in later, Seattle years wrote a biography of her, authorized by the Fielde Memorial Committee. Stevens had daily contact with her, and they shared confidences and philosophies, so that her book is a personal account. While it is very good, and bears the stamp of a kind of authority, it is a genteel, elegiac work, somewhat old-fashioned, and not quite suitable for modern tastes. She used documents and letters to which she was privy, but unfortunately these cannot be located today. Attempts at locating scrap-books and notes of Fielde and Stevens have met with little success, and I have had no choice but to use Stevens' account of them, many verbatim. A second work from which I have borrowed is *The Missionary Writing of Adele M. Fielde* by Ginny Seabrook (1993), a thesis for a Master of Arts degree. Aside from a very few, scattered notes about Fielde, and the text of a lecture by Frederick B. Hoyt (1977), there is little other commentary on her.

My own enlightenment about the plight of women in evolving America came about in responding to the justified criticisms of the anonymous reviewers of my manuscript, and I thank them. They pointed out that I had not paid attention to feminist writings and history detailing women's struggle for their rights, and that would provide an appropriate background for Adele Fielde's life experiences.

I am most indebted to Nina Long, Librarian and Archivist of the Wistar Institute and master of the computer search, for her unfailing assistance. This book could not have been written without the resources of the Archives of the American Baptist Center at Valley Forge, PA, and the friendly, expert help of its Chief Librarian and Archivist, Beverly Carlson. Naomi Reynolds and Betty Layton of the American Baptist Center library were also most helpful. I am deeply grateful to them for revealing to me the treasures of that institution. The Academy of Natural Sciences of Philadelphia, and its Manuscript/Archives Librarian, Carol M. Spawn and Earle Spamer, provided much information. Much of the book was written in the library of the Marine Biological Laboratory, Woods Hole, MA, where the librarians Heidi Nelson and Cathy Norton provided generous assistance. I am deeply appreciative of the conscientious assistance provided by Brian A. Sullivan of Harvard University Archives, Karyl Winn and Janet Neff of the University of Washington Library and Archives, and by Earl M. Rogers, Archivist of the University of Iowa. Edward O. Wilson, Bert Hölldobler, and James Sprague kindly read parts of the manuscript and offered constructive suggestions; I am the beneficiary of their scholarship. The encouragement and assistance of my wife Eve, an astute editor with an intelligent, critical eye, is gratefully acknowledged.

Chronology

1839 Born March 30, in East Rodman, near Watertown, New York.
1856 Taught school for three years.
1859 Entered Albany Normal College.
1860 Graduated with Teaching Certificate. Taught school on Long Island.
1864 Proposal of marriage by Cyrus Chilcott, a Baptist missionary.
1865 Sailed for Hong Kong to marry Chilcott, learned of his death, decided to stay on. Proceeded to Bangkok for missionary work, beginning in 1866.
1872 Returned to America. Successfully defended herself against charges of misbehavior.
1873 After one year of travel, arrived in Swatow, China, where she established a school for Bible-women, in which Chinese women were trained to become evangelists and health educators in their villages.
1878 Published *First Lessons in the Swatow Dialect.*
1883 Published her Chinese–English dictionary; resided in Philadelphia for two years to learn obstetrical techniques at the Medical College of Pennsylvania, and to obtain scientific training at the Academy of Natural Sciences of Philadelphia. Began to publish scientific papers on scattered subjects.
1884 Published *Pagoda Shadows.*
1885 Returned to Swatow mission.
1889 Resigned as a Baptist missionary teacher. Left China for the last time. Travelled westward to America through India, the Near East, and Europe.
1891 Witnessed a pogrom in Moscow, and reported it.
1892 Arrived in New York after two years of travel.
1893 Began lecturing, and giving courses on civil government and parliamentary procedure. Published *The Stray Arrow or Chinese Nights Entertainments.* Began spending summers taking courses and doing research at the Marine Biological Laboratory in Woods Hole, MA.
1894 Participated in unsuccessful drive to enfranchise women, at the Constitutional Convention of the New York State Legislature in Albany.
1895 Helped establish the League for Political Education, and was its major teacher.

1897 Published *A Political Primer of New York City and State.*
1899 Published *Parliamentary Procedure.*
1901 Began publishing the results of research on ants, their culture and behavior.
1907 Moved to Seattle where she soon began to lecture. Became involved in several causes: public health issues, building a hospital, control of tuberculosis, political reform, passage of Direct Legislation Amendment to the Constitution in the city and state of Washington, Seattle Fine Arts Association, the temperance movement, control of prostitution. Actively organized women's groups, lecturing and writing on the suffragist cause.
1910 Enfranchisement of women in the state of Washington.
1912 Fielde became a trustee of the Seattle Public Library (the first political appointment of a woman in Seattle).
1914 Passage of Temperance law.
1916 Died February 23, in Seattle.

Prologue

The exemplary life of Adele Marion Fielde came to a gracious close more than eighty years ago, and we are now able to appreciate the entire range of her endeavors, knowing with a kind of certainty the outcome of each chapter of the narrative. The completeness, the finality, is a haunting and poignant lesson for us all. Truly, her pilgrimage was a fit subject for a heroic chronicle. From meager beginnings she astonishes us by her intellectual growth, her fine intelligence and her prodigious energy. The making of a reformer can be traced in the experiences of her life, for she quickly perceived that there was little difference between the egregious exploitation of black people and the oppression of women – denial of education and rights, both in China and in her own country. Above all, this indomitable woman was possessed of a moral certitude, a knowledge of what was right and what was wrong, that was the fuel for her mighty engine. When she perceived suffering and injustice, wherever she was on this globe, she entered the battle unconditionally, with her acts and her words. As a single woman in a man's world she strove mightily, and achieved so much as a teacher, an evangelizer in foreign lands, a social activist, scientist, lexicographer, writer, and lecturer.

Fielde did not begin her career as a missionary with a burning desire to serve the Lord. Rather, she was a teacher who by chance found herself in the East committed to missionary work. In time her narrow Baptist viewpoint, which never melded comfortably with her restless intellect, fell away as she seized elements of Christianity and other religions, and fashioned a very personal system of belief. To her, God the Creator and Jesus were still central, but good works, helping others, were more important than faith alone; human effort could be of greater benefit to suffering humanity than could divine intervention. Still profoundly religious, she lost interest in religious organizations (or their representatives) – all male-dominated institutions which had so abused her. She could hardly escape the conclusion that organized religion, however lofty its aims, was a means by which men dominated and exploited women, and it angered her that there was not equality of the sexes. Still, she could not be called a radical, militant feminist like Elizabeth Cady Stanton or Charlotte Perkins Gilman, and her relationships with men were often warm and affectionate. But she would not take nonsense from anyone.

Her extraordinary energy and intelligence craved release from narrow, sectarian religion, and there were astonishing outbursts of widespread interests. She was strong, forceful, and independent – a tough person – who offended some of her colleagues in her drive to achieve an end. Explicit criticism is rarely recorded among the polite people with whom she interacted (except for certain male missionaries in Swatow, China), but her associates must have shaken their heads in wonder as they witnessed her unstoppable activity, obliged, whether they wanted to or not, to follow along. With such determination, she must have stepped on many toes, but for the most part she was forgiven because her demands were to achieve a common end, sparing none, herself least of all.

As a missionary in China she organized a movement to realize the dream of conversion to Christ of the Chinese people, an impossible task for Westerners alone. Fielde established a school to train Chinese women from various parts of the country to become preachers, and she educated them in public health as well. These *Bible-women* were then sent back to their own villages to do good works, and periodically they came back to school for refresher courses. The plan was extremely successful and was adopted by many Protestant sects. As an expert in the Chinese language, she took it upon herself to write a truly impressive Chinese–English dictionary.

Fielde retired to the U.S.A., presumably for reasons of health, where she could do as she pleased. She chose to become involved in scientific research, the delivery of infant and medical care, adult education, the temperance crusade, the abolition of prostitution, and the suffragist cause – disparate interests that had in common the struggle of women to ease their lot and to compete equally in a man's world. This included the scientific field, where productive women scientists and naturalists were rendered invisible, and unacknowledged – Adele Fielde included. Fielde became a productive, imaginative entomologist who worked on the sensory system of the ant, and she used her knowledge to inform the public about the spread of plague by the flea.

While scientific research was an almost solitary search after the truth, the fight for the vote was a political struggle that entailed dealing with dishonest politicians and special interest groups. Knowing that the only hope for better government was to educate the public, she lectured and wrote extensively on civic and state government. Despite her exposure to greed and corruption, she still believed that humans were rational beings and if they only knew the facts they would do the right thing. She also focused on the right of women to vote, immersing herself in grass-roots politics. Issue oriented, she never indulged in partisan politics or made deals with dishonest politicians to win votes for her cause – she appealed directly to the voter whom she hoped she had educated properly.

When her weighty concerns were set aside, Fielde was sociable, a fine conversationalist, full of fun, capable of not taking herself too seriously, and in her missionary days, perfectly willing to ignore stringent proscriptions of Baptist orthodoxy which she judged to be of a trivial nature. She was always surrounded by warm and affectionate friends who recognized her unique qualities, and wanted to be with her, and when she died, convinced that she would meet her Creator and be taken up in the arms of Jesus, they felt that their world without her would never be quite the same again.

1 Beginnings[1]

Adele Marion Fielde was born in 1839, when the world of Jefferson and Andrew Jackson was fading, and Queen Victoria was embarking on a long reign that marked a new era. American science and technology were beginning to come of age; during the 1830s and 1840s, crossing the Atlantic Ocean by steamboat became commonplace, and the railroad was becoming a standard mode of travel. The year 1839 had witnessed the passage of the steam packet *Britannia* from Halifax to Liverpool in a mere ten days, and trains had achieved the astonishing speed of thirty-nine miles per hour. Charles Darwin's voyage on the *Beagle* had come to an end, but it was the beginning of a revolution in biology, and Theodore Schwann published his seminal theory that all plants and animals were constructed of a fundamental unit, the cell. An ever increasing number of prodigies – Emerson, Hawthorne, Melville, Poe, Whitman – was beginning to fulfill the Democratic Republic's promise. Young America was in the grip of a financial panic that could only make life harder for Fielde's parents. A besieged President Martin Van Buren was finishing his first term at a time of profound and prolonged economic depression. Hard times in a country dependent for its growth on European capital cost this able New Yorker a second term.

The Industrial Revolution gained momentum as Americans overran the West. Burgeoning cities were peopled with boatloads of newly arrived immigrants who brought with them unfamiliar values and languages that countered the dominant, Victorian certitudes – the beginnings of populism, mass culture, and egalitarianism. America took its familiar political shape as the two-party system evolved, and the North and South of the U.S.A. became defined entities of conflicting interests – the South with its economy based on cotton and slavery, and the North, on industry and free men. The problem of slavery and race relations festered as the U.S.A., led by vacillating presidents, exploded into a Civil War that jump-started American industry and manufacturing. Whatever the self-doubts and professed shortcomings of Americans, their nationalistic ardor flourished, their energy was without limit, their hopes for a triumphant republican democracy boundless, for they *knew* their democracy was special and exceptional. Both North and South were united in their disdain of the old tired monarchies of Europe, despite their submission to its perceived intellectual superiority.

America had begun as a provincial, junior partner with European powers, particularly Britain, both culturally and economically, but by the time Adele Fielde died (February 23, 1916) the U.S.A. was a nation of enormous cities, with pre-eminent industrial and manufacturing might. She had witnessed the growth of an infant nation into a giant power of immense wealth, attended by dreadful poverty, appalling corruption, and social injustice. Still, the Republic had a remarkable capacity to change and to better itself with the prompting of zealous reformers, never in short supply.

Adele Marion Fielde was christened Adelia Field at her birth in East Rodman, Jefferson County, New York State, a village in the marches bordering the St. Lawrence River and Canada to the north, and Lake Ontario to the west. When Adelia was 5 years old, the family moved to Tylersville, New York (now called South Rutland), a few miles away, where for the next twenty years she lived with her parents and three older sisters, Celinda, Clarinda, and Orinda, and an older brother, Albert. The town, was set in a fertile valley by the Sandy River, which ran westward into Lake Ontario. Like many other communities typical of the new Republic, the community bustled with tradesmen, busy factories, a woollen mill and tannery powered by flowing water. A scattering of impressive homes belonging to manufacturers and distinguished citizens was tangible evidence that earnest effort was rewarded in America. Farmers who worked the surrounding lands brought in their produce, and bought their supplies from the town merchants. Whatever amusements and cultural events there were – lectures, concerts, recitals, political meetings, etc. – were centered in the town which was graced by a town hall, a school for the children of the larger community, and a church, freely used by various Protestant sects (Baptists, Methodists, Universalists), but most certainly not by Catholics, echoing an intolerant Puritan past. The locals were the descendants of stern Calvinist New Englanders who had migrated inland, ever westward, through northern New York to the Western Reserve, to Ohio, Indiana, Illinois, and beyond. Miss Fielde's people had left New England to live a hard, pioneering life in the uppermost reaches of New York, a beautiful but cold Arcadia, while some of their distant cousins, who gave rise to the Marshall Fields, pushed on to the midwest, and fared much better.

Adelia was a country girl, inheriting the Protestant values of a rural and small town society that had not changed much since before the Revolution, but she grew up in a time when newly established railroads, telegraphs, and inexpensive printing methods were bringing the changing views of urban society to the backwoods. The old conservative values of Fielde's world were under siege by populist and feminist movements that challenged the social order as the nation became ferociously industrial and capitalistic. Americans were becoming both secular and eclectic with regard to other religions, while at the same time a vigorous Protestant evangelical revival came into full flower in this bourgeois Victorian society.[2] Protestant values found a

Figure 1.1 Fielde's parents, Sophia and Leighton Field

receptive acolyte in Adelia – lofty moral concerns, a sense of duty, hard work, competitiveness, sacrifice, and the secondary importance of immediate gratification – the values of a rather earnest and self-righteous young woman. How much she was exposed to early feminist thinking, which in fact emanated from Elizabeth Cady Stanton and Susan B. Anthony in Seneca Falls, nearby in northern New York, is unknown.

Miss Fielde's father, Leighton, scratched out a living as a painter and carpenter, jobs which could barely support his family above the level of subsistence. Dignified, reserved, and generous, a natural leader of the community, he lived to the age of 84 (d. 1878). Her mother, Sophia (Tiffany), born to some refinement, settled for a hard, demanding life but remained cheerful, maintained a good sense of humor, and always hoped that her children would have a better life than she and her husband. She was a voracious reader of Shakespeare, Sir Walter Scott, John Milton, Charles Dickens, William M. Thackery, James Fenimore Cooper, and Nathaniel Hawthorne – all subjects of family conversation, though mother and father had little formal education. Mrs. Field died in her eighty-seventh year (1880). Of the five children, three were talented; Albert had a promising career as a writer, cut short by his early death, Clarinda became an astronomer, married and had four children; all but one, Adele, died. The family portrait can be completed with "Grandfather Tiffany," Mrs. Field's father (d. 1849), a veteran of the Revolutionary War, who amused the children with tales of his military adventures.

If blood will tell, the Field children were marvelously endowed despite the cruel fact that this impoverished branch of the extended family had stumbled into the wilderness. On her father's side she was directly descended seven generations back from Zacharia Field and Sarah (Thornton) Field of the Rhode Island Colony, the progenitors of innumerable, renowned individuals including Cyrus W. Field, financier and promoter of the first TransAtlantic cable, Marshall Field, merchant and philanthropist, James B. Field, editor of the *Atlantic Monthly*, Eugene Field, the journalist and writer, Justice Stephen A. Field, and David Dudley Field, the author of *Field's Code of Civil Procedure*, an important and widely adopted codification of common law. The English branch of the Field family could also boast of its luminaries, including some minor nobility. The mother's side was no less distinguished, descending from the brilliant Jonathan Edwards, an eighteenth-century Protestant divine who instigated the *Awakening*, a revival of Calvinism in eighteenth-century America, and became the first president of Princeton University, known then as the College of New Jersey. His wife Sarah was a Pierpont descended from Sir Robert de Pierrepont, a participant in the Norman Conquest. Other nineteenth-century descendants included a duke, members of the peerage in England, and several prominent citizens in colonial America.

At a time when eugenics was formulated and admired as a discipline, and the genetic history of an individual and place of birth were criteria of worth,

Miss Fielde, although proud of her illustrious pedigree, never became a member of the elite patriotic societies for which she was eligible. She felt that credit should be given for individual achievement, for high aesthetic and ethical standards rather than for any accident of birth, and that true aristocracy and "social congeniality" would be

> apparent to all regardless of the record, by the behaviour and the actions of the individual . . . character is the one unchanging thing in the world. . . . I have friends in many countries, and among the most exquisite of body and soul, I reckon a high caste Hindu lady; a Chinese peasant's daughter; the wife of a Russian tanner; and an Irish nurse. . . . Consorting with congenial spirits such as these aristocrats, is the acme of earthly enjoyment, [while] . . . coteries found on place of birth, national preferences or convictional prejudice, ignore the fundamental bases for congeniality. They tend to narrow the mental horizon, and to limit the sphere of social delight. Congenial souls come to us from all points of the compass, and from diverse lines of parentage.

Her room-mate at Normal School, Lucretia Chilcott reveals more about her intimate friend:

> Miss Fielde was an intense lover of humanity, if not especially a respecter of individual persons. To her, human dignity, in its true sense, was a source of genuine pride; something to be cherished and maintained – something sacred. That "man was made in the image of his Maker," was a thought that impressed her above all others; and, in reality, was the one that exerted the dominant moral influence upon her whole career.[3]

Adelia Field's name is absent from some of the genealogical records, a missing twig, because as a 16 year old she adopted a *nom de plume*, Adele Marion Fielde, which was entered in the registry of the Baptist church, and the added *e* seemed to confound the genealogists. Eugenicists delighted in the fact that not one of many hundreds of this family had ever resided in a prison, mental hospital, or poorhouse – strong evidence in support of their theories!

Miss Fielde's parents were the kind of people who astonished Alexis de Tocqueville, with his European sensibility. As he traveled in the wilderness of northern New York in the 1830s, he encountered settlers whose new homes were built in fresh clearings of virgin forest, far away from civilized city life, yet reading newspapers and books, keenly interested in what was going on in the world, and who plied him for the latest tidings.[4] American pioneers like the Fields who so impressed him were unique in his experience. Despite their rude life, they were confident people of high principle, and considerable intellectual refinement – anything but coarsened, craven peasants.

Adelia, her father's favorite, was not a particularly attractive child, and indeed her appearance did not improve with age. She was described by a friend as having a

> very large head, masculine in its proportions, and her features were decidedly irregular . . . positively homely; but her looks improved as acquaintance with her became more extended. Her face was singularly expressive, seldom in repose, and in moments of inspirational excitement it reflected the grandeur of her character to such an extent that it was exceptionally attractive.

In maturity she was 5.5 feet tall, a large, stout woman despite vigorous exercise – walking, boating, and horseback riding. She was self-conscious about her obesity, and she was known to say that she could never reduce her weight to "known standards of gentility." Yet she could take a joke about her adiposity. She wrote in a letter that as the ship carrying her and others to the Far East passed the Solomon Islands, her fellow passengers "solemnly requested" that she remain out of view of the natives, who were cannibals, for fear that she might stimulate their appetite.[5]

The Fields were Baptists, of the tolerant New England kind, who affirmed the importance of education while their church functioned as a unifying center of authority and social order. But Adelia, a serious, observant Christian, with her parent's blessing, chose to be a Universalist, a more tolerant sect which believed in universal redemption, the salvation of all human beings by a loving God who would not exclude anyone for any reason. When, as a girl, she began to write, and used the name of Adele Marion Fielde to hide her identity, there was no protest from her parents, who quite possibly encouraged her independence.[6] It would seem that Adelia's tolerant parents permitted her to construct a persona of her own, and as her history unfolds, a separation from her childhood community becomes apparent. Her feeble, almost comical attempt to avoid drawing any association with her writing by changing her name (slightly) suggests a desire for anonymity, and yet she had to contend with her strong and irrepressible ego; Adele M. Fielde was the compromise. Perhaps her change of name, and separation from her parents' church, were ways of distancing herself from the debilitating poverty of her parents. Both actions suggest a willful, independent nature, unafraid to challenge authority, traits that became more apparent in later years. Once she left South Rutland, she rarely visited her old home, though she was always solicitous of her parents – from afar. In 1911, she wrote to her old schoolteacher: "You have lately been back to those old scenes; I do not think I could now bear the stress of a return to them. The things that are no more wrack one too severely."[7] Though she lived for many years in alien lands, she never seemed to be homesick, as were many of her colleagues, nor did she sentimentalize small town American life; the bitter struggle of her parents to survive, and to stay "respectable", colored her views. Out of this background emerged a cosmopolite, a traveler who preferred to inhabit the great cities of America, and a reformer who, through education, wanted to lighten the burdens of the oppressed.

Taking on the views of the townspeople (and the rest of Protestant America), she at first grew up intolerant of Catholicism and Popery. However, although she quickly shed her prejudices when confronted by Catholics whom she befriended and admired, she always retained a critical attitude toward Catholicism for its dogma and ritual. She deplored raw, emotional anti-Catholicism, the kind responsible for riots, murder, and the burning of churches and nunneries that had taken place in most of the large cities of America. One of her Catholic friends was Edward J. Nolan, Librarian of the Academy of Natural Sciences of Philadelphia who was instrumental in obtaining a place for her to work and study for her scientific career. Early in their relationship their discussions of religion induced her to believe, erroneously, that he was trying to convert her. The incident was recounted by Helen N. Stevens, her friend and biographer.[8] She had been to a Catholic service and when she met Dr. Nolan she said: "Dr. Nolan, do you know where I have been? . . . I have been to *your* church; and I have witnessed the 'Elevation of the Host.' During the performance I could not help but wonder if in the light of the twentieth century civilization, such an exhibition of superstition could possibly appeal to the reverential in man." Dr. Nolan, not openly provoked, took leave of her and returned in an hour. "Miss Fielde, do you know where I have been? I have been to *my* church and on *my* knees I have prayed to *my* Lord to forgive you for the insult you offered Him." A few hours later Miss Fielde approached Dr. Nolan. "Dr. Nolan, do you know where I have been? . . . I have been to *your* church, and on *my* knees have prayed *our* Lord to forgive me for the wicked insult I offered *you*."

She was a serious, attentive student at the South Rutland school, eager to learn, and though friendly and pleasant, she seemed to have little interest in social life. Excelling in her studies and easily the best student, she graduated from secondary school in her sixteenth year, planning to continue her education at the State Normal College at Albany to prepare for a career in teaching, one of the very few opportunities for a woman to become a "professional" and earn an independent living. Young women graduates gained entry to teaching, but they could not compete with their male counterparts who had graduated from universities and real colleges (where females were not admitted) for the better positions. At a time when free, compulsory public schools did not exist, the Fields, taxed to the limit educating all their children, could not afford to support Adele, even at the State Normal College, created by the state to train teachers, and far less costly than many other colleges in the region (Colgate, Hamilton, Union). There was nothing for her to do but earn enough money to go to Albany, and this she did for the next three years teaching in the local school, doing it so well that by the time she left she was earning the highest salary ever of any female teacher. Undoubtedly, the disparity in pay between men and women for comparable work did not escape her attention. Living simply, she had saved enough to pay for her education. At 19 years of age, in 1858, she left home for Albany, the first time she had ventured more than ten miles from her place of birth; a lifelong exile had begun, and, for whatever reason, she looked away from her place of origin to become an eager pilgrim in the greater world.

2 Out of the nest

Miss Fielde found herself in a new and unfamiliar world in Albany, on a miserable and rainy day, her very first day away, alone in her room and wrenched from all that was familiar. This small town girl wept, but her tears were soon interrupted by the arrival of Miss Lucretia M. Chilcott, who had been assigned to be her room-mate. Sadness came to an end as the two earnest spirits began their lifelong friendship in the magic days independent of family. Deep, probing conversation revealed that they had much in common except for their sectarian beliefs; "Dell" was a Universalist, while Lucretia was a Baptist. They resolved that religion would not come between them and that they would not argue about church doctrine. If, however, either could demonstrate by example through the excellence of her living that she was closer to the *Truth*, the other might be convinced, and so might change. Each of these unblemished young women held to her creed, but a few years later, Adele did become a Baptist for a more compelling reason.

A buoyant Dell was popular with her teachers and a few of her class-mates at Albany – fondly remembered by fellow students for her humorous antics, sometimes self-deprecating. She was a serious student whose literary talent soon became evident, and with her natural confidence, flair for leadership, and exceptional scholastic record, she was usually the speaker for the class. A perceptive Lucretia Chilcott reminisced:

> In one respect she was peculiar, if not somewhat contradictory. Although of world-wide sympathies and genuinely democratic, she was exceedingly choice of the selection of her intimate friends. No human being was too insignificant or too humble for whom she would not make any reasonable self-sacrifice; but she positively would not permit herself to be bored by the companionship of mediocre or commonplace individuals. As a consequence she was very much alone in early life; and not at all popular with persons of either sex. However she was very fond of taking part in social gatherings. She was a brilliant conversationalist, an appreciative listener, a person of exquisite manners, and possessed a strong sense of humor. Also she was deeply averse to anything that partook of the nature of a practical joke – to anything that made a

> human being seem ridiculous. . . . To her, human dignity, in its true sense, was a source of genuine pride; something to be cherished and maintained – something sacred.[1]

After two years of training, she was awarded a teacher's certificate in 1860, and began what appeared to be her life's work, teaching at Watertown, NY, a larger town a few miles north of East Rodman. The following year she moved to Mamaroneck, NY, near the Connecticut border, where she continued to instruct, probably for higher pay. The Baptist missionary register noted that she became Principal of the Ladies Seminary at Astoria, Long Island, an institution that no longer exists. It may be no accident that Fielde taught at Astoria because the ancient Field farm dating from the seventeenth century was nearby and there were numerous Field descendents in the area, distant cousins about whom she might have been curious.[2]

In those days, free public school education did not exist, and colleges and universities denied young women entry. In a society that did not provide girls with a good education, the establishment of Female Seminaries was a major advance, for they provided young women with a good education, and in doing so they turned out many teachers and abolitionists. In the early part of the century Elizabeth Cady Stanton, one of the founders of the American feminist movement, had been educated at the Troy Female Seminary, the first such institution.[3]

The war years were spent teaching at Astoria where Fielde was an ardent abolitionist, although her efforts go undescribed. Many years later, she wrote: "I lived through the war, and worked as hard as I well could for the freeing of the black people," and she often spoke about the utter evil of slavery.[4] The oppression of black people, so obvious and egregious, started Fielde thinking about the many injustices endured by women, and gave rise to her reformist, feminist convictions. She must have been conscious of the fact that the school in which she taught had been established to correct a wrong – the denial of education based on gender – and that great numbers of young girls were still unable to obtain an education.

The great social and feminist issues of the nineteenth century with which Fielde's name has been associated had been gathering momentum while she came of age. Even before she was born, Catherine Beecher and Emma Willard had established schools for the education of young ladies, and there were many brave women such as Frances Wright, Lucy Stone, and the Grimké sisters, Sarah and Angelina, who had traveled around the country lecturing on the evils of slavery, a calling that was not without danger. The Grimkés, daughters of a southern slaveowner, moved to Philadelphia and became Quakers; eventually Angelina wrote *An Appeal to the Christian Women of the South*.[5]

In the early part of the nineteenth century the major concerns of social reformers were improvement in the state of prisons and asylums for the insane, and the emancipation of slaves, while the rights of women and the suffragist cause were considered of secondary importance. Despite the large number of dedicated women in abolitionist societies, these organizations were run by men burning to redress the abuse of black people, but barely disposed to heed the voices of women struggling to improve their status.[6] Feminist and abolitionist causes were always intertwined, but gradually, after discouraging experiences in which women's claims were set aside in favor of the anti-slavery movement, tensions arose that led to a separation of efforts as feminist leaders concluded that they had to fight their own battles for their own rights.

In 1848, when Adele Fielde was 9 years of age, an organized feminist movement was born at a convention held at Seneca Falls in Upper New York State not very far from Fielde's home town of East Rodman. The convention, whose major organizers and leaders were Elizabeth Cady Stanton, Susan B. Anthony and Lucretia Mott, ended with a Declaration of Principles that embodied the hopes and aspirations of women. The declaration was not only a call to arms, the rallying point of future struggle, it also outlined legitimate feminist and social grievances, above all the denial of suffrage to women. Surprisingly, the demand for the vote was not high on the list for many women.[7] A very young Adele Fielde was probably unaware of this momentous assembly. But as this intelligent girl grew up, she could have hardly avoided discussing matters of concern to a perceptive young woman, one who participated in the struggle to realize the declared intentions of the movement.

In the spring of 1864, before returning home for school vacation, she made a wide detour across the state to visit Lucretia Chilcott in Buffalo, and there the detour changed her life, for she fell in love with Lucretia's brother Cyrus. This earnest young man, "unselfish, self-sacrificing, and devoted to high ideals," had prepared himself for missionary work in the Far East at the Rochester Theological Seminary, and had become a Baptist minister at Fredonia, NY. He was now preparing to depart for his posting in Bangkok, Siam (now called Thailand), burning to bring the Word to the heathens. The comments, made many years later by her intimate friend Lucretia are particularly informative:

> It was love at first sight with both of them . . . Miss Fielde was a person of intense affections and her desire for love were equally strong. She was fitted by nature for wifehood and motherhood and to be a wife and mother was the chief ambition of her life. Because of her humble home-surroundings, heretofore she had not come into social contact with anyone of the opposite sex who would make a suitable matrimonial match for a woman of her superior endowment; and already her friends began to regard her as a "confirmed old maid."

Engaged to Cyrus at the age of 26, she spent much of the summer of 1865 in Buffalo, planning their future together. In the glow of first love, the spirit of accommodation and compromise prevailed. The two lovers had no difficulty

Figure 2.1 Adele Fielde in 1864

arriving at a common understanding of doctrinal beliefs. She assented to becoming a Baptist (again), a bridgeable distance from her Universalist sectarian convictions. But Adele was the main support of her aging parents, and any arrangement would have to provide for them.[8] Despite their protestations that they could look after themselves (which they could not), Adele and Cyrus decided that Adele would become a salaried missionary teacher, and that some of her income would go to the elder Fields. Adele would follow her fiancé to Thailand within the year when all was settled. She would sail for Hong Kong where they would marry, and together they would travel to Bangkok. If no paid position was available she would wait for him in America, and continue with her teaching.

Cyrus sailed for Bangkok in August 1864 and arrived on Christmas Eve, pleased with what he saw: a large city of 300,000 inhabitants teeming with potential Chinese converts. Adele was baptized in the Calvary Baptist Church in Washington, DC in January 1865, and became a missionary teacher, agreeing to spend at least five years at her post. Almost a year passed before she was able to book a passage for the East, finally setting sail on December 20, 1865. There were no passenger steamers across the Pacific Ocean at that time, and so she sailed on a tea-clipper with sixteen passengers from New York. After an appalling voyage that lasted 149 days, having been given up for lost, they finally arrived at Hong Kong with a crew depleted by fever, and an ailing Miss Fielde. This was the voyage of her life, often perilous, and it ended with a catastrophe. Many years later, a running account of the adventure was published by Miss Fielde:

> The *N.B. Palmer* of New York was of proven speed and soundness, and her captain was of notable standing among his peers. Most of the passengers, of whom I was one, had waited for months upon the movements of this particular ship, whose route was to be around the southern point of Africa, without stopping at any port, and with the expectation that a hundred days would suffice for her transit to the other side of the world. Two mission boards had placed nine persons among its passengers. . . .
>
> Great flakes of snow fell slowly on the deck as we stood watching the receding shore of native land, wondering when and whether it would ever again be of our beholding. Hope prevented heartbreak. . . . Miss Sands, slightly my junior, introduced to me as my cabinmate, straightaway won my regard by proposing that we each occupy the lower of the two berths a week at a time alternately, and by insisting upon an absolutely just allotment of the brass hooks that must serve us as wardrobe. . . .
>
> A cursory survey of the ship made us acquainted with the after deck, our prospective area for open-air exercise; with the middle deck, which we were not to cross save with the captain's permission; and with the forecastle, the dormitory of the sailors. . . .

Figure 2.2 Fielde's fiancé, Cyrus Chilcott, a Baptist missionary ministering to the Chinese in Bangkok, Thailand (Siam)

Gradually we learned the vocabulary of the sea, and knew the names of all the sails and spars, the location of the scuppers, and the use of belaying pins, bitts and binnacle. We soon prided ourselves on fluency and accuracy in nautical terminology. I learned to take the sun and to keep the ship's log.

Early in our voyage, Miss Sands suggested that its length and leisure ought to conduce to our higher education. That very day we elaborated a programme requiring exercise on deck for an hour after breakfast, then an hour in the study of French, and an hour in the reading of history. In the afternoon we were to sew, and were to take turns in playing chess with the invalid, for whom chess was the sole palliative of misery in a sea-voyage. The next day we achieved our programme perfectly; but during the ensuing night the waves rose high and for many consecutive days we were unable to leave our bunks. Then in early dawn Miss Sands, peering through our single port-hole over the upper berth, called blithely, Oh Miss Fielde, the sun is shining, the sea is calm. To-day we can return to our regular habits! And so did we; but hourly changes in latitude and longitude bring vicissitudes that greatly interfere with regular habits.

There were frequent calls to the after deck for the inspection of strange denizens of the deep. The propeller of a steamer frightens these creatures away; but our sailing vessel was to them only another water bird disporting itself on their domain. Close to her sides came schools of leviathans and of gay jelly-fish. We seemed to meet all the inhabitants of the ocean, except the sea-serpent. Sometimes a shark, a porpoise, or a turtle was captured and examined on deck. Once a passenger caught on a fish-hook, a stormy petrel and kept it on board until the sailors demanded its release. The crew had declared from the beginning of the voyage that bad luck would come to a ship carrying so many sky pilots, and the capture of the stormy petrel further aroused their abiding superstitions and established a grouch that had no palliative.

There was little communication between the passengers and the crew, but an exception was made in favor of the old quartermaster, Joe, during his long illness, when I was permitted to carry to his cabin such tidbits as I might secure, after dinner, from the captain's table. Another exception was made for young Shaw, a Boston lad of seventeen years, whose mother had sent to Captain Steele a touching appeal, begging him to guard the morals of her boy. . . . Many hours did I sit with Shaw. . . . Had I myself been rightly educated, I might have warned him against the contagion from the strange sores that I saw on many of the sailors, but I was ignorant of their terrible significance.

Mr. Sands edited a weekly newspaper, *The Hurricane*, filled by anonymous communications from the passengers and read aloud to them at evening assemblages in the dining saloon. The entertainment was sometimes enlivened by singing. Little Miss Wheeler was often called upon for a hymn, and she never failed to respond with her whole repertoire. . . . If the encore was loud she would sing it again. . . . Original dramas, charades and tableaux were presented. . . .

We crossed the line on a sunny day, and Neptune, with many attendant sea gods, came on board, over the stern. The gods all bore a striking resemblance to Santa Claus. . . . We were constant in our lookout for other ships, whether they passed by day or in moonlighted nights. Leaning against the bulwark, we discerned on the horizon the tops of masts. Sometimes the masts seemed to rise until the hull came into view, and the signal flags entered into conversation. The name of the ship, the last port of call, the destination, the recorded latitude and longitude, the sort of cargo, the number of passengers, and as many other facts as the distance or the light would reveal, were made by each ship to the other as it sped by. The signal for goodbye was always raised at parting. If the passing vessel flew old glory at its stern, as did the *N.B. Palmer*, we did not thereafter look at one another for a while. It is not polite to observe furtive tears.

Of land we saw only the coast of Brazil and the islands of Tristan da Cunha in the distance. Then the tanks rusted, and our drinking water became scant, so that the captain decided to go into Cape Town for fresh supplies. . . . During the five days that our ship remained at Cape Town, its passengers were entertained in the homes of resident Americans, and we thus escaped the dangers of a mutiny quelled with bloodshed, on its decks. The removal of the second mate and the restoration of order preceded the continuance of our voyage.

In the Indian Ocean we encountered a typhoon that mauled and drove our ship for days, spent in bunks by the prostrated passengers, and in terrific exertion by the crew. Upon its abatement we returned to our charted course and in a shining calm lingered near enchanting coral beds. These tempted some of our men to go off in small boats for the gathering of multicolored sprays, which were brought on board and were cherished on the roof of the deck-house until their unbearable stench compelled their return to the ocean.

By the time we reached Anjer, a town then at the west end of Java, the condition of our water tanks necessitated our entrance into its harbor. The passengers had experience of a sweltering night at a hotel on shore, and of some delightful daylight hours in a wonderful tropical garden. The old Anjer is no longer extant. In 1883 it was cast to the bottom of the sea by a volcanic earthquake. . . .

As our ship passed slowly through the straits between Java and Sumatra, strong perfumes from jungle flowers were wafted to us on the night breezes. A strange insomnia followed the inhalation of these scents, and then jungle fever seized all on board save the captain and the colored steward and stewardess. There were degrees in the severity of the fever and some of its victims were scarcely disabled while others

> were scarcely alive. A chill like that of ice in the veins was followed by scorching fever, accompanied by unusual strength and wild delirium, succeeded by collapse, utter helplessness and possible coma. While in a state of coma, I was thought to have died. The distress of resuscitation remains in my memory. There were no doctors on board, and no quinine in the ship's medicine chest. Sailors, mad with fever, were locked in the cabins to prevent them jumping overboard. The water tanks were rusty and the water foul. One night there was a slight shower, and the first mate, by setting pans on the deck, caught half a teacupful of rain water which he brought to me. I know how nectar tasted to the gods on Olympus.
>
> We were three weeks in traversing the China Sea. As Victoria Peak came into view, the second mate, an old whaler, in the delirium of fever, jumped overboard and was rescued after long pursuit in the rowboats, only to die the same day. . . . On a clear morning in May we entered the harbor of Hongkong. Ten of the crew were carried ashore for burial. All the passengers survived. . . . I was barely able to stand, and Miss Sands, who had partially recovered arrayed me in white.[9]

In Hong Kong harbor, a frail Adele in a wedding dress awaited the arrival of her betrothed. For this exquisite moment she had endured the menacing high seas for five months, had experienced a typhoon, witnessed a mutiny, and was brought to the point of coma by "jungle" fever. Miss Sands, her cabin mate, had discreetly vacated the cabin for the reunion, and was on deck watching the approach of two men rowing to the ship. Neither answered to the description of Cyrus Chilcott. They were dark heralds, despatched to inform Miss Fielde that Chilcott would never come, for he had died of typhoid fever in Bangkok on December 30, ten days after they had set sail from New York. Captain Steele and his passengers, who had lived through hazardous times together and had forged a close friendship, were to have celebrated the consummation of the love affair, and the joyous union was to be officiated by the captain on his ship. Now, no one could muster the courage to break the dreadful news to Fielde, and it was left to Dr. Legge, a physician from Hong Kong, to inform Adele of Chilcott's death. Numbed, she seemed to take the catastrophic news calmly, and asked what her course of action should be. Captain Steele insisted that she return to New York with him, and several of the passengers agreed with the plan. Thanking her friends for their concern, she delayed her decision, but an hour later she informed everyone that she would continue on to Bangkok, her final destination which had been so long in her thoughts and dreams. If she did not see and experience the mission where her lover had died and lay buried, she would forever be burdened by a sense of incompleteness. Her choice to go forward rather than to retreat at a time of catastrophe was characteristic of her behavior. Her positive decision opened up new worlds for her and permitted the full expression of her talents, though the path she chose was not easy, for there was only a grudging place for single women in the mission to the heathen.

No sooner had she made her agonized decision than she broke down, collapsing into unconsciousness. Fielde was removed to a hospital where she remained for three weeks, oblivious to the world, constantly attended by her fellow passengers, some delaying continuation of their journey until she recovered. Her hopes for a home and family were shattered, and yet characteristically, she was neither embittered nor self-pitying; rather, she simply changed her plans. Many years later Fielde recalled, "I then resolved to live less myself that others might live more through me." She had become a teacher to earn a living, and a missionary to be with her husband, but now in a time of despair and bleak prospects, her path would be one of self-sacrifice – to live for others, an apostolic mission that was not born of a burning religious faith. Rather, her decision to dedicate her life, and give herself entirely to a mission, was not without an element of rationality and calculation.

Adele Fielde remained faithful to Chilcott's memory, for in the course of time she declined several proposals of marriage. Though reserved, she occasionally recounted the sad, romantic events to her intimate friends – Chilcott's perfection growing with each telling. A friend has raised the legitimate question whether her married life would have been so perfect, given Miss Fielde's driving and exacting nature.[10] What conflicts would have tested this Victorian marriage if she had become a great success (which did occur), and her husband remained in her shadow? He was an admirable and courageous person, clearly superior, but no mortal could match Miss Fielde's idealized image of her lover, and time would not diminish his luster.

3 Bangkok

> And all that one can do is like setting the faintest taper to light a wilderness in a stormy night.[1]

The voyage from Hong Kong to Bangkok, Siam, her final destination, lasted for thirty-four days, and though tranquil it was not without its moments of high adventure – a threatened attack by pirates was averted by outspeeding them. After being tossed on churning seas she was cast upon Asian shores, bereft of husband, children, and home. Her careful plans were in tatters for she had wanted to become a wife and mother, and as her friend wrote: "She was disappointed beyond measure. She was naturally domestic, and it was simply out of the question for her to conceive of a successful life for herself that was not based upon conjugal love, the care of a home and the rearing of children."[2] Fielde was described by William Dean, Head of the Bangkok Baptist mission,[3] as

> wonderfully sustained under her overwhelming bereavement and [she] affords by her personal cheerfulness, in this hour of dire calamity, another proof of the divinity of the religion she has come to teach. . . . She takes the house fitted up for her reception by Mr. Chilcott, her husband during the last weeks of his glowing life. Her first introduction into the room where he died, and to the house as it was in his health, seemed too much for her to endure and live; but after a few hours, the objects most familiar to him in health, and the room that witnessed his dying struggle, seemed to speak to her. . . . She finds a warm companionship in my family. . . . We went with her yesterday to Mr. Chilcott's grave. At first sight she fainted but soon recovered, and after spending a little time at the sacred resting place of her chosen husband, she came away with great calmness and gave directions for a monument to be erected over his grave.

Miss Fielde, devastated and physically weakened, a "widow," living in the empty house her fiancé had prepared, expressed her torment in a surprisingly confessional letter published in the *Baptist Missionary Magazine* (*BMM*):

> I have journeyed seven weary months over tempestuous seas and in strange lands to meet my beloved and I found his grave with the grass upon it seven months old. I have come to my house; it is left unto me desolate. While I stood holding out my hand for a cup of happiness, one of fearful bitterness was pressed violently to my lips. I looked joyfully to Providence and it turned upon me a face of inexpressible darkness. And because I believe in God I have been able to endure it.[4]

Such a public cry of despair, a barely contained anger and sorrow, was unusual for this private person. Quickly, she seemed to gather her courage, to end her biblical lamentation on a note of defiance, and gratitude to the Almighty, although it is hardly possible that she did not feel violated by higher powers, or by fate. After living in Chilcott's rooms for a month she wrote:

> I am cheerful and content. Surrounded by things sanctified by his use of them, engaged in the work for which he freely gave his life, I am happier than I should be any where else where he is not. If I waken every morning to the same sorrow, I also find every morning the same consolation. There is always the same consolation. There is always the same bosom of Infinite Love on which to rest my head, the same unfailing promises on which to stay my heart.[5]

Comforted by both Dean, and Chinese Christians in the mission so moved by the tragedy, she could say, "There is no doubt that I have something to do here." Fielde had many close friends, but never again did she have a serious, romantic relationship.

The Bangkok mission, founded by William Dean in the 1830s, and still under his charge, remained small. With Dean were his wife, and three children, two young boys and an older daughter, and a second family, the Smiths, who had been at the mission for twenty years. Earlier in the century the Chinese Imperial power had prevented the entry of Westerners, and so missions run by sixty Protestant missionaries had been established among Chinese immigrants in locations at the southern fringes of China – Bangkok, Malacca, Batavia, and Singapore. However, since the Opium Wars of 1842, Chinese mainland ports had been opened to Westerners by military persuasion, and religious missions followed closely in the wake of conquest. For thirty years, the resistance of the Siamese to Christianity in Bangkok had been almost total, while the Chinese immigrant laborers were more receptive. Despite the Siamese location, the mission was essentially directed toward the Chinese.

Later, when permitted entry, an energized missionary effort was quickly transferred to China, fifty additional staff were added in the next five years, and by 1876 there were 266 missionaries (not including wives), of whom thirty-eight were single women – one evangelizer for every 1,600,000 inhabitants.[6]

During this time, the Bangkok mission was relegated to secondary importance – not very attractive to bright young male missionaries.

Chilcott had worked with the Deans, and it was natural for Miss Fielde to begin working with them – father, and daughter Fanny – who had learned the local Tie-chiu Chinese dialect, and were attempting to convert the numerous Chinese of Bangkok. Missionary work at the time was considered arduous and dangerous, not fitting for single women unless they were associated with and protected by a man. Missionary boards, fearing public criticism for sending young women into dangerous situations without protection, were reluctant to send them into the field. With periodic uprisings and massacres of Westerners, as occurred in Tientsin,[7] the title "missionary" was regarded in the same category as "martyr." Oddly, missionary boards did not hesitate to send single women to the American frontier to evangelize the Native Americans. In China, evangelists were laughed at, ridiculed, stoned, and threatened as they went from house to house and street to street; it was said that to preach the Gospel and withstand the abuse required "fire in the bones." In 1885, the Presbyterian mission in Swatow was attacked by an angry mob who beat the preacher, destroyed the chapel and stole everything owned by the mission. The Baptist mission reported that despite the open hostility of the Chinese, the local magistrates could not (or would not) provide protection.[8] The suffering and martyrdom of missionaries were not rare occurrences, as described by Barr in *To China With Love* (1973), although Fielde was fortunate enough to escape the worst of the wars, famines, and peasant uprisings that periodically beset China in the second half of the nineteenth century.

Only single men and married couples were recruited for the calling, and so Adele's prospects were not promising in this unfamiliar land. While Catholics demanded celibacy of male missionaries, Protestants preferred married males and females. Though Dean was sympathetic to Adele's plight, he did not consider her to be a suitable addition to the Bangkok mission. For some time, he did not treat her as a single woman but as a widow, and he hoped that she might attract a young male missionary, a vexation that could sometimes evaporate through the matchmaking skills of the missionary's wife. He made desperate appeals to the Board of Baptist Missionaries in Boston to send young males, always in short supply, for they preferred the more fertile, promising field of China, rather than the struggling mission of Bangkok.[9] The Chinese of China rather than those of Siam were the preferred target.

Since the beginning of the nineteenth century, there had always been women volunteers, especially in New England, dedicated to spreading the Christian Gospel to save both body and soul, and to abolish devilish heathen practice.[10] But Victorian society and missionary administrations were imbued with the Pauline doctrine of male dominance, and gender-determined division of labor. According to Blackstone, English Common Law stated that "the personality of the married woman was entirely merged in that of her husband," and that whatever she had to suffer was for her own protection and benefit. More relevant to Fielde's experience, J.N. Murdock, Corresponding Secretary of the ABMU, Fielde's superior and friend, expressed his belief at the London Missionary Conference in 1888: "Women's work in the foreign field must be careful to recognize the headship of man in ordering the affairs of the kingdom of God."[11] It was *natural* that men should run things, and be the decision-makers – single women could not operate by themselves without guidance and direction, prone as they were to hysteria and fainting. In the civilized Western world, they had no vote, nor could they testify in court. Once married they owned nothing and their husbands had complete, legal control of all possessions, including their children – punishment for the sins of Eve, which began to be redressed in the mid-nineteenth century.[12] Though women were not without some power by exploiting their "feminine wiles," the opportunities for marginalized single women and widows in America were limited – dressmaking, teaching school, helping in the homes of married brothers and sisters, being a household servant or a governess, and to this short list could be added the evangelical call: the spreading of God's word in the lands of the heathen.[13]

In 1834, an American missionary, the Reverend David Abeel, troubled by the wretched conditions of women in the East, spoke of their plight to a group of women in England.[14] He emphasized that the alleviation of their condition, and the conversion of women and children, could take place only if they could be reached in their homes, and he concluded that only single Christian women could have this access. By custom, male missionaries were excluded from dealing with Chinese females, and the wives of missionaries, the unsung heroes of the evangelical movement, were already overworked.[15] Men could be reached, but the critical social problems could only be solved by converting and educating women. The English were enthusiastic, and formed a non-denominational Society for Promoting Female Education in the East. In America, the response was quite different, for there was a delay of many years for the establishment of similar societies. It was only in 1871 that Women Baptist Foreign Missionary Societies were formed in Boston and Chicago with the hope that they would raise their own money for women to work in foreign lands without support from the male-dominated Baptist Missionary Union. However, all donations would go into the Union's treasury, and while the women's societies could recommend young ladies for appointments, the Union would have the final word, and money for their support would be disbursed from the Union's treasury.[16]

In the mid-nineteenth century, women had acquired a confidence and sense of empowerment through the demands made on them in the Civil War. Beginning to insist on their rights, they organized themselves into networks of women's circles, independent of masculine organizations, and they collected significantly large amounts of money by asking for only pennies from widespread numbers of people. Individual women could be dominated by male-directed organizations, but when intelligent women with financial means organized themselves, their wishes could not be ignored. Even so, over decades, they had to be vigilant in defending their rightful privileges against a male society whose belief in male dominance was sanctified by their religion. Now women could focus on matters that concerned them most, among which was the abuse of women in Chinese, Hindu, and Moslem countries, which they believed was an integral component of Eastern religions and cultures. As the missionary, Eliza Bridgman, so eloquently pleaded:

> But who shall teach the women of China? The missionary – the ordained minister of the gospel, who goes forth to preach, cannot gain access to the daughters of the land. The usages of society debar these from public assembly. Woman in all ordinary cases, is secluded, and cannot come out to hear the preaching of the bible. Shall woman then be there neglected?[17]

Enlightened, activist mission women and their organizations heeded the call, and, because they were concerned with problems abroad rather than at home in the U.S.A., they did not meet with serious opposition as did suffragists and reformers. Their concerns were not with the vote, reconstruction, slavery, drink, labor unrest, poverty, nor with any emotionally charged issues that might cause trouble in the U.S.A., and arouse opposition. Women missionaries were concerned with righteous issues – women's education, the abolishment of footbinding in China, and the enhancement of women's welfare. The principal objection to women's organizations was that women were not sufficiently competent for the task "unsupported by male wisdom," but a little experience could easily dispel this notion. Though the number of Protestant women's missionary societies and participating women increased rapidly, recognition of their contributions by male leadership was slow in coming.[18]

There was no shortage of young women offering themselves for a great crusade which would give meaning to their lives, for China was a new frontier upon which moral order must be imposed, a burden that was both heroic and romantic. The single American woman found a kind of liberation and fulfillment, a legitimate profession ordained from on high that permitted some measure of economic independence. An opportunity for a new life presented itself, not without an element of danger, and perhaps a respectable escape from an unhappy situation at home. The young woman was given responsibilities, and authority over other adults (servants whom she may never have had at home). In a sense, the young woman's work placed her on a par with her single male colleagues, and, once in foreign missions, missionaries "found unexpected authority in their status as Westerners in colonial China."[19] In this situation she acquired a taste for independence, and she lost a timidity appropriate for a young Victorian woman; old habits of subordination to the dictates of men weakened, and in the process the demarcation between male and female was blurred.[20] Still, the unmarried female carried the stigma of second-class status; she might be regarded as a spinster or "old maid" who, through desperation, seeking a last chance, became a missionary, removing herself from her society.

Christian feminists and women missionaries believed that since Christianity in America had done so much for them it would surely be a liberalizing, emancipating, democratic force of great appeal to women who suffered so terribly – "woman's sure friend in all countries and ages."[21] The task was formidable, for "heathen" women had been downtrodden, isolated, and in a state of total ignorance for so long that they found it difficult to learn, they were prey to superstition, and prone to misinterpret: "Woman is sitting in darkness, without love to shelter her head, or hope to illumine her solitude."[22]

However, a radical, contrasting perception of what Christianity had done for women was provided by one of the founders of the American feminist movement, Elizabeth Cady Stanton, who insisted that in fact, Christianity was at the very heart of the oppression of women, that male-dominated organized religion prevented women from attaining any position of authority or of being able to make decisions.[23] Adele Fielde's experience was to confirm the essential correctness of this view.

Missionary testimonials always stressed the enthusiasm of converts, and the relief, both spiritual and physical, felt by those who embraced Christianity, for their new beliefs justified escape from an intolerable situation. It meant, for Chinese women, the end of infanticide, and the footbinding of their daughters; the custom of child marriage had to be discouraged as well for it brought the education of girls to an abrupt halt. The potential convert was most impressed by the benefits of Western medicine – the alleviation of pain and suffering, hitherto considered one's fate.

Yet, in some respects, Chinese women were not as deprived as the women of other cultures such as those of India, where the crippling problem of caste was an extra burden, or of Turkey, where women were confined to a harem, or of Tibet, where an un-Western polyandry flourished. Fielde believed that environment could also lead to the devaluation of women as in Siam where they were scantily clad because of the warm climate. In China, the virtue of women was esteemed, and there was more equality between men and women. According to Fielde, a Victorian small town prude, the virtue of young Chinese women was as good as could be expected from heathens, guarded more in the French than in the American style.[24]

Though Fielde's religion at that time, and her condemnation of pagan religions were conventional, the same as those of Dean, most of her revulsion arose from the appalling social and economic conditions which confronted her, and especially the pitiful condition of women. The zeal of this fledgling missionary was directed toward the betterment of life for the Chinese woman. The conversion of men and boys was also a high priority, but inherent in Christian belief was the insistence that the masculine world of the East be deprived of ancient privileges that permitted it to benefit at the expense of women. There would be a measure of independence from husbands; polygamy and adultery would no longer be tolerated, and women, heretofore considered worthless, would not be forced to live on the leavings of men. As females tended to embrace Christianity, males would see it as a threat. Even if women were capable of learning, husbands did not want "silly notions" put into their heads. Whatever its success, Christianity would create a central tension, a disruption of ancient habits and beliefs, and Western missionaries had no qualms about destroying the old order; to them, native religions were hardly more than superstitions. Although Fielde admired certain aspects of Chinese culture, she was more impressed by the terrible life of the average Chinese: "There is no Romance in the life of a Chinese woman, and nothing chivalrous in the character of a Chinese man."[25]

Missionaries were convinced that the adoption of Western ways and Christianity would improve the lot of the converts; embracing the new religion would mean more than a new religious practice, it would change their culture and their way of life. However much the Evangelist had the best interests of the Chinese at heart, some aggressive missionaries were so intolerant that they roused the ire of the natives who resisted the Word of Christ, and were "half devil, half child," cursed for having "dark and narrow minds." Evangelists were sometimes regarded as a nuisance by citizens and by officials, protected only by the force of arms of Western nations. They had to be tolerated, but their presence was resented, and particularly galling was their purchase of Chinese property. In their relentless attempts to overturn ancient ways and disrupt the family, their presence was an irritant, sometimes leading to disturbances and riots that Chinese and Siamese officialdom quelled with little enthusiasm because missionaries preached a doctrine that led to a diminishment of their power over converted, Chinese Christians.[26]

Just as the Chinese resented the ownership of their land by outsiders, North American Indians became embittered when they saw white settlers (who accompanied missionaries) acquire extensive tracts of their land after resident Indians had died from diseases brought by the white man. In 1847, thirteen settlers were massacred, among whom was Narcissa Whitman, a young missionary whose story is much like that of Adele Fielde's. Born in northern New York State in 1808, she became a teacher, and in 1835 married a missionary with whom she journeyed west over the Oregon Trail to evangelize Native Americans in the western territories, now Washington State and Oregon.[27]

So fervent and dogmatic were many missionaries that they could not or would not appreciate the magnificence of the complex and ancient civilizations they planned to enlighten; Chinese belief was demonized. Upon arriving in the East, Fielde's dismissive, intolerant views were quite typical of her colleagues, but in time, her insight into Chinese civilization matured, and her concern was more with people than with doctrine. After years of study and intimate contact, her perspective broadened, she acquired a remarkable knowledge of the Chinese, their culture, language and religions, and she regarded China as her second home. Possessing great writing and oratorical skills, she became an intermediary between China and America.

Adele Fielde's predicament was uncommon, and rather special. The American Baptist Missionary Union had hired a "married" woman, but through chance, had on its hands a strong, persuasive, single woman already in place in a foreign mission, one of the very first unmarried women to become a missionary, a calling that was not really her first choice. She was permitted to remain, though it was against their policy. Before she was transferred to the mission at Swatow, China,[28] she had answered only to a masculine governing board, fed information from half a world away by a male head of a mission. In 1866, when Adele arrived in Siam, boards controlled by women were just starting to emerge, and increasingly they became a policy-setting force, with the result that young women missionaries entering the service were increasingly being directed by women (by 1890, 60 percent of board members were women, single or married, and over half the women in the field were women).

Whatever the denomination, and whatever the country, the central mission was to evangelize, to convert the local "heathen" populace to become followers of Jesus. The establishment of schools and the training of converts to spread the Word among their own people was the highest priority. Teaching the heathen about cleanliness and hygiene was also important, so that the establishment of churches, meeting places, hospitals, and dispensaries soon followed. The situation was challenging, for the missionary was continually confronted with unfamiliar situations and problems, and sometimes with hostility. With few established procedures, problems had to be solved innovatively as they arose. Adele Fielde, deeply religious, a teacher by training and experience, considered her primary mission to be the establishment of schools and to teach. To do this she would have to learn the language of her pupils, gain acceptance in the community, find students, and build schools.

To learn a new language such as Chinese, especially as an adult, is a formidable undertaking. The novice is confronted by a bewildering multiplicity of definitions of words and figures, mysterious inflections that confer new meanings, and a sheer absence of words (missionaries to Hawaii found no words for *weather* or *chastity*). Fielde hired a teacher to instruct her in the local Tie-chiu dialect, but she confessed that she learned less from books than from mingling with the Chinese, especially in the countryside and villages. Devoid of reticence and self-consciousness, she practiced her clumsy speech, evangelizing, holding services with local Christian converts, teaching students, and instructing the country people in sanitation. She usually traveled with her teacher, and sometimes with Fanny Dean, whose language was more advanced than Fielde's. They would talk to women in their homes and in the street, teach them, and hold services in the evening. Later, when fluent, Fielde would travel alone, boarding in Christian Chinese homes.

After three months she wrote: "I rejoice in the hope of sometime being able to help these heathens. When my tongue is loosened, I will praise God in Chinese." She was aware that much conviction and inspiration was lost by her halting language, and that her speech must flow if she was to be persuasive.

Boredom and despair were kept at bay by cultivation of a rose garden in which she pottered on summer evenings. The care of a rose garden brought a little bit of America into her life, a soothing diversion from the chaos of the surrounding world with its appalling filth and squalor. The transplantation of a rose-bush provided her with a lesson in the form of a parable. She apologized to the plant for pruning it and destroying new buds and flowers – its "pride and glory" – but she explains that the maiming was done so that it "may live, and grow fairer and much more luxuriant than before" just as "we human creatures cry out under God's pruning hand, when our hopes are cut off." If we could hear God he would say, "O my Beloved, I do this only that your soul may live."[29] Fielde placed herself in the hands of God, whom she does not presume to understand.

After ten months in Bangkok, she wrote:

> I have been very happy in finding myself able to tell the people a few gospel truths. It is with much difficulty on my part and much patience on theirs. . . . The face of heathenism was not so dreadful as I had expected to see; but as I day by day look into its heart, I find it more terrible than all I had thought. Their souls are in the blackest darkness, and have been there so long that they have even ceased to remember or hope for the blessed light. . . . The great need of the people, as I feel it, is that some one who knows the common language of the common people, who understands their every-day thoughts and life, should go to them and tell them the truth, personally and particularly. I fear that even here, where good and earnest missionaries have lived for thirty years, very few natives have really heard and understood gospel truth from living lips.[30]

The "darkest blackness" she writes about was not only Chinese ignorance of the one true God, but the abysmal condition of their lives, the consequence of their ancient, "defective" religion and philosophy. Enlightenment would come only after the missionaries had attained intimate knowledge of the Chinese language and thinking.

> As these people will not come to me, I must go to them. I go and sit down with them in their houses, or workshops or in places where they sit idle by the wayside, and teach them as much of the gospel as they have time to listen to, or I have the ability to speak. In this way I visit from three to ten houses in a forenoon, and talk with from ten to thirty people, giving books to those who can read. The houses are hovels; the

> people are half naked; they are ignorant and unclean, but no one of them has ever addressed to me an unkind or a disrespectful word. This kind of work and no other appears practicable to me, here.[31]

While spending her days evangelizing, and learning Chinese, Fielde maintained an active correspondence with friends, and contributed to the widely read *Baptist Missionary Magazine*. Board members considered her letters interesting enough to be published in the house organ – usually four per year – and they were pleased that her letters were imbued with the religious fervor of an orthodox Baptist along with factual and intriguing detail. Others sent letters, but Fielde's were distinguished by their refreshing candor, and forthright opinion. They had a fine narrative ring to them, and, by bringing the unknown Far East to Americans in their living rooms, she became fairly well known in America.

She wrote of her voyage to Hong Kong and Bangkok, the tragic news upon her arrival (as shocking a drama as could be found in novels or the theater), life in Siam – *Darkness of the heathen mind, Missionary housekeeping – Teaching the doctrine, A Good field – Its fruits, The transplanted rose*, and *Death of the king – his successors*. In some the voice is impersonal, written as scholarly dissertations, while in others when appropriate, such as in accounts of travels, the voice is in the first-person singular.[32] Fielde was skillful in targeting her audience (men, women or both) and maintaining their interest with little stories, and interesting facts.

The letters fascinated the public, drew attention to the missionary movement, and elicited numerous small donations from readers. By the time Fielde returned to America in 1872, she was a kind of hero, in great demand as a speaker by various missionary societies run mainly by women, for she communicated with an appealing feminine voice.

Fielde was happy to travel to the countryside around Bangkok, to explore the land and its people, and shed the authority of Dean. In a letter published in the *Baptist Missionary Magazine* (*BMM*), she recounted one such experience that provided an intimate insight into life in backwoods China:

> Banplasoi, April 24 – . . . Chek Leng's wife gave us the use of a small house. . . . We spread our carpets, made our beds, put up a line to hang our clothes on, and hung a curtain at the door, while our Chinese boys set out our dishes in a shed in front, bought some earthen pots to boil rice in, and set up three stones on a heap of mud for a fireplace. . . . Our house, sides and roof, is of atap leaves, tied to bamboo posts and rafters with bark strings – the whole supported, about twelve feet above the mud and water, by teak piles. The floor is of poles laid side by side. On the north, west and south we have an extensive view of mud flats; on the east we see the mountains looking over atap roofs. To-day we have been out through the market trying to teach the true doctrines. Miss Dean stops at one house and I at the next, where the people seem to wish to

> hear. They listen willingly, sometimes eagerly. I asked a man this morning if he thought Jesus' word were true. He said, "My heart is dark – I do not understand; but if you go on and teach me, perhaps I shall believe . . .[33]

On more than one occasion Fielde described her daily life in the mission as one of contentment, though "monotonous," immersing herself in the intricacies of the Chinese language during the rainy season. After three years in Siam she summarized her experience:

> I found that I had spent one-third of my time at the outstations and other villages, the remainder in Bangkok, and had distributed several hundreds of books, talking as I was able, of the Gospel to those to whom I gave the books. . . . Can I be content to work as I am now doing? It seems to me wise and right that I should work as I am now doing. I cannot unloose the cords that hold me to Bangkok. I do not think I could live anywhere else now.

She described a typical day in a humorous letter to her friend, Miss Sands, with whom she had crossed the Pacific Ocean.[34] Her day began with chapel, where she played "the squeakiest of melodeons," the unintentional discordant notes and off-key sounds attracting the Chinese, whom she jokingly claimed had educated ears. The music continued until enough passers-by had gathered for her Chinese assistant to preach. Afternoons were reserved for the learning of Chinese, and on the occasional evening she went out to dinner – a quiet life, which she increasingly found unsatisfactory, claiming that as she grew older she "cared more for living things and less for books, though I still prefer a lively book to some live people." In a land where help was very cheap she had a cook who unfortunately was an alcoholic, known to have drunk the preserving fluid of reptiles: "unhappily for me, to keep his spirits up, he takes some spirits down. When this happens, as it did tonight, I get a burned cutlet for dinner." Croquet was played almost every evening except Wednesdays, which were taken up with choir practice.

The balm of travel was permitted for reasons of health only, and since Fielde enjoyed exceptional health, she was kept working. She still managed to visit distant heathens, the Buddhist temples at Anghin, and she observed a total eclipse of the Sun on the Malaysian peninsula, an impressive event attended by the King of Siam, many nobles, Europeans, and the Governor of Singapore. Not long after, the King died of a fever leaving 250 widows, and seventy children. Her letter to Miss Sands ends with characteristic charm: "If you see anyone I love please tell them so. The nearest and only duty you need perform to fill my request is to turn to the mirror."

Though William Dean was a kindly, decent man, solicitous of Fielde's "best interests," his attitude toward women was similar to that of the

Baptist Board to which he answered. In his view, women should be married and in the home raising children, and the role of women missionaries should be restricted and supervised. Dean's strong views reinforced the Baptist stereotype held by other Christian missionaries, summarized by Barr: "Nineteenth-century Baptists, with their rigid Calvinism and bald liturgy, were seldom renowned for tolerance or magnanimity."[35] Dean did not approve of Fielde's unaccompanied expeditions, where she spent months in the homes of Christian Chinese, perfecting her knowledge of the language and of Chinese ways, but she continued to do so, escaping Dean's direct supervision in distant villages, and flouting his authority. As her facility with the language left Dean's far behind, and her sympathy, understanding, and admiration of the Chinese grew, the rift between them increased. Seabrook has commented that "It must have frustrated Fielde that the better equipped she became to do missionary work, the more Dean tried to restrict her."[36] In contrast to Fielde's increasing sensitivity to the ordinary Chinese, Dean looked upon them condescendingly, and almost as adversaries, to be set right for their own good. The language of this "warrior for God" was replete with military metaphors and allusions[37] – "the war has not ended," "needed reinforcements," he will persevere until he is in a "soldier's grave."[38] In more concrete matters of forceful persuasion, he wrote: "The presence of a ship-of-war from the United States has done much to improve the nations respect for our country . . . [and the mission]," testimony to the fact that Western missionaries operated under the protection of Western arms.[39]

As a worker, Fielde was irreproachable, thorough, and tireless. Dean's early letters are filled with praise of her cheerfulness and total commitment. But Fielde did not take instructions or advice without examination, for she had ideas of her own, and from time to time confrontations, albeit polite, arose which in time erupted into open warfare. While Fielde's communications to the Board and the *BMM* were intriguing, Dean continued to appeal for help, for young men to aid in the great cause, complaining that he was sent *only* young women (Fielde). He emphasized that they operated in a land of "pirates and pestilence, of robbers and rapine" particularly dangerous to young ladies,[40] – utterly un-American – but he sang the praises of the land, its beauty, and its healthful climate, trying to sell his struggling mission to prospective male missionaries; uplifting stories of successful conversions abounded in his letters.

After observing the entire missionary effort in Bangkok, and studying the records, Fielde wrote two letters to the *BMM* with information that could only be described as devastating, and they were sent, quite obviously, without Dean's blessings. In October 1868 she reported that over the thirty-six years of their existence (since Dean's arrival), Christian missions in Siam employed fifteen missionaries for an average of thirteen years each, resulting in fewer than three native Christians (of dubious conviction) per missionary. The performance was poor, Buddhism was as strong as ever among all classes, the Prime Minister was a "rank infidel," and the King signed letters to a missionary: "Your friend, but a sincere hater of Christianity."[41] Reports of successful conversions of Siamese by missionaries were naively optimistic and sad – one Laos man at Wongtako was baptized, another half-dozen young men were converted (but missionaries soon learned that at least two were then executed). To straighten things out with the King the missionaries attended Court, were graciously received, and afterward the king acted as he saw fit – quixotically, unpredictably, and with no regard for the Christian faith and its representatives. Unsettled, they still remained confident of the ultimate triumph of Christianity.[42]

> *Statistics of Missions in Bangkok*. In considering what has been done for the Chinese here, I find that fourteen Protestant missionaries, under various Societies have labored among the Chinese in Bangkok. Of this number, three have died, and three have returned to the United States, in less than two years from their arrival here. Of the remainder, six have removed from here to China. Omitting all those who have lived in the country less than two years, there have been seven male missionaries, averaging eight years each, who have worked here among the Chinese, between the years 1834 and 1869. The present number of nominal Chinese Christians is eighty.
>
> Of these, I fear some would not bear any true test of their Christianity. To the eyes of those who look at missions from the other side of the world, increase of members means progress; but sometimes persons are added to the church, when there is little in their habit of thought and course of action, to distinguish them from the heathen.[43]

Fielde's critical mind can be seen at work. In scientific fashion, she gathered the data, and the numbers she assembled made for a harsh judgment. Her statistical approach, however simple, was effective, and prefigured her later involvement in science. Fielde's shrewd analysis was a tonic for the many letters sent in by enthusiastic missionaries, rejoicing that in the past month they had succeeded in converting two or ten Chinese – a rather sad score-card. In fact, the reporting to missionary boards of numbers of conversions, "missionary arithmetic," was an intimidating exercise for field missionaries, one that "terrorized" them because their continued existence depended on this index of success.[44] One can only imagine Dean's reaction to these open letters, written by a novice, and a female at that! Looking at the numbers, Fielde was not sanguine about the victory of the evangelical movement in Asia, and particularly in China:

> It took an army of two millions of men and cost six billions of dollars to set free three million bondmen in America. Here in China and Siam alone are four hundred millions of people in a thraldom far more dreadful than any African slave – that of a living soul bound to a dead god,

> with all the powers of darkness holding the chain. Against them are arrayed a force of two hundred men and women. . . . It cannot be done.[45]

Still, she was hopeful, fueled by the credo embodied in her pronouncements, "Go and teach," and "I do not believe our Lord sends His servants on useless errands." Perhaps modest success could be won through innovations which she was beginning to formulate.

Though Fielde was in a vulnerable situation, she would not compromise her principles to establish peace with her superior. Fearless, shrewd, and able to communicate, she knew how to look after herself; by nature, she was not a passive victim. Fielde established a regular correspondence with Josiah Warren, the Corresponding Secretary for the Executive Committee of the American Baptist Missionary Union ABMU in Boston, the organization that supported and oversaw the Bangkok mission. Obviously, through him, Dean was circumvented. The Board could be informed of what was going on in Bangkok from a second source, so that the Board was placed in the position of mediating between Dean and Fielde. Fielde became friendly and almost personal with Warren, her correspondent, and, while he was not openly partisan, he was sympathetic to her views. Despite the fact that she was a woman meddling in men's affairs, she made sensible suggestions born of her own experience, which she knew would reach the Board – novice missionaries should learn the Chinese language in China *before* coming to Siam, since in Bangkok they might be confused by four spoken dialects of Chinese, and Siamese itself.[46] She also suggested that a better system of acquiring information about travel to and from the Orient should be organized – people waited months for a booking while ships with empty cabins plied the route.[47]

The issue of salary arose soon after Fielde's arrival. She was allotted $300 annually, plus $100 for medical expenses and travel which, if needed, could also be considered as salary. She had made three times as much as a teacher in New York State. Fielde pointed out that with expenses being at least as great in Bangkok as at home, and her expenses being the same as those of a man, she needed at least $600 a year, ($500 + $100), the salary that her "husband" Cyrus Chilcott had found necessary. Routinely, single women were paid 60 percent of a man's salary. Fielde sent a detailed account of her expenses, and wrote: "I cannot see why an unmarried woman giving all her time to missionary work, paying all her own expenses, having precisely the same or equal expenses – does not require and should not receive the same salary as an unmarried man."[48] After two years of deliberation she was informed by Warren that her salary was to be $500 plus $100 for medical expenses, retroactive for one year, and that the pay scale for all single women in Asian missions would be similarly adjusted. Fielde answered that she would not need all of the retroactive pay since she survived by selling some of her unneeded household goods, for she had no financial reserves to draw on. Part of Fielde's salary was sent back to America to support her mother and father. The generous medical allowance would suggest that affliction of missionaries by fevers and other mysterious diseases was common, and to be expected.

In contrast to the usual procedure of single women living with a couple, Fielde had been living by herself in quarters originally assigned to Chilcott. The arrangement was to come to an end with Dean's decision that a new missionary couple with a child, the Lisles, were to share Fielde's space. An alarmed Fielde wrote a letter of protest to Warren and the Committee. She argued that at the end of a day's work everyone was entitled to a quiet time of privacy, to renew one's self. She pleaded not to be inflicted on the Lisles, and for the time being, she won this battle.[49] Increasingly thwarted by Dean and the Committee, who were opposed to her desire to evangelize in the country and to live with the Chinese, she was relegated to handing out religious literature to the illiterate, and making pathetic attempts at playing a musical instrument at evangelical meetings – monotonous labors which Dean believed were fit for a "widow," a single woman.

Very few single women taken up with the noble evangelical mission would have insisted on higher pay, however little the pay might be. They were expected to live without, to submit to guidance, and not to complain. Living with a married couple was usually a suitable arrangement, since living alone was felt to be an unhealthy situation for a single woman. Fielde was quite different: a superior, independent intellect, a natural organizer and thinker who stood up for what she thought to be right – for her own good and that of her cause. She cherished her hours alone, thinking, reading, gardening, writing articles for publications, and letters to her many friends, and she saw her friends when she chose to – just like a man. Considering the time and place, and the certain beliefs of the people with whom she worked, Fielde was playing a risky game, one from which she could not refrain, for compliance for her meant suffocation.

Threatened both personally and professionally, Fielde continued to communicate with Warren. She expressed herself clearly, firmly, and politely, the embodiment of reason, rarely rising to passionate polemic. Since letters to Warren were her only means of defending herself, she carefully thought out, and constructed her messages to have their maximum effect. In matters of business, she removed herself – the "I" – and spoke "objectively" in the third person.[50] Her arguments, based on facts, and views, were models of felicitous diplomacy, and coming from a woman, they were unprecedented, and unsettling. Her persuasive letters were a subtle mix of clear-cut demands and suggestions, and a passiveness and submission to the will of Warren and the Committee. Without irony, she thanked them for the "perfect kindness" with which they had always regarded her. In another letter to Warren, a despairing Fielde wrote: "And because in your letters you are so good to me, you tempt me strongly to say 'I am wrong; I repent; I will reform.' . . . But in my heart I do not think I am wrong." She ends the message with a pathetic "What *can* I do?" Perhaps, intuitively, she was a master manipulator and strategist, a daughter dealing with an omniscient father figure, Warren, and later with his successor, John N. Murdock – at one moment helpless and passive, and at another demanding and galvanized to action – a blend of vulnerability and strength. It was the only way a strong-willed, opinionated female could survive.

Much to Dean's chagrin, Fielde's writing, so popular in America, induced many single women to write to him requesting to come to Bangkok, and the problem of how best to employ single women became pressing. Though few in number in the Baptist mission in the late 1860s, increasingly they wanted entry into the missionary movement. Fielde outlined a plan whereby a mission could be run effectively by a team of four women, with a man to do the preaching. "These women must be of very thorough education, of very great intellect – of very brave heart, and very strong in body. If then they are willing to forsake the high positions they might adorn in cultured society, to live alone among filthy, unclothed barbarians, their missionary spirit is beyond questioning."

The word of a male pastor in China was apparently far more convincing than that of a female, but all other functions could be carried out by women. It was not fitting for females to preach to males. Fielde pointed out that since wives of missionaries, burdened as they were with children, and "regarded as extensions of their husband," made little direct contribution to evangelism, two single females were more valuable, per dollar spent, than a married couple in which only one could interact with the Chinese. In remote missions, married women were placed in jeopardy by giving birth under poor conditions. Of the four women in the unit, one could assist the Pastor, and could teach native assistants, a second would keep house, and look after medical matters, a third would be responsible for the teaching of children, and a fourth would visit and teach in the homes.[51] A stable domicile for single women was thereby formed, comparable to a married household. Ludicrously, since single women who lived with a married couple were often regarded by the Chinese (perhaps with a wink) as concubines of the husband, this undermined the missionaries' argument against concubinage and polygamy whereas four women living together would be considered an irreproachable arrangement. By 1919, 13 percent of all missions in China were run solely by women living in stable residences.[52]

However much Fielde wrote and presented her reasoned argument, Dean, Warren, and the Board would not change their entrenched beliefs, and so Fielde came to realize that she was fighting a losing battle. Well aware of her abilities, Warren greatly admired her and had her letters published in the *BMM*. Writing to William Ashmore, a missionary in China, he commented:

> Miss Fielde is a very able woman, and very decided in her preferences. I hope she will be useful. If she had a strong companion by her side, a man her equal, the prospects of her usefulness would not be impaired.

> Some of her letters indicate a breadth of view, together with a degree of penetration, and quick intuitive insight, which I seldom see elsewhere. She uses the English language with uncommon power, and has a most refreshing way of putting things. One conscious of so much power, would not easily be put into leading strings.[53]

Warren did not deny Fielde's ability. His praise, which he kept from Fielde, is unstinting, but he revealed a masculine bias. He, the Board, and Dean felt that women could not operate alone, however talented and intelligent, for like children they should be seen but not heard, and that communications should only be between men, intelligent as Fielde's comments were. Warren also felt that for Fielde to be a good missionary, she would have to learn to take orders. If only she was the wife of a missionary, busy with children, she would fit into an established role, and her word could be conveyed through her husband. The plight of women was brilliantly delineated by the suffragist Julia Ward Howe, author of *The Battle Hymn of the Republic*:

> The cruel kindness of the old doctrine that women should be worked for, and should not work, that their influence should be felt, but not recognized, that they should hear and see, but neither appear nor speak – all this belongs now to the record of things which, once measurably true, have become fabulous.[54]

Fielde was deeply troubled by the threat of change in her living arrangements, and by the duties she was expected to perform. What was her "special mission" to be in Bangkok? She had come to Siam to teach, and if necessary to build a school, but she found that most Chinese in Bangkok were single males, laborers, and that in the few Chinese families she could reach, the wives and children spoke Siamese, a language she and other missionaries did not know. There was no future here, since education was not in demand, prompting Fielde to write: "Without presuming to criticize or disparage anyone's plans, it seems to me there is a vast deal of strength expended for nought among us by taking very remote routes to an immediate point." Despite Dean's objections, Warren and the Committee were inclined to agree with Fielde who insisted that Bangkok was not the place to build schools. It was a victory of sorts that effectively eliminated her own job. Warren, realizing how unhappy she was in Bangkok, mentioned that perhaps she would do better in a mission in Swatow, China, whose head was William Ashmore. Fielde had already been corresponding with Ashmore, and had found him to be enlightened and sympathetic, but she never formally requested a transfer.

In the continuing conflict between Dean and Fielde, she was not only a sharper, more effective communicator; she also had the stronger arguments. Though her information convinced Warren and the Committee that perhaps the missionary effort among the Chinese of Bangkok should be reduced, no immediate action was taken. Dean and a newly arrived ally, Sylvester B. Partridge, felt that hostilities could end only with the recall of Fielde, who they believed was a disruptive element in the small mission, "dangerous to the interests of the cause." She "takes councel only of herself, and her independent action in the mission works like a wheel out of gear."[55] Providing reasons for sending her home, they informed the Committee that Fielde was not a true Baptist but a Universalist who chose to consort with the European community, bankers, diplomats, and other "unbelievers" not affiliated with the Church, rather than with members of the mission. She indulged in card-playing and attended dancing parties, forbidden by Baptists. She shocked them by saying "I desire to be *good*, but I do not wish to be *Pious*," and "I cannot admit in my heart that Jesus Christ, an innocent being, should suffer for my sins. . . . She does not seem to understand how anything that is not in itself wrong can become wrong by association or other circumstances."[56] Clearly, Fielde's views on religious doctrine were either changing or being expressed for the first time, deviating substantially from the Baptist orthodoxy of her superiors.

While Dean's attitude toward Easterners and Westerners not associated with the mission was guarded, Fielde was open and friendly. Dean acknowledged that she was popular outside the mission community. His letter had been sent to the Committee through the Reverend B. Stowe, the Committee's Chairman, rather than through the normal channel – Corresponding Secretary Warren – because he felt that Warren was biased in Fielde's favor. Warren wrote to Fielde that the "incredible" charges placed her in "extreme peril."[57]

In response to the accusations, Fielde wrote Warren a lengthy letter of carefully chosen words, playing upon Warren's interest in her, asking him for guidance and, in a sense, giving him the satisfaction of confirming his belief that women could not operate without a strong (masculine), guiding hand. Explicitly, she threw herself on his mercy, a confused and errant child, all interwoven with a strong rebuttal of the accusations.[58]

Fielde claimed that the people with whom she associated were of the highest quality and virtue, despite the fact that they did not belong to the church – doctors and consular officials, their wives and daughters. However, justifying playing cards and dancing, which Fielde believed were not morally wrong, was a more difficult task. She expressed herself delicately, but she was made to squirm – a naughty girl justifying her misdemeanors. Fielde stated that she played cards only once, when she was confined to bed through illness. She dismissed card-playing as a trivial activity, "stupid" and "stupifying," an activity hardly worth thinking about. As for dancing, she felt that it was a wholesome activity, good exercise, on a par with croquet or hoops, which were approved of by Baptists. She had danced only with religious and respectable people – an "innocent and easy way of being happy." "If the Baptist Church condemns dancing *per se* – then I think the Baptist church is wrong in that particular. That is Puritanism, not religion . . . the capacity to be happy in so childish a thing as dancing seems to me almost a virtue." She always liked to dance, and felt as close to God when dancing as when she was on her knees praying.

Despite Fielde's image as a strong, independent woman, her errant behavior had arisen through her loneliness and isolation, something Warren could understand. She insisted on her privacy, but she also needed society because there were no galleries, concerts or lectures, not much to do, and no companionship for her. "In the regular order of things, I *sleep*, I *eat*, I *work*, I *live alone*." She was unhappy, unappreciated, living in a hostile setting where there were

> petty envies, the small back-bitings, the great jealousies, the conscientious wickedness of the "saints". . . . Between Dr. Dean and myself there is a radical and irreconcilable difference of life-purpose . . . the sentiment. "*I am the mission*," is so strong in him as to result in a disregard, not only for the just consideration due an associate, but a violation of the common rights of property. . . . He has always rendered it impossible to me to make my *house* a *home*.[59]

Stoically, she accepted the reproach, and the humiliating affair came to an end, but resentment lingered. Her letter had been convincing, and sufficiently conciliatory to permit her to stay, but she was to refrain from card-playing and dancing. In effect, she was told that she should keep her beliefs to herself, but she must fit in if she wished to remain in the mission. Since Fielde had gone astray because of isolation and loneliness, the Committee implored her, the Deans and Partridges to make amends and live in harmony.[60] Once again Dean was frustrated, convinced that Fielde was protected by Warren. Clearly, Fielde's religion and social behavior were evolving in ways that could only lead to conflict with a male-dominated, Baptist orthodoxy.

Miserable and isolated, she took less care to conceal her blasphemous opinions, and she engaged in an activity that would have truly shocked her superiors. Baptist credo forbade smoking and the drinking of alcohol – how would they have judged one of their own (female) missionaries who smoked hashish? Realizing that this activity would be utterly and absolutely unacceptable to the Board, Fielde had enough sense to conceal her secret until many years later when she was no longer under their control. Hashish provided her with unique pleasures in her time of despair, but it did not take command of this disciplined woman, and in the end it was hardly more than a pharmacological experiment.

Her curiosity had been aroused by the sight of natives under the influence of hashish, and she wondered exactly what they were experiencing and what the mental state of these "sufferers" was. Finding herself in a small village away from the mission where there were no Westerners, which assured her complete isolation, she fashioned a pipe with which she "smoked six thimblefuls of the *kang cha*. The smoke was stifling, but I persevered in puffing until I felt luxuriously quiet." She "became conscious of dual being," her double standing in a radiant, pillared hall of great beauty. "I was infinitely joyous. Every atom in me quivered in unspeakable spiritual bliss . . . I am now in Heaven," and then she fell into a deep sleep.

Two weeks later she repeated the experiment. This time, before finishing smoking, she "began to respire loudly with gaspings, accompanied with violent but painless involuntary contraction states of the muscles." She seemed to pass back and forth through sleeping and waking so that dreams melded with conciousness; again, she was aware of a dual state.

> My duplicate became a boundless sea, ravishingly cool, utterly free, rising in vast billows under an illimitable sky, and feeling in every drop of every wave the transport of my own pulsations. Then I became a continent with wide meadows and verdant forests. A breeze swept over me and rustled all my leaves; I felt my vital forces waking in every blade of grass and every spreading tree, sending them gently upward. The thrill of growth was in them all, and growth was ecstasy. This ended in profound slumber.

It hardly takes a psychiatrist to divine the meaning of this efflorescence.

A few days later she smoked *kang cha* again, but it had no effect. One month later she took twice the usual dose, determined to record her experiences with pencil in hand. Though spatial judgment seemed normal, judgment of time was distorted. Her "mind was exalted by an indescribable increase of consciousness. Thoughts crowded upon me in numbers sufficient, could they have been recorded, to have filled the world with new books. The causes of clairvoyance, hypnotism, and other psychic phenomena became temporarily plain to me. . . . I had not dual but multiple existence . . . passing from dream to dream with such speed as to make several distinct dreams seem each to be unbroken." After a long sleep she awoke to find she had written only parts of words, words with little relationship to each other, and a pregnant "Spiritualism comprehended."

Mindful of the dangers of addiction to hashish, a curious but disciplined Fielde never smoked again, and in later years she was shocked that she had indulged in such a foolish and dangerous activity. She admitted that "during many years thereafter, drudgery or monotony always made me unwisely meditate on this beatification, and then, wisely, on its accompanying perdition." Two decades later she published a detailed account of hashish intoxication in the medical journal *Therapeutic Gazette*, hoping that it would contribute to an understanding of consciousness. The article was widely reproduced in European journals.[61]

With Dean trying to unearth violation of Baptist orthodoxy, and Fielde not hiding her despair, it was inevitable that the truce at the Bangkok mission would break down. Although she was under surveillance, Fielde continued to see her "unbelieving," secular friends, but she did not play cards or dance. She did however stoke the fire of piety by becoming friendly with the American Consul, sometimes visiting him for lengthy times, even when his wife was away, playing the role of hostess at Consular Washington's birthday party, and remaining well into the morning after guests had left. Outraged by this indiscreet behavior, a letter was dispatched by Dean to the Corresponding Secretary informing him of Fielde's egregious behaviour.[62] The grievance did not go to the Committee through the hands of a sympathetic Warren because he was seriously ill at the time, and had been replaced by the Reverend John N. Murdock. The shocking charges led to the desired response. She was ordered to return home – "rise up and come away, quietly but quickly."[63] This outraged indictment seems strange in view of the fact that male missionaries did not object to women being accompanied by Chinese men without an appropriate chaperone.

Fielde, the first and only single female missionary at the Bangkok station, left Siam in November 1871, never to return, and indeed uncertain about her future as a Baptist missionary. She had spent five years in the mission, a period of learning and preparation for the following decades she was to spend in China. On her way home to America, not really knowing what the future would bring, she spent a week in Swatow, on the South China Sea, almost two hundred miles north of Hong Kong, where they spoke the same Chinese dialect as in Bangkok. In contrast to the hostility of Dr. Dean, her hosts in Swatow, William Ashmore, a humane, liberal scholar, and head of the mission, and his wife Eliza, were warm and welcoming, "unexpectedly" impressed by her ability, "high motives," her facility with the Chinese language, and her cheerful personality.[64] Fielde and Mrs. Ashmore became close, lifelong friends. Discussions with Fielde convinced Ashmore that Fielde's religious beliefs were deep, sincere, and compatible with the tenets of Baptist orthodoxy on such matters as "Love of Christ and Love of Man," though Fielde tended to emphasize man over religious belief. She needed something beyond "serving Christ alone."[65] The other missionaries, and converts of Swatow were open and friendly, and urged Fielde to return to their mission. Taken with their sincerity, she promised to do so if it was at all possible. She spoke to many Chinese women, and concluded that they could be the focus of her efforts, a useful undertaking fully approved of by Ashmore. Sympathy for the Chinese and physical stamina were required – both were plentiful in Fielde. But before her lay the daunting task of convincing the Committee in Boston that she was fit for the missionary calling.

4 Passage through America

Fielde had been away for six years. When she had sailed for Bangkok in late 1865, the Civil War had just ended, the nation was still in shock over Lincoln's assassination, and a hapless Andrew Johnson was President. The Reconstruction period was being set in place, and the Fourteenth and Fifteenth Amendments of the Constitution were passed giving citizenship and the right to vote to all who were born in the U.S.A., or were naturalized; this included blacks, but women's suffrage was set aside, an act that alienated many feminist leaders from male-dominated radical Republican and reformist organizations. Women's suffrage would come about only through women's efforts and leadership.[1] The U.S.A. was bursting with energy, rife with corruption, and in turmoil over Reconstruction.

The errant missionary reached Boston on January 17, 1872, and the very next day a full hearing on the Bangkok affair was held by the Baptist Executive Committee at its headquarters, Missionary Rooms, 12 Bedford Street. Ashmore had prepared the way for the accused by writing a strong letter of support to help the Committee understand Fielde's predicament, and to provide a perspective that might counter Dean's charges. Having been Dean's student, Ashmore was familiar with his heavy-handed, authoritarian ways that were bound to antagonize Fielde. He wrote approvingly of her religious beliefs, and of her "painful awareness" of some of her transgressions; she knew she had made "mistakes" of a social nature, which Ashmore said, frankly, she would probably make again in Swatow. He assured the Committee that if she was permitted to remain a missionary, she would find a home in Swatow where she would be of great use.[2]

A penitential Fielde defended herself against Dean's charges with remarkable rhetorical skill. She was popular with the members of the Committee, and they were willing to bend, to give her the benefit of any doubt. As if in a court of law, letters from Baptist and Presbyterian missionaries were presented attesting to Fielde's high moral character. No one had ever heard Fielde actually berate Dean in public. A letter from the American Consul stated that he spent time with Miss Fielde because she gave him French lessons for a fee that was set by Dean himself. A journey with the Consul and his children while his wife was in America sounded deplorable, until the

Consul pointed out to the Committee that his children were adults. With a degree of repentance that satisfied the Committee, and with the respected Ashmore's backing, Fielde was hastily cleared of all charges. The Committee concluded that "Miss Fielde has not been involved in greater imperfections in judgment and conduct than are common to Christians everywhere."[3] Although there must have been lingering doubts about her tendency to follow the dictates of her own conscience at the peril of deviating from strict Baptist dogma, the Committee was probably pleased to permit someone so appealing and effective, a celebrity in America, to return to Swatow. Fielde was now the first unmarried female evangelist at the mission with an official appointment of her own, unlike her position in Siam which was unofficial, tentative, and the result of chance.

However favorable the outcome, Fielde must have realized that she had been cleared by a jury of men of charges brought against her by men, and it was they who defined what was proper behavior for a woman. There were no real female models in the missionary field who might serve as a guide.[4] Though she asserted herself in some ways, there was no alternative for a strong, self-confident woman but to fit in and operate as best she could. There was nothing radical about this small town girl, nor was she boastful, but she did express her opinions, and was openly critical, something new in the male-dominated missionary field. Even she, at times, felt it necessary to convey the illusion of helplessness, and dependency, and an eagerness to comply with male dictates – a device for survival of the dominated among the dominant, females among males.

The exoneration of Fielde could also be attributed to the growing influence of women in the evangelical movement. Womens' boards, which were first organized in the early 1870s, raised significant amounts of money for the missions, and with the dollars came a voice that was heeded by male leaders.[5] Young women of quality and stamina were volunteering for missionary work in increasing numbers. They were now welcomed, a great source of help, especially since male volunteers were always in short supply. With women looking over its shoulder, the Committee was inclined to treat Fielde gently and fairly. But there may have been another motive for sending Fielde back to China, since she was so independent and articulate, and not above urging innovation on a conservative Executive Committee, which may have preferred to have Fielde far away, a kind of banishment to neutralize a troublemaker. The leadership of the Baptist mission was grappling with an unfamiliar problem. One senses that they were in a panic, for they had never been challenged by anyone like Fielde, the forerunner of a new kind of person – intelligent, with opinions of her own, who could defend herself, and could not be easily silenced. Though devout, she seemed to be oblivious of some rules of her church which were considered sacred doctrine. As a woman she was supposed to be the standard-bearer of decorum and morality, and to accept the decisions of masculine authority without complaint.

Dean was now in a difficult position, for his dictatorial style, his passion, and his narrow view of a woman's place in the world (albeit rather conventional) had prompted him to trifle with the truth. Dean had been enraged that this woman with "the attractive smile and the enticing words of a card-playing dance girl," was so influential.[6] He was rebuked by Murdock for his behavior, and charged with overstepping "the courtesy due to your bretheren." Murdock mentioned that during the hearing the Committee was disturbed to learn that Dean had personally flogged two native men, one of them Fielde's teacher, and the other a carpenter who worked at the mission. A dismayed Fielde had informed the Committee that her relationship with Dean had been destroyed by these violent acts. She also revealed that Dean insisted on knowing what she was writing to the Executive Committee. The Committee, hinting at chastisement, discussed the possibility of closing the Bangkok mission, and asked for detailed and accurate information about its activities and the nature of the converts, upon which members could evaluate the efficiency of the enterprise.[7] The conclusions Fielde had reached were found to be correct, and the Bangkok mission was again perilously close to being abandoned, although it managed to survive through Dean's efforts.

Fielde spent the next half-year in America traveling, and speaking to men and women about missionary life in China, and the Eastern experience. She enthralled her large audiences with colorful accounts of China, the suffering of its people, and their great need to accept Christ. The Board was delighted with her efforts, not only for the funds generated, but for the broadcast of information on the evangelical movement. While members of the Board would not take the opinions and suggestions of a single woman too seriously, they were happy to have her represent the Baptist Missionary Union to the public. Through her appealing lectures, and writing, both in English and Chinese, Fielde became a major publicist for the missionary effort and for the Baptist Union during the next few decades. She made many new woman friends, some wealthy, with whom she maintained contact amidst assurances that she would not lack funds for her work. In New York, after speaking at the Fifth Avenue Baptist Church, she met and became a close, lifelong friend of Mrs. E.M. Cauldwell, who generously supported her and the Swatow mission.

With her speaking engagements over, she returned to China with some hope, having earned an official position following a turmoil that could have ended her career as a missionary. Her superior, Ashmore, was highly supportive of her "special mission" – a new approach to the conversion of the Chinese to Christianity, and the improvement of the wretched lot of Chinese women, goals to which she was passionately devoted. For a goose who was laying golden eggs, the Committee provided the mission with $500 to construct suitable living quarters for Fielde, attached to Ashmore's house. Still, she felt "hedged in," writing "With my strong body in its prime, with my mind at the peak of its power, with an intense and unvarying desire to be used by God – for whatever object is most really His . . . [yet] . . . I am involved in doubt."[8] The rigid code of the Baptist church, which she felt had little to do with true religion, seemed to be a harassment. Could she carry out good works, to which she was dedicated, despite the obstacle of narrow dogma?

An extensive correspondence between Fielde and Ashmore, Murdock, Partridge, and Warren attests to their concern for the spiritual welfare of this dancing and card-playing woman. These devout men, who had a great concern for her, agonized over the dilemma. They recognized her remarkable abilities which could be put to good use in the evangelical movement, they believed in her deep religious feeling and high motives, but they found her to be willful and defiant in her desire to do as she pleased in her private life, and her persistence in scandalous behavior could reduce her effectiveness in the conversion of the heathen. Ashmore felt that the subject was disturbing and "painful."[9] Sometimes, Murdock could not sleep; he woke up at night and prayed for her, crying out loud, and he was thunderstruck when he learned *after* the Committee inquiry that she had danced on the ship taking her home to America. He had written to her: "It is a marvel to me how you can receive a married gentleman to your house day after day and remain with him for hours together at each meeting, and that when his wife is thousands of miles away, without being aware that it would be considered an impropriety."[10] At another time Murdock wrote: "we all cherish confidence in the purity of your life and the righteousness of your motives."[11]

She erred only in society, and they were all willing to accept her for what she was. In a letter to Partridge, Murdock summarized the situation:

> If she should be sustained in her present sincere purpose to know nothing but her work among the poor heathen and if Christ should bestow upon her his meek and teachable and self-denying spirit, she will be greatly useful. Her powers are of no common order; she is eminently tender-hearted; she is ready to labor and to suffer, if need be; she believes in God and wishes to do His will. And yet I see there is something in her that may thwart all these powers and tendencies, unless a tender and loving human interest shall hold her in a gentle restraint.[12]

This restraint would be the task of Ashmore and Partridge at Swatow. An undaunted Fielde wrote to Murdock, "I think it very probable that we shall dance in heaven."

Fielde began her long eastward trip to the Orient on the steamship *Australia* in New York, bound for Dublin, the first part of a long journey through Europe and Asia to Swatow. When she left, Ulysses S. Grant was beginning his second term as a Republican president of a country in turmoil, beset with rampant corruption in high places. Fielde's opinions on political and economic problems were never recorded in articles or letters; we can only guess that, like everyone else, she was troubled by the scandal in Washington. The financial panic of 1873 and the subsequent depression created great difficulties for charitable institutions such as the Baptist Missionary Board, but these matters did not seem to be of noticeable concern to Fielde.

By the early 1870s, a growing boldness among women was finding expression in the agitation of suffragists; respectable middle- and upper-class ladies were becoming involved in reform. Women were now organized into national groups with chapters in most cities, and these groups were communicating with similar groups in Europe.[13] Increasing numbers of women, one of whom was Adele Fielde, were traveling without benefit of male companionship and protection.[14] Oddly, all details, including selection of her berth, had been left to a devoted Dr. Murdock. When she boarded the *Australia* she had a plan for an incredibly ambitious tour of several European countries, beginning with Ireland, but she had only the vaguest idea of who her traveling companions would be. "When I left America, I thought Providence had provided all that was necessary for my long desired visit to Europe, except a traveling companion, and lo! I found her, all cut-out and equipped for me, ensconced in my room on board the *Australia*. Miss Ritchie is to travel with me." Miss Carol Agatha Ritchie of Pittsburgh was just the right person, a most compatible room-mate, but without Fielde's stamina.

Fielde's European trip, begun on July 13, 1872, was fully documented in a diary with detailed commentaries richly enhanced by etchings and photographs of churches, cathedrals, castles, and monuments. It was in fact a long letter that could have been converted into a publishable travelog, but this was never done. The account revealed her discerning eye, her intelligence, and her wit.[15] The hilarity and fun that her college room-mate Lucretia Chilcott spoke of become apparent in descriptions of her shipboard companions, most of whom were ill because of rough seas:

> The thirty five sea-sick ladies are attended by the stewardess, Mrs. Spence – she, much to her own comfort – in her office, but greatly to the disadvantage of her patients, lost the senses of taste and smell in falling down a hatch last year. The dear old creature's memory suffered too in the fall, and after much discipline, my wants were subdued one morning to a cold potato for breakfast – at noon. Mrs. Spence came and said she forgot to bring the potato in the morning, and would I try it for lunch! The only amusing thing about the ship during those sea-sick days, was the remarks of the sufferers. . . . We have seven clergymen on board besides a Mormon missionary in steerage. One sits at the prow and composes *very* blank verse . . . one goes about with a countenance which says "Lord receive my spirit" at every pitch of the vessel; one preaches several times Sunday with a huge bass voice, and speaks in a small treble all the rest of the week; one is going to England for his bride, and has told each of his fellow passengers, separately and confidentially how the courting was done; one looks as if he would flee before a mouse – and tells a good story of his overcoming bears and sharks in Australia and California; one is sick in his head, and one is a little disordered in his

> heart. With such variety in the greater lights – no need to describe the lesser. Were it not that I have *known* a preacher who was a grand specimen of manhood, I should say piety, when it becomes chronic, is dangerous.

She was, of course, referring to her dead fiancé Cyrus Chilcott, whose excellence was beyond compare.

Ireland was sighted on the afternoon of July 24, and by the next day they were touring Londonderry in a two-wheeled carriage to visit the Giant's Causeway. Fielde's enthusiastic but slightly musty account of this, as with all other tourist attractions, included descriptions of major monuments, cathedrals and buildings, historical events, legends, and myths. Special mention was always made of birthplaces and graves of poets, writers, and historic personages – Swift, Goldsmith, Wellington. The quintessential tourist, her account would rival that of a knowledgable local guide with a flair for the dramatic. She was indefatigable as she wore out her companions at the Giant's Causeway:

> and while Miss Ritchie rested, I went and had a bath in the chill salt waves – then walked over the sand hills. In that hour – walking and lying alone on the heath, how I thanked God that he had let me come to see Europe . . . I was very happy in that fresh sea air, on the billowy hills among the heather.

At Belfast and Dublin, they encountered other American tourists with whom friendships were instantly established as the usual, formal barriers were dropped. In this new situation, reserve gave way to the need to reassure each other in a foreign land, to lessen their sense of vulnerability, and to get quick advice from the experience of others. Networks of travelers meeting here and there were established, and invariably, no matter from where in the U.S.A. they came, someone learned that their close friend back home was a second cousin of someone's Aunt Mary – an extended American family.

There were comments in Fielde's diary that would not appear in the usual travel guide. Inevitably, the tourist is a natural prey of the poor of the country, and in Ireland so many were very poor. Fielde's experience led to unflattering remarks which reflected the open disdain many Americans expressed against impoverished Irish immigrants: "Something halfway between beggary and extortion marks the intercourse of travelers with the Irish. . . . The ignorance of the common people is amazing."

Then on to Limerick, and to Killarney, where she was enraptured by the beauty, music, and history there. She "came to a blind piper concealed under a rock . . . a group of peasants, old and ugly and wretched were dancing to his piping for the entertainment of a party of travelers. It seems to me there is no more pathetic sight than beggars dancing for pay." However, she spoke approvingly of a guide, a "very clever fellow – but seldom showed a disposition to exercise his powers in the games that others delighted in." Visiting Blarney Castle, it was *de rigueur* to kiss the Blarney Stone, but to Fielde's horror, the stone lay on two iron stanchions beneath the cornice 125 feet above the ground. To reach it one had to lean out through an aperture "just large enough to fall comfortably through." She was content to touch the stone with her fingertips. "The language of the inhabitants of the tight little island had not so charmed me that I was willing to risk my life for the sake of being like them by kissing the Blarney Stone." After visiting Cork, she wrote of the appalling beggars who beset the tourist, and "spoil the island," who, when given what they asked, demanded more, and if this was denied they cursed – "Bad luck to ye."

On August 6 they arrived at the walled city of Chester, enchanted with what they saw ("indescribably charming"), but they complained of the tea ("undrinkable"), the food (unavailability of beefsteak), and the slow service in restaurants and inns. Impishly, she wrote: "Agatha's temper is best when she is well fed. When she is hungry it is dreadful – so we try to eat well – but the bill of fair is very short and plain, even at the most stylish hotels." This recently chastized Baptist missionary was not above having a pint of ale now and again in European inns. Fielde's highly informative report describes places of historical interest in the region, the walls and battlements of Chester (with measurements), its Roman associations, and later, the defeat of the army of Charles I in nearby Rowton Moor.

From Chester the travelers ventured into Wales – Conway and Cernarvon Castles and Llanberis. She climbed Mount Snowdon on a perfect, sunny day, and reveled in the magnificent view while being served buttered bread and hot coffee. The Lake District was next, and here she visited the house of Wordsworth, drawing its ferns and ivy, sketching the flowers along Wordsworth's favorite walk, and the grass over his grave. Fielde was especially attracted to remembrances of literary people such as Southey and Burns – birthplaces, homes, churches where they worshipped, and their graves.

Fielde and her companion proceeded to Glasgow, were favorably impressed, and found it was the first city they had ever seen built entirely of one material – gray sandstone. "The Salt Market – the worst part of Glasgow is so much better than the slums of other cities that the Scotch must be a decent people." Here they were entertained by friendly hosts with whom they viewed the surrounding countryside, and made the customary pilgrimage to Robert Burns and Sir Walter Scott country. Her wanderings through northern Scotland and the Islands with their spectacular vistas were recorded in detail, and her extended comments constitute a short textbook of Scottish history.

The diary winds down with a visit to the grave of Charlotte Brontë and her family in Haworth, Yorkshire, and then on to Shakespeare country – Stratford-on-Avon. A furious pace had been set by Fielde that a worn-out Miss Ritchie could not sustain. Consequently she frequently rested or slept late while Fielde visited yet another castle or church, and learned more of local legends. She visited the graves of countless political and literary figures, and from their places of final rest she plucked leaves of ivy, grass, or flowers, which she carefully drew and preserved. These were powerful mementoes that linked her to the long-dead heroes whom she so admired. Fielde the tourist had fully indulged her interest in natural and political history, literature, and culture in general, and at the beginning of October, after ten weeks of dogged sightseeing, they arrived in London. This marks the end of the first leg of her long return to the Orient.

The diary ends in England, and there is no further record of her travels to Rouen, Paris, Naples, and other cities. She arrived in Venice where she boarded a steamer for China, and after a further three months sailed into Swatow harbor, having been out of sight for almost a year, a period for which there is little record. Fielde was to spend the next ten years in Southern China, before returning to her native country.

5 Swatow, China

> What a time we live in! What a privilege to live in such a time! and to be employed as willing agents in the fulfillment of the Divine purpose, in the final triumph of the kingdom which must stand![1]

Fielde had been living well, an eager American wandering about Europe, exposed for the first time to the wondrous creations of an old Western civilization. Now that she was back in China, the exhilaration was tempered by a feeling that the good times were over, and her memories of Europe would have to fortify her against "the time of intellectual famine that is coming." Europe so appealed to her that she thought she might stay, suggesting to Murdock that perhaps she could found a mission school in France or Spain, especially if she was judged not fit for missionary work in China, but the proposal quickly died, and she did not pursue it. She knew what lay ahead of her in China and she had half-heartedly tried to avoid the formidable task that was her lot. By the time she arrived in Swatow, in early 1873, she had embraced her "special mission" that would consume her every waking hour. In Bangkok, much of her evangelical work had been with men; in Swatow, women would be the focus of her efforts.

At the beginning of the seventeenth century a few Jesuit missionaries had evangelized in the East, but it was not until 1843 that the first Protestant (Baptist) mission was established in Hong Kong. Imperial China had proven stubborn in its resistance to entry of Western merchants and missionaries. The Chinese dumped 20,000 chests of opium into the sea and had destroyed cauldrons for processing opium. They sent a letter to Queen Victoria pleading with her to stop the trade that was devastating the Chinese, but British businessmen prevailed, and military forces were dispatched to punish the Chinese. After military action – two opium wars – terminated by the Treaty of Nanking (1842), and the Treaties of Tientsin, and of Peking (1856–1860), Westerners gained access to almost all of China, a country in tatters, run by a corrupt, ineffective government that was called upon to manage an armed conflict. By an agreement framed by the victors, Chinese had the right to become Christians if they chose, and missionaries had the legal right to preach. Several ports, including Swatow, were opened to ships from the West which brought opium from British India for sale to the Chinese masses, an enormously profitable business, but one that was destroying the Chinese people. The opium trade was in fact so lucrative that it largely sustained the economies of Britain and France which were quite willing to go to war to protect their interests in this enterprise.

Missionaries deplored the commerce but were joyful that they were now able to enter the country to save Chinese souls, protected by powerful European forces. In effect Western missionaries, like other Western constituencies, were sovereign powers within the land. It was apparent to many Chinese that they were helpless in the face of Western forces with their deadly weapons and stern justice; perhaps, if they went to church, they would reap some benefit. However, protection of missionaries by arms was still essential, as outlined by a missionary, Mr. Knowlton:

> without force, that is, a show of military force for protection, the position of foreigners of every class would not be tenable in China a month . . . force is the only thing that can give us even a footing here, to say nothing of expansion. . . . No treaty can for a moment be maintained without it. Thanks to British guns and the Providence of God for all the privileges that we peaceful Americans enjoy.[2]

This was a disturbing fact of missionary life, since missionaries were in China to evangelize, not to further the political and economic interests of the U.S.A. Indeed, missionary and governmental activities were sometimes in conflict. Still, whenever the natives threatened, they knew they could rely on the military for protection. On the other hand, many government officials in the field did not seem to appreciate the activities of the evangelizers who were prone to accept the Word of God rather than civil law as their authority. A missionary in Swatow wrote: "Mr. Wingate, the American Consul, was one of the few Consuls in China who can see that God has a work among this people."

Just as businessmen have always appreciated the importance of massive Chinese markets, so Western leaders of the evangelical movement have realized the central importance of China in their efforts to spread the Word:

> All things considered, this [China] is the field of supreme difficulty, and at the same time it is the field of supreme interest. The Chinese are manifestly the governing race of eastern and central Asia; their national qualities and their geographical position make them so; they evidently hold the key to the future of almost one-half the unevangelized people of the globe; so long as they remain without the Gospel the great bulk of Asia will be pagan; when they are evangelized the continent will be Christian and the world will be won.[3]

Ashmore, head of the Swatow mission, also believed that China, with its 400 million people, was by far the most important field mission in the world, although it was known to be the most difficult of all fields because of its complexity, its numerous ancient cultures and religions, its political leadership, and the pervasive poverty and corruption in the land. Apostolic missions to Africa, India, and the South Seas were considered more successful. Based on his broad knowledge of Confucianism, he was convinced that this ancient philosophy was the great obstacle to the acceptance of Christianity, and that "the age of collision of the hard death-grapple with Confucianism is beginning."[4] However, there had also been infusions of Buddhism and Taoism into the religious life of China, so that according to missionaries, a vague and confusing blend of religions existed, without mutual contradictions or conflicts, and none compelling fierce adherence; indeed, most literati were atheistic. Taoism was based on an overarching idea about the origin and workings of the universe – without immediate interest to the potential convert, or challenge to the evangelist.

Confucianism, which venerated the past, concerned itself with the functioning and the regulation of society and the state, almost devoid of a spiritual element or an interest in the future life, a lack that was partly filled by Buddhism.[5] The Confucian "develops the individual desire for perfection in the moral and ceremonial, but has no doctrine of the higher idealism, no belief in God, or self-sacrifice."[6] Through Buddhism, an imported religion, idolatry had been introduced, there being as many as 30,000 distinct deities and 300,000 idol temples, much to the disapproval of the Confucians, the government, and the missionaries. Still, it was admitted by missionaries that this idolatry had "no lascivious rites . . . less power to degrade . . . is more favorable to morality and religion than that of other heathen nations . . . once won to Christ, they [Chinese converts] may be expected to furnish a high type of Christian."[7]

However, beyond these formalized systems of religious beliefs lay the greatest obstacle to Christianity that manifested itself in religious practice – the deep conservatism of the Chinese people, profoundly imbued with ancient animalistic beliefs and superstitions which gave rise to ancestor worship, and a crippling veneration of the father.[8] The Chinese found it almost impossible to renounce the worship of their ancestors, and their most compelling and pervasive law was that one must obey one's elders. The family and each of its members had to endure the strains imposed by these beliefs, and women were the special victims, since they were of no value except to bear sons to create descendants. A woman's success was measured by how many sons she had produced.

Because of the tight, convoluted interdependencies of the individual with the family, the family with the clan, and the clan with the community, all bound together by ancestor worship, self-interest and custom, rejection of ancestor worship in favor of Christ had far-reaching consequences. Those who converted to Christianity paid a heavy price because so many people were affected. Evangelists fought an uphill battle against the dogmas of the

Chinese heathen. Clearly, the Chinese were different from Westerners, confounding them and presenting the missionary with special problems:

> We must understand the peculiar character of the Chinese: (1) They have hazy ideas about gods. A Chinese who went to the United States was written to by his father that his sixth mother was well. What can a man who has six mothers know of a mother's love? (2) The Chinese have hazy ideas about sin, which they confound with crime, treading on one's toes, being late to dinner – the same character for all. (3) They have hazy ideas about a future life. At a Chinese death-bed there is never a word about future happiness, but only about mourning and money. If they did not think the gods could affect men's bodies the temples would be deserted, and ancestral worship would decline. They are not to blame. It is their misfortune and not their fault. The Chinese cannot see Christianity as we see it.[9]

Ashmore believed that for Christ to triumph in China, both "people of standing" as well as the "humble" would have to be won away from Confucianism, in the countryside (where missionaries must live to be effective), and in Shanghai and Hankow, "the great citadels of paganism." He could already see signs of uncertainty in the Chinese, who had never questioned the primacy of their ancient culture. Nineteenth-century missionaries were supremely optimistic, and confident about the coming triumph of Christianity in pagan lands. William Ashmore wrote of *Signs of the Coming Dawn in China.*[10] Missionaries were "winning splendid victories," and, like Puritan revolutionaries in England, "entering no battle but to conquer. . . . Hinduism, Buddhism, Confucianism, are but the shadows of their former strength, and seem on the point of extinction." Opposition to the grand crusade was brushed aside as "petty criticism and thoughtless ridicule." The magnitude of their task, rather than discouraging evangelists, seemed to exhilarate them. The avowed aim of the missionary was to fill the void by providing 400 million Chinese with the Truth that set men free, and establish a healthy, balanced family in which boys and girls are treated and taught alike. Their incessant premature declarations of victory were part of the pep talk – self-encouragement in the face of impossible odds. "Win China to Christ, and the most powerful stronghold of Satan on Earth will have fallen."[11]

When peasants saw no use in education, and refused offers of instruction for their children, missionaries were not above paying parents to send their young to missionary schools. In the long run, education of young men and women proved to be the most important and lasting consequence of missionary activity. Though the education of young people assured a future for Christianity in China, there were some who felt that the missionary's charge was only to evangelize in the narrowest sense.

Ashmore, a scholar, believed that Confucianism was "the ground-work of all Chinese education," the source of profound insights, and remarkable in some ways. Still, he felt it was fatally flawed ("one of the most stupendous failures in history") in that its only concern was man – an "abiding love of man." It rejected the spiritual, which, according to Ashmore, was absolutely essential for society to survive in a healthy state – witness the plight of China and the traits of the Chinese – "dishonesty, trickery, falsehood, covenant breaking, pride, revenge." The great failure of Confucianism was that it served the creature, not the Creator, and that men could not be made upright, conscientious members of society through science and politics alone.[12]

Missionaries had prided themselves on the spectacular growth of the evangelical movement in foreign countries. There had been a few Protestant missionaries scattered about the globe, but an organized movement began in 1792 when William Carey founded the English Baptist Missionary Society, and by 1901 there were over four hundred Protestant societies, with 14,000 missionaries and 74,000 native helpers in 5000 stations throughout the world. To spread the Gospel, the Bible had been translated into hundreds of languages and dialects. They took pride in the establishment of many hospitals and dispensaries that tended 2.5 million patients every year, a genuinely good work that offset some of the damage done by commerce.

Nineteenth-century missionaries were, on the whole, courageous, idealistic, and of a high caliber. Some discredited the missionary movement because they were so intensely ethnocentric, so fervid in the belief in their benevolent God, and the absolute superiority of Christianity over all other beliefs, that they found it difficult to appreciate virtue in religious views (pagan beliefs), customs, and cultures other than their own. Indeed, some were prone to regard nonbelievers as evil – unwitting or perverse. China was often viewed as a degenerate monster that had to be tamed.

On the other hand, there were sympathetic observers who marveled at China, the largest, most populous country on Earth with one-third of the Earth's inhabitants. The Chinese had a 4000-year history, with the oldest government of any nation, at peace for hundreds of years until destabilized by Westerners. Admirers saw an authority that derived from the people, the family, and the clan rather than from a distant capital. The nation's prosperity was dependent on a widespread literacy, and the education of a large number of people who lived exemplary, moral lives. While missionaries' judgment of the Chinese was often unflattering (small brown creatures), and their educated members were arrogant and chauvinistic, these people were described by some Western observers as frugal, sober, industrious, skillful, polite, provident, conservative, and peaceable, in a society based on filial and parental piety.

To the Chinese, Christianity was "the disturber of the old order of things," and in a parochial way they let no one forget that they had invented or thought of everything first, and that Confucius had lived 500 years before Christ. Consequently, the Chinese, who revered the ancient, regarded Christ and the Bible with contempt, dismissing them as "modern" newcomers.[13]

Despite their conviction that Western science was borrowed from China, their civilization showed signs of grievous decay. Westerners, particularly

Americans, were overwhelming them with wondrous inventions to which the Chinese could not realistically lay claim. Still, Westerners were amazed at the outrageous assertions of priority by Chinese, perhaps the consequence of a different conception of truth. When the telegraph and the railroad were presented as recent Western inventions, the Chinese would shrug, and claim that they had invented them centuries before but had no use for them. In general, the literati and the elite considered themselves the superiors of Westerners and their missionaries, and they proved to be resistant to the blandishments of Christ and the promise of everlasting life. Some considered the Christian message to be good – the problem was the Western messenger.

While the mechanical clock, a Western invention of major importance, was never considered more than a bauble, and precision in time unnecessary, steamships were another matter, for they carried impoverished Chinese to a rich America in only a month, and sometimes returned them safely with undreamed of wealth in their pockets. Many Chinese came to recognize the merit of Western ways, and were not unwilling to adopt them – both the tangible and the intangible, the truth of the Bible with the demonstrable truth of science and technology. The benefits of Western medicine were also becoming apparent, but Ashmore was convinced that the most important part of the missionary's job was to persuade the Chinese that it was Christianity that was the most desirable Western import, with its moral code, and its spirituality; a great opportunity was at hand for missionaries to "enter their hearts." Conversion might become "contagious and assume epidemic proportions."[14]

Ashmore, who wrote extensively on the Chinese people, their economics and religions, had an affectionate understanding of the natives – a mixture of admiration and what can only be called contempt and exasperation – as revealed in his writing: "Chinese conceit and pride have been proverbial. Their arrogant claims to superiority to all the rest of mankind have ever been pressed forward with a pertinacity and obtrusiveness that have tried the tempers of foreign diplomatists more than all things else combined. . . . This arrogant and exclusive China must fall."[15] He called them a "money-loving people."[16] The "Chinaman" in his natural state is "phlegmatic . . . excessively practical and mercenary." They have a "passion'" and an "addiction" for gambling, and are prone to "petty resentments . . . and when he becomes a Christian, these characteristics stand in the way of his spiritual growth."[17]

Perhaps the most intolerant of missionaries was the Reverend George L. Mason, whose denunciation of everything Chinese did not staunch his passion to save this incorrigible people: "Whether or not falsehood is universal in all heathen lands, it certainly is the most common vice of the Chinese . . . and it is not thought to be a vice. . . . It is no insult to be called a liar, for they do not expect from each other either truth or sincerity." However, he conceded that the Chinese believed "falsehood is wrong only when it hurts another. . . . Chinese military power is a ludicrous pretence. . . . The judicial system is a cruel fraud. No one expects justice. . . . Chinese education is a sham. To discover truth is not the aim. To remember is everything, to think is nothing. . . . Most of Chinese religion in its practical working is a conscious sham." Generously, he concludes: "But we must not think the Chinese irreclaimably untruthful, and their institutions all sham. . . . We know not a few Chinamen who have received the love of the truth, and whose characters and lives are notably different from the heathen around them. Therefore we rejoice, and toil on."[18] Scattered throughout the missionaries' narratives are references to the utter corruption and incompetency of the government and its officials – both high and low – where "extortion is the chief use of office, and fear of it the main spur of obedience."[19] Why couldn't the Chinese be like Westerners?

Critical views, and harsh judgments by Western missionaries, born of their feeling of natural superiority, were reinforced by the fact that the heathen Chinese they dealt with were those at the bottom of the social and economic scale – peasants, farmers, and small merchants. Not infrequently they were addicted to opium and alcohol, and periodically they were ravaged by famine, pestilence, and war. Over 90 percent of Chinese converts were illiterate, and of the lowest class.[20] Education and refinement had not filtered down to this abject level, and there was little will or ability to counter the opinions of the evangelist. Fielde's writings rarely refer to educated, middle-class women who in fact tended to remain aloof from missionaries. Had the target been the more affluent class of Chinese, beneficiaries of a "moral education," evangelists might have been resisted by lengthy argument in which "scriptural promises" would be set against a religious system based upon Chinese moral precepts.[21]

The worst of missionaries were humorless and tyrannical, absolutely convinced of the *Truth* of their religion and the superiority of their views. They were not interested in turning their movement into a forum for debate but in saving as many human souls as quickly as possible. In doing so, the quality of Christian conviction of many of the converts was questionable, a constant concern to some evangelists in the field, although it was the number of conversions reported, a comprehensible measure, that impressed the missionary boards back home. Fielde had written about this disparity as it existed in Bangkok. To some, it was difficult to see how ignorant Chinese could even conceive of a single God, while it must have required great effort on the part of Chinese to comprehend why an unknown man, Jesus, should die for their sins. What was a sin? Who was this incredible man? If Christianity was so superior, with its high moral preachments, why were the actions of Christian nations so murderous and unjust? Yet, acceptance of Christianity might not be difficult; it was yet another religion the Chinese might add to the others in their syncretic approach to theology – and it might help them obtain food and medicine.

Missionaries were sometimes callous in their evaluation of converts – they were still Chinese with all their faults, who "showed no signs of grafting their old civilization to our civilization."[22] Though they believed that sin and ignorance could be overcome, and heavenly redemption achieved by adoption of the True Faith, missionaries often regarded those who converted as childlike, and they were not fully respectful of their understanding of Christianity, a frustration and a sin that justified the beating of adult Chinese for their own good. Missionaries were frustrated in their aim to bring this vast and ancient people into the green pastures of their own Christian world, and they were not tolerant of the existing religious beliefs of their flocks. Yet, Ashmore admitted that the Chinese people were "cheerful givers." In the midst of poverty, a town of 6000 families freely raised $60,000 for their temple – vastly more than could be raised in a prosperous American town.[23] Should not Americans provide more generous support for outstations where "multitudes" of Chinese heathens could be reached?

Ashmore and Dean were strong, intelligent, righteous men, certain in their belief, moral and religious, and urgent in their desire to save souls, but their views on women and "heathens" were condescending and paternalistic, views they had brought from home. They came from a land of growing power, with a deeply ingrained sense of natural superiority, viewing the benighted Chinese as paying for sins imposed by a just and loving God. Though they gladly endured hardship and danger for Christ, they left all manual labor to the heathen. In disputes with natives, Westerners would almost always close ranks, and in transgressions of the heathen, punishment was swift. Yet, on the whole, the quality of missionaries in foreign lands was very high, though, in a group such as this, there were also a few "bad apples," fodder for those unsympathetic to the missionary movement.[24] Ashmore, head of the mission, warned Murdock of the trouble they could do, and advised him that they should be dealt with firmly on an individual basis.[25]

At a time when Darwinism, and Spencer's notion of the "survival of the fittest" were widely discussed, and some thinkers predicted that "inferior" races would soon be eliminated through the operation of biological law, missionaries insisted with some urgency that all of mankind must be exposed to the Word of Christ and that the soul of the heathen must be saved before their inevitable extinction. Christianity would endow them with the capacity to cope. Brave missionaries felt it worthwhile to endure hardship and expose themselves to danger, and yet there remained a competitive element – their culture against that of China – that fueled their mission to convert the misguided to a superior belief – in effect, to remake their society.

Swatow, a treaty port to the south, had long been known to be hostile to foreigners, the consequence of raids upon the city for young males who were transported to other lands for enforced labor.[26] A Mr. Burns had been caged like a bird and was transported to Canton, several hundred miles away, and even the British Consul was at one time driven away, despite an armed accompaniment. Fielde was fortunate that throughout her years in China during war and peace, she was never in mortal danger at the hands of bandits or soldiers.

The city, in the Tie-chiu Department of Kuang Tung Province of Southern China, was a commercial center of 30,000, and, despite harassment, had a foreign population of 120.[27] The city served the hinterland of eight million people who spoke the Swatow dialect, a relatively minor fraction of the Chinese people. Above all, the city, whose wealth derived from the exportation of silk and tea, and the importation of Indian opium, was considered a center of culture; yet shocking reminders of the hard, rough life of the Chinese were everywhere. The city square was a place of execution where thieves were crucified, or buried alive. Fielde never ate pork after seeing a pig devour the corpse of an abandoned baby.

The main Baptist station, in the hills that formed the south side of the bay, across from the city itself, consisted of two, large, typhoon-resistant houses for the staff, and between them was a chapel. Over the years, since its founding in 1859 by William Ashmore, the missionaries had fashioned a small oasis by beautifying the rocky compound with winding walks in a park of trees and shrubs, a little island of America in China, physically and psychologically separated from the vast Chinese engulfment. The climate was mild enough to permit roses to bloom in midwinter, but the long summer brought a stifling heat that wilted flowers, and was considered unhealthy – not to be endured by Westerners for more than seven years. Fielde described the area as "low, slimy and flat," and "utterly monotonous." The entire staff of Westerners consisted of six men and women, which included Mr. Ashmore, the head of the mission, and his wife, Eliza, and Sylvester B. Partridge and his wife, late of the Bangkok mission, who were as happy as Fielde to have escaped from the control of the patriarchal William Dean. The rest of the mission consisted of Mrs. J.W. Johnson, recently widowed, Adele Fielde, and a relatively large staff of natives. No new single Western male had been added to the Swatow staff in five years. Like the Bangkok mission, it could not be called thriving, perhaps because the mission was in a backwater of China, whose relatively small population was isolated by their spoken language.

Ringing the home base were eight stations, all of which were within sight from the top of a hill near which the mission stood, the furthest being thirty-five miles distant.[28] The Swatow mission field covered the eastern part of Kuang Tung province, an area radiating for sixty miles around Swatow, populated by poor but industrious farmers living in villages, mostly walled to discourage marauders during the night. Walled towns and residences were unfamiliar to American missionaries who had been raised in open spaces with vistas. Still, they found that walls were of benefit, providing privacy and separation from overcrowded and unattractive surroundings.[29] The area was covered with very small farms, heavily cultivated to yield three crops each year, which were barely enough to feed the populace. This compact configuration permitted Western missionaries to preach in the countryside during the day and to return to the Swatow mission in the evening, while from the scattered bases, vast numbers of Chinese could be contacted by native assistants.

The despair of Chinese life affected Fielde deeply. Of Swatow and its people, she later wrote:

> there is no exhilaration in the view [of the harbor]; for visible to the eye within its range, and visible to the heart, whose perceptions extend to the limits of the empire, on and on from the southern border of the land away to Siberia, lie thickly the low gray villages, made up of filthy huts and dingy alleys, and in each men count themselves fortunate, if by daily toil like beasts, they win daily bread; and women weep for wrongs that no one thinks of rectifying; and children seldom smile, because unconsciously they face the vast burden of life and are awed by it into solemnity. . . . Nature lacks exalting charm. The beauteous scenery loses power to delight, when haunted by base, sad souls. So it comes to pass that the bright waters and ferny mountains of China communicate no joy.[30]

Working with Chinese women was her preference because they were by far in the greatest need. Indeed, women missionaries and their supporters were particularly motivated by the abuse of the women, indigenous to Eastern cultures and sanctioned by their religions. To abolish the abuse, their religion had to be negated.

> The lot of Chinese womankind is a hard one. If a little girl comes into a family where there are already more than one or two daughters, she is destroyed at her birth. Public opinion not only sustains but almost demands this. . . . The people are so poor; the mouths to be fed are so many in proportion to the extent of arable land; the uselessness of one whose feet are bound; the fact that after marriage she will owe no filial duty to her own parents . . . all go to explain the common crime of infanticide. When a father tells his friend the number of his children, he does not count his daughter.[31]

In a society which believed that a stupid son was better than a smart daughter, suicide was not uncommon among women.[32]

Fielde describes her visit to a foundling asylum in Kui Su, set up by the Chinese government for the purpose of sheltering unwanted babies. Male babies were never brought to it, but about two hundred females were left each year, a small fraction of those cast away.

> Twenty-five old women at Kui Su, from whom I ascertained this fact concerning their domestic life, had destroyed fifty-two girls at their birth. . . . Those who take their infant girls to the asylum are more tender-hearted, or so near by that it is less trouble to take them there than to the river. . . . When the baby is twelve days old, it is, if healthy and plump, put into a basket with three or four others, and carried off

> several miles to other villages, to be given away. The man who totes the babies around in this way gets twenty cents a day. He takes a basket of babies on each end of a pole over his shoulder, and carries them as he might fruit or puppies instead. Women who want one look over the lot, select one they fancy, and bring it up as a son's wife. . . . The sickly children brought to the asylum are kept by their nurses until they get well, or die, as no one would wish to take them for son's wives.[33]

An outraged Fielde reported the alarming truth in a calm, journalistic style which shocks, even today; one can imagine the effect they had on Americans of the 1870s. To Fielde, the only hope for Chinese peasants was for them to become Christian, so that they might win some measure of control of their own destiny; child marriage, concubinage, female slavery and infanticide, and footbinding would be stopped, education would be stressed, and women would achieve a respected status in the world.

However, it took great courage for Chinese, especially women, to declare themselves Christian, and to place themselves outside the belief system of their family and neighbors. In one instance thirteen converts were attacked by a mob with hoes, sickles, kitchen knives, and canes, who bound and beat their captives, and decapitated one man,[34] but Chinese Christians were generally tolerated and left in peace. Westerners, who were regarded as outsiders and curiosities, were so few in number, and often with imperfect linguistic abilities, that hope of their converting significant numbers of Chinese heathens was small. What did the Chinese think of these large, pale-skinned, assertive Western women who were trying to induce them to accept an almost incomprehensible, alien set of beliefs? What were they up to?[35] Missionaries were confronted by bland-faced, impassive students, resisting friendly advances with a shield of formal, almost ritualistic behavior. However, Fielde's experience with adult students was more direct and emotional as she quickly became friends with the special women she sought out.

Upon her arrival, Fielde the schoolteacher took over and organized the instruction of children, relieving married women of the task, and as an independent agent she was free to put together an evangelical program of her own. Aware of the inadequacy of the existing missionary effort, she instituted a plan that would maximize efficiency by increasing the number of effective workers reaching the natives. Chinese women would be educated and trained so that they could return to the countryside from which they came, and preach the Word without supervision from Westerners. Only women could enter the dank, windowless homes of other women, talk with them, and perhaps start them thinking about their salvation and their physical betterment. There was more to life than bearing male children, feeding pigs, and surviving under the total domination of a mother-in-law. It was said that the conversion of one woman was worth the conversion of twenty men, and if women could not be reached, there was no hope for the evangelical movement in China "for generations to come." In effect, Fielde planned to convince Chinese women to do a kind of work, based on a set of beliefs unknown to them.

Fielde had been raised in a Victorian culture that believed in education, and in the power of persuasion, and as a gifted communicator she was an extremely effective teacher. The Committee approved of her plan to create a special kind of school in Swatow that would train a corp of literate preachers who were called "Bible-women." The training of natives for missionary work was not new, and indeed, native missionaries were called "Bible-women," so that the plan was not exactly original in principle.[36] But Fielde institutionalized the program, explicitly defining its structure, mode of operation, and aims, and she implemented the plan with vigor, fully employing her organizational skills, and her capacity for hard work. The enterprise virtually constituted a new approach to Evangelism – a model to be copied. As E.F. Merriam, historian of the American Baptist Missions, wrote, after twenty years of experience at the Swatow mission: "By these methods Miss Fielde built up an organized corps of Bible-women whose work, under her direction, has been a model for the work of Bible-women throughout China."[37] Mrs. William M. Lisle, a former missionary to China, commented: "Miss Fielde was the mother of our Bible-women and also the mother of our Bible schools." The one in Swatow was "the oldest institution of its kind in the world" and out of it grew the children's school, for the children of Bible-women, and later a school for boys and then for girls.[38] Mrs. Lisle, who had been with Fielde in Bangkok, admired her, for she had done a "man's work." Despite inadequate resources, a determined Fielde achieved this great *tour de force*.

Traveling from village to village by foot, boat, or horseback, Fielde sought out the most intelligent Chinese women of which not more than one in a thousand was literate, brought them back to Swatow, and taught them to read. She instructed them in the Bible, the only book they studied as a lifetime commitment, because it was the only one they would be required to teach. Her strategy of teaching a crash course did not provide for a general education, or instruction in the English language, which under the circumstances might have been considered an extravagance and a distraction. It was a plan that facilitated the placing of an army of evangelists in operation in a relatively short period of time. Fielde said that her model was that of Jesus who selected his disciples from the unlearned, and taught them Scripture only, before sending them into the world to proselytize.

The demanding, total-immersion course she devised that went on all year long without vacations was only the first stage in an ongoing process, for after serving in the field, Bible-women returned to Swatow every two months for a refresher course lasting one week to learn, compare experiences, and encourage one another. If they wanted, Bible-women could spend a second week at home with their families, but few did. Fielde was worried about the effects of isolation in the country on the faith of her evangelicals, for "perpetual contact with the heathen benumbs their consciousness, so they need a quickening influence of a new view of their Lord." The Westerner in such a foreign situation was even more at risk of drying up and withdrawing, becoming frustrated preaching their narrowed beliefs.

She avoided volunteers because she insisted that selection be based entirely on her own standards. The women she chose were already Christian, of good health and pleasant disposition, who were "seeking the Truth." Most of the women were between 40 and 50 years of age, and one was in her seventies. Critics who believed that middle-aged women could not be taught were proved wrong. In fact, age carried with it a measure of respect that Fielde considered an asset in influencing people. According to Chinese custom, older women could move freely between villages and from house to house where they would converse with their hosts, especially at mealtimes and at night. Younger Bible-women were never sent alone to villages.[39]

Fielde had created a bizarre school filled with hobbling, footbound women, many advanced in years, who lived at the mission as an almost isolated unit, and, although their living quarters were spare, they were heavenly compared to their own houses. In the house were classrooms that accommodated thirty persons, presided over by a house mother and part-time teacher, Chin Po. While they lived together and learned, separated from their communities and the distractions of their non-Christian neighbors, students could learn in peace as their Christian faith and group solidarity matured.

Within months of her arrival in Swatow, Fielde wrote of Bible-women assisting her.[40] Her pupils were paid by the mission, and with money that Fielde was given by her many women friends in America. Students received $1.5 per month while the graduate Bible-woman earned $2 per month plus traveling expenses, enough to sustain them but not enough to attract people for the money involved. Once established in a village, Bible-women were supported by local Christians. The Board was delighted that this new program would cost so little.

A typical day at the school was described by Miss Norwood, a young Canadian missionary who assisted Fielde:

> A little before nine Miss Fielde and I repair to the large upper room of the "Womens' House" where we find all the "sisters," as they are accustomed to call themselves, seated and ready for the morning exercises. A strange-looking assemblage they surely are. The most of them are brown and sunburned; nearly all are wrinkled, more from hardship than old age: but all have that in their faces that make them different from any similar company of heathen women – an indescribable something that is peculiar to the faces of those whose names are written in the Book of Life. I know not how any Christian could look at these women, and not thank God for the command, "Go ye into all the world," &c. The work of the day begins by one of the sisters reading a hymn, which someone else is asked to explain, and then all unite in singing it. Then perhaps Miss Fielde speaks of the difficulties that are liable to arise where there

Figure 5.1 Bible-women in the Swatow Mission, trained by Adele Fielde

> are so many together, and the need of the exercise of a spirit of love on the part of each. She asks if there are any special subjects for prayer, whereupon a number of sisters at once respond. One or more asks that some bodily ailment which interferes with her ability to study be removed; one, that she may not draw back from following her Saviour; another refers to the great number of women in her city, and asks that prayer be made for them, that they may hear the Gospel and be saved; one asks prayer for an aged parent, another for a husband, &c; and then two sisters are asked to remember these requests in prayer.

Students are asked to repeat, in their own words, the Gospel story they heard the previous day. "Miss Fielde explains the succeeding chapter, and once a week gives them a story from some other part of the Bible, which each in turn tells to the others . . . after listening to Miss Fielde's recital of the entire book of Esther, A Kue (or Speed) . . . gave the whole without a mistake and with scarcely any prompting." At 10 a.m. beginners were taught reading, and in two months "they had mastered the hymn book, consisting of forty hymns." At 11 a.m. they were taught some doctrine such as Genesis, explicated by Dr. Ashmore. At 11.30 a.m. they went to lunch, except for those who wanted to talk to Fielde, their "great mother." The oldest in the class was 74, the youngest, 23.[41]

In 1876, three years after she arrived in Swatow, Fielde explained her mode of operation:

> I send no Bible-woman to any place where I have not myself been, and with the locality and condition of which I am not acquainted. . . . There are one hundred and fifty women connected with our church and I have visited nearly all of them in their homes, and know their personal circumstances. Those who are of suitable age, and whose domestic relations are such that they can be absent without neglecting any home duty, I invite to come and learn to read for two months. If during the two months she manifests the character and ability desirable in a Bible-woman, I invite her to stay and read two months more, and I take her with me to some of the heathen villages and make practical experiment of her aptness in telling others what she knows of Christianity. By the end of four months I am sufficiently acquainted with her to judge whether it is advisable to spend more labor upon her.

In her annual report of 1880, Fielde stated that she had spent sixty-one days visiting each of fourteen outstations twice, and in doing so she had traveled over a thousand miles.

Women who had finished their coursework were accompanied by Fielde when they began preaching in neighboring villages. She would analyze their delivery and their conversations with women, and make suggestions for improvement, and would provide encouragement, especially after being rebuffed.

When ready, they went off to villages and the countryside without supervisors, but they were never sent to places where they had no personal acquaintances to vouch for them because Chinese villagers were so distrustful of strangers. The goal was to make them independent missionaries, not just assistants. After about ten years, Fielde had personally trained about fifty Bible-women (a 50 percent rate of success), of whom about one-third were capable of training others.[42] The intelligence of so many of the pupils, their loving nature, and their receptivity to new ideas was striking. Most had begun "dirty, sullen, suspicious, and mendacious," and, under her tutelage and genuine interest, Pygmalion-like, they were transformed into "cheerful, clean, and honest women," disciplined, responsible, and self-reliant, qualities that were so admired by Victorian society. Fielde must have taken special satisfaction in her work, for she had shown that if women – Eastern as well as Western – are given the opportunity, they can excel. She spoke of how they grew in grace, and in "knowledge of the truth."

> I now rely much upon their helpful wisdom and patience in the management of all trying cases as they arise. They are a perpetual joy to me. Their abilities and nobilities have increased with the passage of time and I have a score, at least, of Chinese women within my sphere of life, who are engaging and estimable associates in all good work and aspiration.

The aim of the school was to free Chinese women from the burdens long suffered through acceptance of Christ, but also, they were to remain good wives and mothers.

The conservative agenda of the school was designed to produce evangelists, and not to remodel Chinese peasant women into middle-class, Christian home-makers, for this would be an impossible goal to achieve, and Fielde certainly did not plan to convert them into disruptive revolutionaries.[43] In a sense, the establishment of schools for boys and girls was tacit acknowledgment of the fact that the process of meaningful conversion was a long-term affair that would take generations. However, she urgently desired that the intellectual deprivation and domestic oppression of women should come to an end.[44]

On one occasion, Fielde and a newcomer, Miss Thompson, made a tour of eight stations in the relatively prosperous agricultural Kit-Ie district. A letter to the *Baptist Missionary Magazine* gives some idea of local economic conditions. Land, from which there are two harvests of rice per year, was worth $600 an acre. A strong, active man can manage one-and-a-half acres from which he could make $50 per year. Middle-class people could live on $1 per month per person, and each person, apart from the old and the young, was expected to earn $1 per month. On the tour she

> opened a day-school in the new chapel, with one of the oldest boys from my school here as teacher, and twenty-four boys, all Christians, or the

> sons of Christians as pupils. The parents furnished the benches and desks for the school, and six dollars toward the teachers wages . . . these same parents subscribed fifteen dollars for the painting of the chapel, and eighty cents per month towards a Bible-woman's wages.

Fielde insisted that Christianity could only succeed if Chinese Christians supported their own church and its schools, rather than depend on the pittance afforded by missionaries.[45]

Her travels were sometimes dangerous, reminiscent of the menace underlying *Heart of Darkness*. In May 1873, she and some of her native assistants had visited a pagoda on a trip to Kui-Lu, in the mountains, forty miles from Swatow. The locals, who had never seen a Western woman, began to gather in large numbers to form a crowd of uncertain, perhaps dangerous temper. Warned of their possible hostility, she surrounded herself with her assistants, and laughed loudly as she casually proceeded to safety. According to a Chinese proverb (and Shakespeare), a man may smile and be a villain, but if he laughs "he does not mean mischief." Apparently the crowd was of the same opinion.[46]

A common pattern emerges in the tales of difficulties encountered by front-line missionaries spreading the Word.[47] Crowds were frequently hostile against praying, singing, and preaching evangelists; they were like Daniel in the lions' den – outsiders, assisted by native preachers. Meetings were often interrupted by jeers, catcalls, and insulting remarks – usually a planned disruption. A drama would unfold: the situation looked hopeless until, at the last moment, one or two individuals showed an interest, though many in the crowd, through social pressures, "lost heart and became ashamed."[48] They had taken the first step toward salvation, gladdening the hearts of the missionaries, and making the effort worthwhile; the story would end optimistically and almost cheerfully. Sometimes, angry, dangerous crowds were pacified by a "good" Chinese, and at times, missionaries rolled out a powerful weapon against aggressive, vocal nonbelievers – the threat of eternal hellfire and damnation. Converts were to be pitied, since so much was asked of them, especially if they became active Christians, for they were ostracized and persecuted by neighbors and government functionaries.[49]

Fielde, at the nexus of two networks of women, was an intermediary between two cultures, one in America, the providers and a source of volunteers, and the other in China, her students, who were the beneficiaries. The American branch she assiduously cultivated by letters and magazine articles. With new classes being organized each year, a sizable corp of Bible-women came into existence – overall, about five hundred passed through the school in a twenty-year period. Bible-women did not wear a uniform, nor was there any change in their dress or their diet. Fielde wanted no distinctions between these women and the people to whom they preached, though being a Christian was in itself a strong basis for distinction and alienation. "The evangelist must be far enough ahead of his people to lead them, yet close enough to take hold of their hands." Though she wanted nothing to "sever them, socially or intellectually," it was hardly possible, for they were becoming educated, and were rising in status among their fellows. They were insiders who knew the Bible and the language, earning their daily bread, and willing to go out among their people, despite the occasional rebuff or beating. Though some Bible-women left the program because of illness or grave domestic problems, none resigned because of hardship, suffering, or fear of violence. Fielde was in awe of courageous Chinese Bible-women, many with small bound feet, laboriously hobbling about with the aid of a pole, a vision that assumed iconic power. Sometimes, kind village women carried crippled Bible-women on their backs. Perhaps most important was the entry of these people into a sisterhood of common interests and respect, of great *esprit*, based upon a doctrine of liberating Christian love – so different from their former deprivations:

> These women need to be taught to use their own language with force and fluency; to read correctly, easily and agreeably; to speak clearly, truthfully; and to pertinently illustrate, by parable, anecdote and proverb, the truth they communicate. They must learn the most effective manner of presenting the idea of a sole and true God, and of the uselessness of idols, and the best ways of removing the fear and dread of demons from ignorant and superstitious minds.[50]

Bible-women were taught to speak effectively, for the spoken word was the only way of influencing illiterate women. It was only after 1877 that Fielde, with a native teacher, taught some of the Bible-women to write, though it was a skill that was not deemed essential for missionary work. After six months, five of the Bible-women could write letters. Through strenuous effort, Fielde's program became enormously successful, the pride of the Swatow mission, as measured by the increase in the number of women working for the church, attendance of natives at church services, and the number of baptisms. Like Ashmore and other missionaries, Fielde believed that once the Chinese began to accept the Gospel, there would be a snowballing effect, and mass conversion would follow; Fielde's Bible-women might just be the essential catalyst. Such fictions, encouraging glints of hope, were indispensable for morale because the evangelical aspirations of the enterprise were so great in the vastness of China with its hundreds of millions of people whose culture they barely understood.

Fielde wrote out *Gospel Lessons* for her students in Chinese, each lesson dealing with one of the great principles of Christianity, or moments in the life of Jesus, and she translated hymns, and books of the Bible including Genesis and Acts. She and Ashmore wrote a *Synopsis of the Gospel In Chinese Popular Language* for the benefit of the students. Stories were to be taught in simple and easily understood language. Bible-women, raised in the Chinese tradition of memorizing and story-telling, proved to be good students who learned quickly. In this one-woman show, Fielde spent many hours with her students, drilling them, explaining the finer points, and smoothing out the apparent contradictions within Christian doctrine. An elucidation of the contrasts between Eastern religions in which they were raised, and Christianity, was an important part of her instruction. They were taught geography and hygiene. The importance of cleanliness and clean water was emphasized by having the student look at samples of water through the eyepiece of a microscope. Monstrous organisms in polluted water provided Bible-women with a new perspective on public health, and convinced them, with Fielde's elaborations, that cleanliness was next to godliness.

With the number of capable hands greatly increased, an expanding network of country churches and outlying mission centers run by Bible-women became an effective evangelical force, discouraging footbinding and urging families to have their daughters marry Christian men, and their sons, Christian women. Bible-women, usually in pairs, ventured as much as sixty miles from Swatow, where they were accepted in villages in which they were known by at least one person who would open doors for them, procure for them room and board, and reassure dangerous, xenophobic Chinese that they were one of their own. Then they would start their conversations. In the course of three months, two Bible-women might visit between ten and thirty villages.

In time, some of the teaching was left in the hands of the best Bible-women, though Fielde continued to instruct. In 1876 Mary Thompson became a member of the staff, and the following year, Fielde was joined by Sophia Norwood, the two single ladies recruited and supported by Women's Baptist societies, somewhat independent of the Board. They traveled with Fielde, and sat in on her teaching sessions for women while they learned Chinese. Eventually, with the blessings of Ashmore, the titular head of the Swatow mission, they took responsibility for mission work in areas surrounding Swatow, and taught at the girls' and boys' school, separated from Fielde. It would seem that, as these women became more proficient, with ideas of their own, irritations and conflicts arose between master and pupils; Fielde could be overbearing and insistent.

Fielde had a great affection for the Chinese. She lived with them, immersed herself in their culture, and was certainly more emotionally involved with them than most Western missionaries. After traveling sixty miles by boat and spending three days with the Hakka people, she thought about their motives:

> When we see "an open door" in this country, we are not always sure that it is set before us by the Lord. The "childlike and bland" Asiatics hold motives in their mind in layers, many as the superimposed villages buried in lava in some spots on the slopes of Vesuvius. Under the evident one there is another concealed, and still deeper ones may be unearthed by sufficient delving.[51]

Fielde sensed that, before an evangelist could convince the heathen of the advantages of Christianity, it was necessary for the evangelist to have a real and sympathetic understanding of the potential convert; preaching to the lowly Chinese peasant from on high was futile. To some Chinese, Christianity espoused admirable doctrines, but these could not be guiding principles in everyday life. Fielde commented, not without sympathy: "it is curious to hear these half-clad salesmen under a leaf shelter offer the same objection to godliness as is made by the proprietors of marble-front emporiums in western cities," and "If I were to be strictly truthful and honest, I should starve."[52]

Studying and describing their food, clothing, customs, legends, and beliefs, gathering unrecorded lore, she might be considered an early cultural anthropologist, ethnologist, and folklorist who wrote fascinating, authoritative articles: *A Chinese Wedding, Chinese Spiritism, Chinese Habitations, Chinese Laws and Customs Concerning Women, The Hakka People, A Chinese Drug Store, Foot-Binding, Chinese Superstitions, Some Chinese Mortuary Customs, Farm-life in China*, a five-part study *China as a Mission Field*, and many essays and journal articles. She interpreted Chinese life for scholars and the reading American middle class.

There is little question that she was an authoritarian master who gave everything, and in return expected the impossible to occur, and at times she could turn on the charm. Her Bible-women understood her and adored her; they were her family, the children she never had. Her pupils bore such endearing names as *Khue* (Speed), *Yong* (Tolerance), *Mui* (Minute), *Kem Pheng* (Tapestry), *Sui Lang* (Herb), *Gek* (Gem), *Ngun Hu* (Silver Flower), *Phie* (Cress), *Chia* (Rectitude), *Gueh Eng* (Moonlight), *Sai Kio* (Grace), *Lau Sit* (Innocence), *Niu* (Button), *Tit Kim* (Goldgetter), *Chut* (Guide), *Long* (Opulence), *Tien Chu* (Pearl), and *Sui Khim* (Lute).[53] Goldgetter was a totally illiterate woman of 42 who, in the course of ten months, was able to read "fluently a hundred hymns, the whole of four Gospels, and the book of Acts, and to tell from memory nearly all she had read."[54] Speed, the daughter of a Christian, was able to "hold the attention of a congregation of heathen women for hours at a time." Fielde had each Bible-woman tell her story, which she translated and published in magazines. Their heart-rending sagas proved enormously appealing to American women, who could sympathize with their suffering Chinese sisters, and needless to say, they were effective in soliciting funds. Several years later, the stories were gathered together and published as a book, *Pagoda Shadows* (1884). They still make good reading, and along with Fielde's other scholarly descriptions of women's lives in China, marriage customs, and footbinding, are a valuable source of information for historians of culture, and anthropologists.[55]

Fielde's Bible-woman project flourished from its very beginning, and elated by her success, Ashmore wrote Murdock, the Corresponding Secretary in Boston: "Miss Fielde's success has gone far beyond my most sanguine expectations." Referring to Fielde's choice of older women for the project, he added, "the 'old folks' have done remarkably well. . . . I cannot refrain from expressing my joy at the Zeal and energy and Christian devotion with which she has given herself to what her hands find to do . . . as for myself, I am so glad she is here. . . . Her experiences of life in Siam were sad and for most of them the blame lies elsewhere than upon herself. But it has made her only the hungrier for doing good."[56] Partridge, equally admiring, found it difficult to believe that Fielde was the same, unhappy person he had known in Bangkok, under Dean. She was now listened to, and she took over some responsibility for the mission, especially regarding women's affairs, when Ashmore was away. He wrote letters to Murdock that were highly complimentary to Fielde, pleased that she studied the Bible on her own, and that it showed in her teaching. He commended her "growth in grace," and was gratified that "she gives herself without reserve to the work among the women of Tie chiu."[57]

Eventually, word of Fielde's success spread beyond Swatow. In 1877, she was selected to be a delegate to the Missionary Conference in Shanghai, and, while there, was asked to speak of her activities. This she did spontaneously, without notes, and it proved to be one of the highlights of the conference. Partridge, who was in attendance, was elated at her triumph, which reflected so well on the Swatow mission. "It is very seldom that our Mission is favored with two such workers as Dr. Ashmore and Miss Fielde." Fielde's approach to the creation of a small army of Bible-women grew in popularity, and was in general adopted by the missionary world. However, the chairman of the session at which Fielde spoke felt that men alone should conduct their business while women should listen in silence. Though he was "gracious" enough not to prevent Fielde from speaking, he stepped down from the podium during the session.[58] Behavior of this kind was not unusual. The great abolitionist William Lloyd Garrison, who led a delegation to an international anti-slavery meeting in London, was unable to have Lucretia Mott and Elizabeth Cady Stanton, the leaders of the American women reform movement, seated at the convention. They were enraged, but to no avail.

Ashmore recognized that Fielde's religion also stressed the Creature, a legacy of her Universalist convictions, and that it would be difficult if not impossible for her to prosper as a missionary if faith was placed only in man. Overwhelming disappointment would inevitably follow unless the missionary was sustained and motivated by an abiding faith in the spiritual. It was more important to *believe* than to do something good to receive the blessing of the Lord. What success could one expect in bettering the lives – both material and spiritual – in a land where: "The great mass of people dwell in mere hovels; and sleep, eat, and live with their pigs and chickens, in a single room. Cholera prevails all summer, smallpox all winter, and vermin through the year"?[59] When Fielde came to China, she expressed reservations about the primacy of faith in the spirit to sustain oneself in the face of unbearable squalor, but after two years' experience, under Ashmore's guidance, she was of his belief.[60] With physically beaten Bible-women in mind, experience had taught her that those whom she wished to save could be "wicked" and "cruel" and "averse to all good." "If we worked for love of *them*, our impulse would soon fail. Working for love of *Christ*, our impetus grows greater as we see how hard *his* work was, and how unlovely those he loved."[61]

Fielde had great respect for Ashmore's scholarship and linguistic gifts, and she admired the fervency of his religious convictions. In return, by understanding Fielde's strong but tender nature and appreciating her extraordinary abilities, he set a dynamo into action. Learning from Dean's failure, he eliminated all possible sources of friction between herself and others at the mission by giving her a free hand in organizing her program; he isolated her.[62] Ashmore and the Board assigned a woman to work in a separate world of women. In America, the image of a woman working outside her home as a professional, doing God's work, on a par with a man, powerfully appealed to young women, and donors. Funds from the Committee for the support of Fielde's work went directly to her, to be spent as she wished. Fielde blossomed in this liberating environment.

Evangelism and trade closely followed the forceful entry of imperialistic Western powers into China, and just as the country was cut up into spheres of influence by each European nation, so Christian evangelicals, "imperialists of the spirit," divided the heathen land into territories according to Christian denomination. While Fielde was convinced that the missionary movement was benign and well intentioned, and could be the very salvation of China, powerful business interests were another matter. There was much money to be made in providing opium and alcohol to the Chinese – in fact, it was actually forced upon them. She was horrified by the rampant alcoholism: "Of all the multitude of things that they might adopt or purchase, for mind or body, for house or land, for luxury or convenience, they have taken only one – and that the worst – Liquors."[63] However opium was the real enemy, China's "destroying angel," which "is fast destroying the population. . . . Blighted lives, pauperized families, depopulated villages and towns. . . . Oh, its terrible ravages are enough to make one weep tears of blood!"[64] Missionaries were aware of the devastation wrought by opium: "in Tai-ku it is commonly reported that nine out of every ten men and all the women are opium smokers." The report goes on to say that children inhaling the smoke of their parents were also victims.[65] Addicts could be easily recognized by their wan, colorless faces, glistening eyes, and rasping voices, and as one walked along the street the air was redolent with opium. In a letter to the staid Corresponding Secretary Warren, Fielde exploded:

> The Chinese conscience is shrewd; it feels the inconsistency of distribution of religious tracts with one hand and selling poison at a good price, from the other. . . . Recent statistics show that China pays a greater amount of money for imported opium, than she receives for all the silks and teas that she exports. Is this Christianity? English are the worst – send missionaries to England to bring it to "righteous conduct in this matter."

> National policy toward the Chinese must be Christian before the Chinese can be Christianized. How is it that we pray "thy Kingdom come", and yet continually lend our strength to prevent its coming? How is it that all over England, its multitudes meet in softly cushioned churches and grand cathedrals, and five times every Sunday unitedly pray "thy Kingdom come", yet make no effort to hinder, nay permit, support or engage in that traffic which prevents half the human family from ever seeing His Kingdom, either in this world or the next?
>
> More and more I see how great the work to be done at home, that the work may be thoroughly done here. To give money and send men to convert the Chinese is not all that is to be done. Direct, constant zealous work on the minds of those, not missionaries, whose thoughts and actions affect the Chinese is to be done, now by those at home. The policy pursued toward the hundred thousand Chinese in California, and toward those who are called to work on the Southern Plantations, acts toward private individuals, hasty words, unremembered tempers, all these will combine and, gathering multifold force as it crosses the Pacific, will tell here, for or against Christianity with a power exceeding that of hundreds of missionaries. No doubt His Kingdom will come; but whether it comes soon or whether generations on generations pass away without seeing it – depends on us. Of this I am sure – The people of that kingdom will not raise, trade in, nor eat opium. If anyone can make the English matter *as it is*, he will do a philanthropic work for the Chinese such as has never been done before. *Will you?*[66]

Burning with outrage, Fielde departed from her format of cool, carefully constructed letters to Warren. Her handwriting lost its neatness, and her language became almost incoherent as she choked with rage. Figuratively, this young woman seized the diplomatic Warren, her superior, by the lapels and screamed, "You are a man of influence, DO SOMETHING!"

Of course nothing could be done. Missionaries, armed with unquestioned faith in the Word, continued their Sisyphean work, knowing that their Christian ideals were counterbalanced by the dead weight of Chinese inertia, and the formidable corrupting elements of the West. The missionary leadership was aware of the egregious treatment of Chinese by Westerners, prompting the declaration: "In view of the wrongs inflicted upon the Chinese at home and in this country, it should also be our special endeavor to show that they are neither approved nor condoned by us; and that, so far as our voice and influence reach, the wrongs of those who suffer unjustly shall be righted."[67] Some Chinese viewed Christianity and the opium trade as one and the same thing, leading an opium smoking lady of 90 years old to push away a proffered Bible: "Take it away. Take it away. I do not want your opium or your Jesus."[68]

While leaders of foreign missionary societies dismissed "petty criticisms and thoughtless ridicule" of their cherished crusade, there were influential critics who could not be easily dismissed. A withering critique by Mark Twain in the *North American Review* (1901) appeared after the violent Boxer rebellion had been put down by a consortium of Western powers whose soldiers looted the countryside and murdered non-Christian Chinese for murdering Christian Chinese, some missionaries, and the German Minister. Not only did this broadside excoriate England, France, Germany, Russia, and America for their immoral Imperialism, it condemned the missionaries, under the protection of Western soldiers, who sought Draconian reparations for Christian Chinese at the expense of their non-Christian brethren.[69] It was pointed out that in the turmoil, the Boxers had not raped white women, but when the avenging Christian soldiers of the West arrived they freely indulged in molesting Chinese women. The rebellion itself was not only a consequence of the corrupt, convoluted politics of a teetering Imperial China, it was an expression of anti-foreign sentiment. Important Chinese factions wanted foreigners with their disruptive Christianity out of their country.[70] They were impotent and inept in their attempt to drive out the Westerner, and they failed miserably. Foreigners were there to stay. However, the Chinese learned that if they were ever to successfully confront the West, they would have to master Western science and technology. The rebellion, which took place more than a decade after Fielde had left China, was a watershed in Chinese history because power shifted from the ancient, conservative elders in the interior of the country to the more progressive, adaptable leaders in the coastal cities.

Within five years, Fielde had mastered the Chinese language. She thought in Chinese and spoke the Swatow, Tei-chiu dialect fluently as very few Westerners could. The written language was particularly important in her teaching because it was common to all of China, unlike the spoken language which was particular to each province. Fielde completed *First Lessons in the Swatow Dialect*, a grammar of over two hundred lessons in simple Chinese that the least informed of her students could understand. By associating the spoken word with the ideograms in her book of grammar, students learned the written language. She wrote *The Compendium of the Gospels, A Hymn Book in Swatow Dialect*, and *An Index to William's Dictionary*, with pronunciation in the Swatow dialect, which made this important standard work accessible both to her students and to missionaries. A book on the life of Jesus and his teachings, from the Synoptic Gospels, sermons, and tracts on the philosophy of Christianity flowed from her pen; she seemed to be as prolific in Chinese as she was in English. In 1914, long after she had ceased being a missionary, Fielde was proud of the fact that some of her leaflets, such as *After Death*, and *The True God*, written in 1873, were still being used by Baptists and Presbyterians in the field – it was "among the durable satisfactions of life. . . . Tokens that I have labored not in vain cheer me as I approach the end of labor."[71] *The True God* is a brief and conventional account of an omniscient God, the only God, Lord of Heaven and Earth, creating the Earth and life upon it. Accommodating to Eastern sensibilities, and appealing to those who practiced ancestral worship, Fielde calls Him "the original ancestor . . . the fountain-head of life." God, who sent a "Savior of the World to redeem men from their sins and save men's souls," rewards the good who will reach the "Heavenly Temple," while He punishes the evil. To worship this "True and Living God" one "need not burn incense nor paper, nor make offerings, nor go to the temple to worship."

The tract *After Death* informs the prospective Christian that after death there are two places one can go: Heaven, where everyone is happy and joyous, or Hell, where "those who enter there are ceaselessly burned with fire, ceaselessly gnawed by worms, and live among sorrows and wicked men." The attractions of the former and the horrors of the latter were portrayed in elementary terms familiar to the Chinese. In the Heavenly Temple the streets were paved with gold, the houses are of jade, "forever imperishable. . . . In that country it is neither cold nor hot. There are no insect pests. . . . They do not get sick, they do not die, there is no suffering, no sorrow, no shedding of tears. There is neither thirst nor hunger nor poverty . . . one has happiness through endless ages." The evangelist's promise of salvation was incredible, but to accept the offer, the wretched Chinese peasant, if reachable, would have to shed the beliefs and customs of a lifetime, and would earn the enmity of neighbors and superiors who had much to lose should Christianity prevail. The fundamentalist doctrine actually preached by Fielde could not be faulted by her superiors, however much she questioned the historical accuracy of the Bible, protested the injustice of Victorian masculine dominion, or deviated from the tenets of Baptist Christianity in her personal behavior.

Despite Fielde's triumphs, her popularity among women in the U.S.A., her ability to raise money, and the admiration of Board members, the 1870s was a time of turmoil – wrangling with the Board – usually restrained, occasionally bursting out. Fielde could not abide perceived error and unfairness without attempting a remedy. Her living arrangements were a constant source of conflict, sometimes arousing her to fury. The Board supposedly had set aside $500 to build Fielde a home of her own in Swatow, but unaccountably it was never built. Fielde demanded that the unused money be placed in her account to be used as she wished, a request that was denied.

Upon arrival at Swatow and not finding living quarters that had been promised, she was forced to share living space with Mrs. Johnson, who, together with her now deceased husband, among the first members of the Swatow mission, had strongly disapproved of a single woman working at the mission. Fielde, so popular and admired, was to live in the home that Mrs. Johnson considered her very own – an intolerable situation that erupted into frequent, bitter quarrels. All sympathized with Fielde, and when Mrs. Johnson, perhaps psychotic by now, tried to enroll the native members of the mission on her own behalf, challenging Ashmore's authority,[72] the situation became intolerable, and she was recalled.[73] Fielde had become so depressed that she wanted to move away and live with a Chinese family, but she was ordered by the Corresponding Secretary that she must remain at the mission and "live as a Christian."[74]

Since her Bangkok days, Fielde had engaged in a long-running battle regarding her pay, resentful that, even after the Board had increased her salary, she still received less than a man for comparable effort. In Boston, far from the fields of action, the Board was trying to satisfy increasing demands on resources that were actually shrinking during the economic depression of the 1870s. From Fielde's perspective, the Board vacillated in its policies, suddenly changing its decisions – for instance, on salaries. Now, in China, she received an annual salary of $500, $250 for medical expenses and local travel, and $150 for the printing of her writing on the Gospels in Chinese.[75] But in her ever-expanding efforts, she needed more money. The more successful she was, the more money she needed, but a hard-pressed Board could not satisfy all her demands, leaving her frustrated. Fielde needed money to build classrooms, to buy or rent boats for travel to outposts, and to pay Bible-women so that they and their families could live ($24 each, per year). She was fortunate that she had another source of income – donations from her many friends, some wealthy, while readers of her popular articles contributed what they could. The money received was specifically earmarked for Fielde's activities.

Not only did her articles appear in the *Baptist Missionary Magazine*, but also in the publications of several missionary societies. Much of her writing has disappeared after a hundred years because it was throw-away literature, printed on paper of the lowest quality. In the Annual Report of 1880 she wrote that she had written 180 letters, most of which were appeals for money, and had sent over four hundred packages of her printed material for use in Sunday schools, and adult discussion groups to foster an interest in the missionary effort. Even her outlay for postage was not inconsiderable, but with the help of her friends and followers she managed to stay afloat – yet there was always a shortage of funds.

Swatow was so sickeningly hot in summer that Westerners were impelled to flee. While Presbyterians maintained a resort on Double Island in Swatow Bay to escape the heat, and had a sabbatical system of leaves for Swatow missionaries, regardless of their state of health, Baptist missions had no such policy. Missionaries worked in Swatow until their health broke down because there were no provisions for paid furloughs that would permit rest and healing. Does one really need to rest doing the Lord's work? Fielde was especially resentful of this policy because her constitution was robust, and for many years her health did not falter, making her ineligible for financial assistance for extended travel, and a furlough to America.

Letters shuttled back and forth about this matter, but to no avail, prompting Fielde, in her frustration, to publish a devastating broadside in the journal *National Baptist.* The critique was of particular moment because it came from a well-known and highly respected missionary in the field, someone in the trenches who knew what she was talking about. She could barely conceal her anger in her clearly thought-out argument. The missionary effort was insufficient and misguided, and at the present time: "If the Chinese were converted at the rate of ten a day, which would be a great ingathering for the number of missionaries now here, it would take a hundred and seventy thousand years for them all to become Christians." The home churches gave just enough to support a few native preachers, and no more, insufficient to generate a critical mass of native Christians who could create a self-sustaining community with its own churches and schools, all within the financial means of the Chinese. This was the only hope of the evangelical movement. The Western contribution, if sufficiently large, should function as a leavening rather than as a permanent day-by-day support – an eating up of precious seed money. "The self-supporting church or school will effect many times more for good among the heathen than one supported by home money. The self-supporting thing is known to have independent root and life of its own, and is believed in as no mere parasite on the national custom can be."

She claimed that by skimping, missionaries in the field were placed at terrible risk:

> Christ was not careless of the physical welfare of his disciples when he sent them to abide in whatsoever house these missionaries went. . . . The houses [where missionaries work] are not such that we could healthfully live in them; the food is not such that we could share it unnauseated. The natives live in houses without windows and floors, and eat things to us unclean. Most of them sleep, eat and perform all their avocations in one room. Cholera prevails all summer, small pox all winter, and unspeakable skin-diseases, vermin and filth all year round.

She accused the Committee of wasting the missionary's time and life maintaining a policy which "deliberately asked that a few young men come out and kill themselves by low diet and overwork, that the home churches might thus have their blunted emotions roused about the work of missions." People back home seemed to get a vicarious feeling of piety from the suffering from afar, as if participating, but "the heathens are not to be saved by our sufferings. . . . Of course, some suffering and danger is inevitable and to be expected." Fielde ended by listing the qualities of the effective missionary – they must be fluent in the local language, they must know the countryside and their flock, they must have "a discriminative discernment of Asiatic human nature, and knowledge of native modes of conducting practical affairs," they must have executive and organizing talent, and finally, foreign missionary work is only for the healthy and strong.[76] Nowhere in the tract are gender-related issues discussed, probably because Fielde decided to focus on only one problem for the present.

The broadside was astonishing, for the denunciation of the sainted elders of the Board of Missions had not been kept within the family, and it had come from an insider – a woman! The Board had been impressed by her work, they enjoyed her stories and anecdotes, they were willing to listen to her as a source of information, but they were not prepared to accept her opinions on matters of policy, the male preserve in the Baptist church. Murdock the Corresponding Secretary, was torn, for he was the voice of the group, but he had formed a warm, personal relationship with Fielde. In the most diplomatic language he stated that he himself had "no personal feelings in this matter," and he acquitted her of "intentional misrepresentation," but he accused her of being imprudent, unfair, and in error. The Committee was shocked that such an emotional outburst should arise from "one of our most intelligent missionaries." However, the rules regarding travel were not changed, and pay scales were not altered.

Despite the turmoil, there was no complaint about Fielde's performance at Swatow; in fact she ran the mission when Ashmore was away, or was incapacitated by "granular ophthalmia" which confined him to a darkened room for six months. Still, she must have harbored feelings of frustration and resentment at being ignored and treated as something of a troublemaker by the higher powers in Boston. Overflowing with energy, she sought satisfaction elsewhere, and having a natural affinity for language, she began to assemble a dictionary of the Swatow dialect, with English equivalents. Fielde had already written a grammar of the Swatow dialect, an index to a dictionary, and had translated several works from Chinese into English, and the reverse, including classical into vernacular Chinese. Now she saw a need for creating a definitive dictionary of the dialect of the region, one she would use every day.

Drifting away from authority and control, resolved to achieve her goal without guidance or interference, she began work on the dictionary in 1879, and completed the task in 1883, a longer time than she had expected. Once again a determined Fielde, in making her own decisions, was stepping on toes – really, an open revolt against confining religious and male codes. Ashmore was annoyed at the prospect of his junior undertaking such a major, time-consuming, and expensive task. He was the acknowledged scholar of the mission and of Westerners in China, and if anyone was to undertake such a work it should be Ashmore. However, he was circumspect in his opposition, the most serious objection to the project being that Fielde was writing the dictionary in mission time, working on the dictionary while neglecting mission responsibilities when the mission was seriously understaffed because of leave-taking and illness. During Fielde's absence, Miss Norwood and Miss Thompson took over the training of Bible-women, the direction of the school, and visits to the outstations where graduate Bible-women operated.

Though a good friend, kind, and helpful, Ashmore was annoyed that Fielde did not follow his lexicographic advice, and refused to delay the expensive printing that would divert funds from needy projects. Despite the criticism, the dictionary was completed, and in the Preface Fielde thanked Ashmore and others for their assistance. She also thanked those who at different times and places had cared for her in her "severe illness." Fielde had continued to proof-read despite her suffering from "purulent ophthalmia" – "weakened eyes" – in which for a few days her eyesight was "imperiled in the extreme." Ashmore wrote to Murdock that after this she would not be able to use her eyes for some time, and that recovery would be slow because of the heat and glare.[77]

The work was printed by the American Presbyterian Mission Press in Shanghai where an undeterred Fielde lived for almost a year, going over the page proofs day after day, correcting, editing, supervising, and dealing with Chinese printers who spoke no English, and did not understand the Swatow dialect. She would not heed Murdock's pleas to save her weakened eyes and return to America. *A Pronouncing and Defining Dictionary of The Swatow Dialect, Arranged According to Syllables and Tones* turned out to be a magnificent, scholarly work, over six hundred pages long with a seventeen-page Introduction, containing 5442 of the most commonly used words (about half the total used by the Swatow people), and "tables of exercises on the tones, sounds, aspirates, nasals, etc." Sylvester Partridge felt the entire effort was "a great waste," and that it was too complicated for the beginner and not adequate for the advanced student,[78] an opinion shared by Scottish missionaries, who expressed their disapproval in "extreme language." Ashmore, however, was generous in his praise: "There is a great deal of valuable matter in the make up of the book, and I am justified in saying it will prove an 'invaluable help to learners.' I have said this in print and now I say it here. It will be of great help to persons who know how to make use of it." Ashmore acknowledged that "Miss Fielde undertook the preparation of this Dictionary from a strong impulse of her own. I do not know that she made any extensive inquiry about what others might think."[79] He felt that it would have been a much better work if she had listened to others. Some critics were unhappy about typographical errors, and others had serious technical objections to the style of romanizing of characters adopted by Fielde.

On the other hand, the dictionary and its author were praised effusively by the editor of an English newspaper in Shanghai. He called her

> one of the most talented and at the same time one of the most devoted and self-denying philanthropists that ever came to China. . . . The Herculean task involved in the preparation and publication of such a book can hardly be conceived by anyone who has never attempted it . . . a work which does the greatest credit to her literary abilities and her indomitable perseverance . . . the people of Swatow are to be envied the possession of a lady of such accomplishments and refinement, coupled with such sensible enthusiasm and self-denial in the missionary cause.[80]

Thousands of copies of the dictionary were sold, and it went through several editions and reprintings. It was still being used thirty years after its publication

(1883), not only by missionaries but also by English-speaking merchants, diplomats, explorers, and travelers. Considering Fielde's rather poor formal education, the work stands as testimony to her brilliance and resolve.

By early 1883, she had earned a rest that would take her back to America, the Women's Society of the West, in Minnesota, eager to pay her way. Fielde was not only seeking respite from an unhappy, if not intolerable situation, she arrived in Philadelphia with a twofold plan of action: to obtain professional training as a scientist, and to become a proficient obstetrician so that she might bring back to China knowledge that would reduce the death rate and suffering of women in childbirth.

6 Philadelphia, 1883–1885

Adele Fielde had labored for ten years in China, often overworked and exhausted, exposed to disease and pestilence in an unhealthy climate. She had lived in a land of primitive sanitation where outbreaks of cholera and deadly fevers were not uncommon, the drinking-water was always suspect, and fruit and vegetables could not be eaten without special preparation. Constant vigilance in China was the key to survival, although even in America the menace of typhoid and cholera were ever present, for these scourges always threatened, and in fact they were epidemic in Philadelphia in 1891 and 1896.

Fielde began her two-year stay in America in early 1883. Chester A. Arthur had succeeded the assassinated President James A. Garfield, and the following year a tainted Grover Cleveland was elected President of America. The post-civil war Reconstruction Period had come to an end, political corruption flourished, and civil service reform was initiated to counter the spoils system of the Republican and Democratic parties. Huge numbers of European immigrants were arriving on American shores, many settling in Philadelphia, while others were lured to the West with the promise of cheap land. The railroads flourished while they brought death and destruction to the native American and the buffalo.

In a country in ferment, fortunes were being made in industry, manufacturing, railroads, mining, and lumbering, and nowhere was American hustle more evident than in Philadelphia, a city of almost one million people of great ethnic diversity, and the second most active port in the country. The city, in its "Iron Age," could boast of foundries, ship and locomotive building second to none. A green town and port redolent with eighteenth-century charm became a sprawling industrial city with endless streets with rows of houses, slums riddled with disease, and political corruption. It was a center of transportation with a vigorous mix of small factories – textiles, brewing, clothing manufacturing, and sugar refining. The city however had long lost its dominant position in finance, politics, and the arts. Still, music and opera thrived and a vigorous school of writers, now largely unknown (S. Wier Mitchell, Agnes Repplier, Owen Wister, George Boker), scholars (Horace Howard Furness, Henry Charles Lea), and scientists (Joseph Leidy, Edward

Drinker Cope) were active. Numerous painters of the time, including Thomas Eakins, actors (the Barrymore family, Otis Skinner), and brilliant architects (William Furness, a teacher of Louis Sullivan) added luster to the city. Relentlessly over the decades, there was a downward trend in the city's fortunes, signified by the remarkable number of talented and creative individuals with deep roots in Philadelphia, who went elsewhere to enable their talents to flourish.[1]

Science was in full flower in Europe, and technology was reaching new levels of achievement. European bacteriologists were establishing the causes of ancient scourges such as tuberculosis and cholera, and Pasteur and Lister were the great heroes of the day. America was coming into its own, with its ingenious inventions that changed the way people lived. The country could boast of a scientific genius, Willard Gibbs, a major poet, Walt Whitman, and of writers of distinction such as Mark Twain, Henry James, and William Dean Howells. A talented group of American painters had appeared, most notably Thomas Eakins, Winslow Homer, and the artists of the Hudson River School. Fielde had arrived in a land bustling with confidence and hope.

Fielde had planned to visit family in New York State, and to rest for a few weeks before proceeding to Philadelphia, but immediately after her arrival in America, she became a willing conscript of the Board of the American Baptist Missionary Union, who arranged a speaking tour for her of marathon proportions that began upon debarkation in San Francisco and proceeded eastward across the continent. The tour not only spread the word about the good works of the missionary movement, it was also a highly profitable venture for the Union. Hardly realizing it, she had become a hero to an American public enthralled by her accounts of the life of a missionary in China, and the odd, sometimes horrific customs of a distant land. In growing demand as a lecturer to women's groups and church gatherings, she recounted her personal experiences, and told of the dreadful plight of women in China. She spoke of the killing of female babies who were considered worthless, the crippling practice of footbinding, arranged marriages of very young females to old men, and of the high incidence of suicide among young brides – surely an effective prologue to an appeal for money for the Christian missionary movement which was trying to put a stop to these ungodly, unAmerican practices. Five months of incessant travel and 150 lectures was all she could endure. This was no rest, and in fact a "nervous breakdown" ended her lecturing for the time being.[2] Though she was on leave to replenish herself, she was filled with other ambitious plans that would take her to Philadelphia.

During long evenings in Swatow translating *Genesis* into Chinese, she began thinking about the origins of life and of man, and though devout, she seemed to have had no qualms about considering alternatives to the biblical version of Creation. A realist and pragmatist, she may have had lurking doubt about the details of the biblical story, and was no doubt aware of the new geological and physical data which clearly contradicted Archbishop Ussher's calculation that the Earth was created in six days, in 4004 B.C. The devout were convinced that they lived in an orderly world presided over by a benevolent and loving God who had created all living things according to His plan, but Fielde, despite her deep involvement in a fundamentalist version of Christianity, was quite willing to examine the basic tenets of her faith.

Charles Darwin's *The Origin of Species by Means of Natural Selection,* published in 1859, and his *The Descent of Man and Selection in Relation to Sex* (1871), considered blasphemous by most orthodox Christians, were radical challenges to accepted belief. Yet Fielde was intrigued by Darwin's rational, alternative explanation of how species, including the human, arose, and she did not recoil from exploring the role of amoral competition in this dynamic process. Evolutionary change was a chance affair, without direction, without a grand plan – raw opportunism in which a presiding Power, and beneficent Love, played no part. Witnessing the great poverty and misery of the Chinese peasant, the terrible battle for survival, the small value placed on human life, and the behavior of Western and Chinese powers, was evidence enough to conclude that raw biological forces were at work in a world without moral law. Darwin's notions were more in keeping with her experience in China than were the words of Jesus. What were the biological and theological implications of the killing of female infants, and the abuse of women? As an intensely curious person, she must have taken into account evolutionary as well as religious arguments in her considerations of nature and society, but there was, in fact, no conflict between science and religion in Fielde's thinking. Whatever scientists discovered or proposed was merely man's uncovering of God's incredible handiwork.

Surrounded by her devout colleagues, there could be no opportunity for open discussion about evolution, but in a secular center of learning in America she could satisfy her curiosity about this revolutionary notion, which she found was often accepted and accommodated in the thinking of many devout scientists. For the first time in years she felt free to follow her interests, but she had been away for so long she knew little of the educational opportunities in the U.S.A. This was soon remedied when she met David Starr Jordan, an ichthyologist (and future first president of Stanford University), who advised her to study at the Academy of Natural Sciences of Philadelphia, to pursue her interest in science and evolution. At the same time she could also acquire training at one of Philadelphia's medical schools, one established for women.

With Western medicine held in esteem in China, Fielde had been called upon to provide medical assistance. In her report of 1880 she stated that she had tended 100 patients, all of whom survived, but she must have been aware of her inadequacy and ignorance in these matters. Contrary to some in the missionary establishment, Fielde held the view that a physician, male or female, should be part of every missionary post, but medical graduates were in very short supply. Consequently, the death rate of Chinese women in childbirth was appalling because men were not permitted to touch these women, and females, usually family members, were utterly ignorant of obstetrical matters, and could do much harm. To remedy the situation, Fielde sought obstetrical training that might be incorporated into the curriculum of the Bible school at Swatow. Bible-women who had midwife experience could save the lives of mothers and infants, even under primitive conditions, by the application of elementary rules of hygiene and obstetrical practice.

The Women's Medical College of Pennsylvania in Philadelphia was the first school in the country to offer women a doctorate in medicine, and women missionaries were now seizing the opportunity to become physicians, or to obtain an abbreviated medical education, as Fielde was doing. In December 1883, she enrolled for the winter session in a course, popular with missionaries, entitled "Principles and Practice of Medicine and Surgery", in which obstetrics was emphasized. On Saturday mornings, three women, including Fielde, and 150 men attended a medical clinic at Blockley Hospital of the University of Pennsylvania. At a time when women were discouraged or prevented from becoming physicians – a male preserve – they were heckled and made to feel unwelcome at lectures. Fielde was outraged, and put a stop to the hectoring with an impassioned and eloquent plea:

> Gentlemen: I have for eighteen years been a missionary in China. The Chinese have no medical science, and superstitious rites are chiefly relied on in the treatment of disease. *All* the people are in need of medical aid, but the *women* are the *neediest.* A Chinese woman would under no circumstances go to a male physician for the treatment of any disease peculiar to her sex. She would be prevented by her own womanly delicacy and by all the notions of modesty held by those around her. She would suffer lifelong agony rather than violate her sense of propriety. Her father, her brothers, and her husband would even let her die rather than allow her to be treated by a male physician. Full of sorrow for the sufferings of these women, I have been looking to Christian America to see what hope of help for them might be here. I have been glad to find that in some of our great medical schools earnest and self-sacrificing young women are fitting themselves for a work of mercy in Asia and other lands. Unless such women learn to do such work well there is no physical salvation for those afflicted ones. And on behalf of those women, who have no medical care while they so sorely need it, I ask from you the courtesy of gentlemen toward ladies who are studying medicine in Philadelphia.

Properly disabused, the entire class cheered, and a spokesperson reassured the ladies that they were welcome, a concession in the battle for women to attain a semblance of equality.[3]

Once her medical training was on course, Fielde looked into the possibility of obtaining an education in biology. With her considerable reputation as a writer and lecturer, and bearing letters of introduction from David Starr Jordan to his Philadelphia colleagues, scientists such as Joseph Leidy, Edward D. Cope, Harrison Allen, and Angelo Heilprin, Fielde visited the Academy of Natural Sciences of Philadelphia to see whether she might obtain instruction. Although the institution was famed for its paleontology and natural history, and prided itself in its magnificent museum and library, it was primarily a specialized institute set up for research, not for the education of students. A formidable lady, she must have impressed the members of the Academy, for this novice was given a place to work and a microscope, and her training was supervised by the geologist and paleontologist Heilprin, and the invertebrate zoologist Benjamin Sharp, all with the blessing of the Academy's president, Joseph Leidy, an enlightened man who had sympathy for women seeking an education. Thereafter, Fielde always considered the Academy her "Alma Mater." Fielde became a close, lifelong friend of Edward J. Nolan, the Academy's librarian and secretary, who later carried on an extensive correspondence with her, advised her, and edited many of her scientific papers.

By her own admission, the two years spent in Philadelphia were the happiest of her life. Living in comfortable quarters at 3933 Pine Street in West Philadelphia near the University of Pennsylvania, she found herself in a society of sophisticated people who welcomed her and recognized her superior qualities. Here, for the first time, her new friends were willing to explore any subject without ideological or theological constraint. For someone who was so driven, and had never enjoyed an easy life, a summer vacation spent with Benjamin Sharp and his family on Nantucket was idyllic – a paradise. In a letter from Nantucket to Edward Nolan, who seemed to be something more than a close friend, she was radiant with pleasure.[4] The letter is particularly interesting because in it she writes: "I am capable of being agreeable through an entire summer: and so are you, though you do not believe it." She seems to suggest that she is aware of the fact that she could be difficult and demanding, characteristics that one suspects from her record. Having always led a demanding life, she almost evoked a feeling of pity for her deprivations when she yearns: "If man in his (or her) normal condition were, like birds, fish and squirrels, what lovely times we could have, without work or worry, and with sunshine, seashore and science. With a bathing dress, some bread and milk, a microscope . . . one would be fully equipped for Happiness." Though ecstatic, it was mere lip-service to an Eden she herself would never inhabit for long.

Fielde suddenly found herself surrounded by kindred spirits as she immersed herself in scientific and medical studies, a dramatic escape from her years of desperate labor, and troubled relationships far from her native land. She thrived in this new situation, and her natural ebullience and sense of humor, so evident in her student days, reappeared. Although Fielde was a determined and serious woman, her lively sense of humor endeared her to her friends, and she had a marvelous sense of fun. In 1885 she attended a meeting of the American Library Association in Milwaukee. A group photograph was taken, and a year later it fell to Fielde to identify each member.[5] Quick to sense pomposity and self-conscious, "proper" behavior, her comments about each person are irreverent and hilarious. One couple whom she liked were "newly married, very devoted and therefore ridiculous, more or less." Another recently married couple, the Fosters, "were infinitely more absurd . . . Fortunately they dropped out early – Mrs Foster caunt stand the fatigue, you know." Another was "an old man with a young wife." A Mr. Barton was "an intense family man and therefore something of a bore. Disposed to always date events by domestic incidents; for instance 'it was the year my Lillie had the whooping cough . . .' and he was always showing photographs of his children. A very nice man doubtless, but of the kind that makes me deathly ill." Another man was "thoroughly respectable, evidently anything but at his ease during the reception at Schlitz park, because of the beer." He was renamed "Mr. Pumblechook," and a Reverend from Milwaukee was renamed "Mr. Creamcheese." Another woman, very old, was "a wonderful example of the dreadnought character of certain American women." Perhaps her tart comments about newly married and devoted couples had their origins in Fielde's tragic, romantic past and her subsequent "free" life unfettered by personal attachment. An imposing Fielde with her sharp wit sometimes antagonized new acquaintances but hostility was soon banished through her honesty and charm. One of the ladies developed a hatred of Fielde, calling her "that horrid old doctor," but she changed her opinion when the two ironed out their differences.

In Philadelphia she learned the fundamentals of laboratory biology by dissection of vertebrates and invertebrates, and by microscopic study of unicellular organisms – all under supervision. Her training was classical and old-fashioned, almost entirely descriptive, with only small mention of the manipulative and intrusive approach of experimental research which was beginning to be more widely appreciated and practiced in America. Almost intuitively, Fielde seemed to understand the necessity of experiment in her work, and that to involve oneself in science meant to manipulate experimental material so that its workings would be revealed. Experimentation rather than passive observation suited Fielde's activist nature.

In 1885 she published her first scientific paper entitled "Observations on Tenacity of Life, and Regeneration of Excised Parts Lumbricus terrestris."[6] In this independently done work on the earthworm, as in many of her later studies on other forms of life, she was concerned with the care and culture of the organism, but this was only a preparation for later experimental work. Fielde, a patient observer, seemed to have the instincts of a born experimenter, developing reliable methods of measurement, establishing basic, standard conditions in which a process can operate, then performing the experiment. By doing this, confounding variability in the process observed is minimized. Fielde seemed to be fascinated by the effects of environment (temperature, air, light and dark, water, and food) on the survival of whole, and parts, of worms. Experienced in the culture of segments of worms, she proceeded to carry out ingenious experiments on the manner of regeneration of the worm, showing that the process takes place in the inner rather than at the terminal segments, and she also demonstrated that brain and nerve ganglions of the earthworm can be regenerated.

Fielde was honored by election to membership of the Academy of Natural Sciences, and became an active participant in their bimonthly meetings as the resident expert on the Orient, the language, literature, and folklore of China, and, after returning to Swatow, she continued to send communications to be read at meetings of the Academy.[7] Part of every meeting of the Academy was taken up with oddities reported from abroad, and one such, "Chinese Women and Spiritism," concerned seances in which women vividly described their encounters with the dead after awakening from trances. Fielde's precise descriptions of the phenomenon were followed by a wry analysis: "They evidently see what they expect to see," and "These seekers after truth in the land of the shades bring back no ideas save those which they took with them when starting on their quest . . . in spite of their disheveled hair, pallor and exhaustion."[8] In another communication, "Fishing Lines and Ligatures from the Silk-glands of Lepidopterous Larvae," Fielde described the process by which country people made thread of great tensile strength for use as fishing lines. Doubting the purported strength of the thread, she tested it and found it wanting.[9] Surrounded by experienced geologists in the Academy, Fielde had developed an interest in the subject, and had learned their language. In an account of a trip up the Han River, which courses between high mountains, she described in some detail the geological characteristics of the exposed strata. Her account was read and discussed by the geologist Angelo Heilprin, and, along with the communication, she sent the Academy eight boxes of rocks, systematically collected from various strata in different regions of the river, to be studied by the Academy.[10]

We see the shadow of one of her mentors Joseph Leidy in a report on fresh-water organisms ("Rhizopods") from streams around Swatow. Leidy had published his classic *Freshwater Rhizopods of North America* in 1879, and Fielde reported that some of the organisms she had found in China were identical to those American species described by Leidy. In the next few years she worked on aquatic insects and larvae,[11] and on a parasitic trematode, *Distoma* in the snail.[12] It is evident that Fielde was both a descriptive naturalist, and an experimentalist, and that she was sufficiently versatile to exploit both approaches in her science.

Fielde was also concerned with how science was taught in schools, and she took it upon herself to describe the status of Chinese science to Americans.[13] While astronomy and mathematics had been studied for thousands of years, no other branches of science, such as biology and chemistry, were known. On the other hand, there were countless volumes of what Fielde called pseudo-science – "myths, fables and superstitions set forth as facts." She was pleased that changes were beginning to take place, for in the past few decades many Western texts had been translated into Chinese, and their sale and distribution were increasing. Competitive civil service examinations, which assured a young man a job for life, covered only the Chinese classics, but in recent years knowledge of geography and natural philosophy had been added to the requirements.

Before returning to America, Fielde, at the urging of friends, gathered several of her essays, many of which had previously appeared in journals, and in 1884 while in Philadelphia, published them as a book – *Pagoda Shadows* – dedicated "to American women." The work informed Americans about the China encountered by Fielde, through a series of authoritative and accurate accounts of the daily lives of Chinese women, their "sorrows and disabilities." With its special emphasis on problems that concern women, her writings, sometimes angry, forged a link between American and Chinese women. Fielde's accounts went far beyond formal history and statistics – these were essays filled with arcane and exotic knowledge which informed the reader about everyday life in China, a narrative enlivened by anecdotes, legends, and lore unknown to most Americans.

The book begins with an account of the status of women in China, which, bad as it was, was not as hopeless as in other pagan countries – women were not oppressed by caste, confined to the harem, or "not in a climate which keeps her bare and lazy, like the women in Siam." Though women were in fact treated with some respect in the home, they had no political rights, but neither did men in a land where "extortion is the chief use of office, and fear of it the main spur of obedience." There were whole chapters describing women's dress, betrothals, wedding ceremonies, divorce, the life of a child, the Chinese language, education, literature, festivals, funerals, religious practices, spiritism, medicine, the law and justice, business, loan associations, farming practices, and modes of travel. Fielde, fluent in the Swatow dialect, was trusted by the Chinese, and so she was privileged to gather information firsthand, an eyewitness, though sometimes discretely, listening from behind a screen.

Fielde returned again and again to the low regard the Chinese had for women. Once married they became an integral part of the male's family, and if unhappy there had no hope of divorce, the only alternatives being acceptance or suicide. Their sole means to attain status and power was to produce male children, and live long enough for their parents and in-laws to die. Women would then be elder mothers of sons in a system where obeying elders was the prime law. The Silver Rule of Confucius – do unto others as you would have others do unto you – was a central moral precept, understandable to Americans. Chinese children were instructed never to steal, in accordance with a well-developed sense of private property, but they were never taught *not* to lie.

Footbinding was given its most detailed clinical description by Fielde in her account of the practice, with all its pain, deformation, and putrefaction, and she was dismayed that 90 percent of Chinese women underwent this crippling torture, willingly or not. Crippled, what kind of mothers could they be? Almost half the population was either immobilized, hobbled about with a walking stick, or was carried on the backs of female slaves (who were so low in the social scale, their feet were large and intact). To Fielde, the insistence on having "fairy feet" was a "mystery of human perversity." The law did not compel the practice, it was desired by most women, but to Fielde it was just another device for maintaining male dominance – "Religion is not the only sentiment which has its martyrs."

To Fielde and other missionaries, the killing and abandonment of female babies was a blatant, horrendous practice not actually punishable by law, and women were not ashamed to admit to the deed. As Fielde traveled about the country, she frequently saw the remains of infants scattered by the roadside. From her own study, and gathering numbers from other missionaries, she could report that the practice varied from region to region, and that in her study overall, 160 women, "all over fifty years of age, had born six hundred and thirty-one sons and five hundred and thirty-eight daughters." Sixty percent of the sons had lived more than ten years while the number for females was 38 percent. "The hundred and sixty women had, according to their own statements, destroyed a hundred and fifty-eight of their daughters; but none had ever destroyed a boy." One woman had killed eleven of her daughters. A Catholic priest in Peking had told Fielde that in 1882, "seven hundred little castaway girls had been gathered up alive from the ruts and pits of the streets," and were taken to a foundling asylum.

Fielde's writing is surprisingly secular and technical, but in the face of such horror, she boldly asserted her opinion that the acceptance of Christianity would put an end to infanticide, footbinding, and other abuses of women. The only hope was for the Chinese to embrace the Gospel. Yet there were numerous skeptical Americans and Chinese who wondered how Christianity and its messengers could cure these social ills, while Christian nations behaved so barbarically toward Asians, native Americans, and Africans.

The second half of *Pagoda Shadows* consists of a series of autobiographies of Chinese women – Bible-women, some very able. Fielde listened to their stories, and translated them into English, each a tale of woe with few moments of happiness that leaves the reader with a profound sadness for these tragic lives. The dead weight of Chinese law and custom that governed the lives of so many people existing at subsistence level had a particularly damaging effect on women. Taken together, these stories are a lexicon of legitimate grievances, illustrations of the abuse of women that pervaded Fielde's writing and lectures. Most of the women came from small villages, often betrothed as children, working as slaves, attending in-laws, literally on their knees, and beaten by husbands who were sometimes alcoholics, drug addicts, or gamblers. Their stories provide vivid insights into the intimate life of the family, and its struggle to make a living.

Each woman told how she stumbled into Christianity by chance, and how a sense of liberation and hope was born in her grim life by accepting the

Word of Christ; redemption and heaven could be hers. But renouncing old beliefs was profoundly disruptive to family and village life, for these women lost the esteem and respect of their neighbors, and their husbands could no longer make a living once they adopted the new religion. Sometimes there was violence, and families were destroyed when some members converted, while others held to the old beliefs. Christians also had a special problem of marrying off their children, for they insisted that their children marry Christians, but there were so few available. On the other hand, Christianity saved some women from the torture of footbinding and suicide as a way out of their intolerable lives, since suicide was no longer possible because they were now "God's property." The Bible-woman Orchid ends her narrative on a plaintive note:

> I have been sorrowful from my childhood up. I have never known a time when I had not reason for anxiety. But during the past year, though my earthly circumstances remain the same, I have been almost happy. I know that there is a Saviour and a heaven, and that has taken away seven-tenths of the weight of my troubles.[14]

Pagoda Shadows ends with an evaluation of Chinese civilization – all classes were devoted to learning, and education was eagerly sought because it was the key to advancement. Success in education was measured by passing brutal, competitive examinations, open to all, which determined the level to which one could rise in government. To Fielde, China was admirable in so many ways, with ancient systems of philosophy, a long history, a fine literature, and sophisticated cultural traditions, but Fielde's vision was colored by the suffering she saw, and the ubiquity of a debilitating belief in demons and superstitions. Along with almost all Westerners, she viewed the country as stagnant – "no important addition to the sum of Western knowledge has been gained" from the Chinese. In contrast to the European and American experience, "for hundreds of years the Chinese have discovered nothing, invented nothing, improved nothing."[15] China's history weighed heavily, the past overwhelming the present.

Pagoda Shadows was a great publishing success. It was a bestseller, and went through six editions, the first selling out in less than a week. Even after the initial excitement, it remained for many years an authoritative work consulted by students of China. Reviewers of the book found it to be an admirable, beautifully written account of Chinese life and culture by an observer with intimate knowledge of the subject.[16]

After three years away from Swatow, the latter two in America, the time came to return, and this Fielde did without hesitation. She had enjoyed a rich life in Philadelphia, and had achieved her goals of becoming competent in biological research and in obstetrics. Far removed from the drudgery of Swatow, she felt rested, and, having come into contact with freethinking people, she was made aware of other ways of looking at the world. Conventional orthodox Christian dogma was no longer sufficient for her, while Darwin's theory of evolution of how species arise was consistent with what she saw and knew. Though it was considered by some a blasphemous alternative to biblical Truth, to Fielde, as to many religious scientists of the time, Darwin had merely revealed a mechanism by which God, the Creator, who most assuredly existed, operated in the natural world. "Nature is not 'an irresponsible force.' The laws of Nature are, to my thinking those of God, who, acting under a sense of responsibility, chooses to exterminate evil. Infinite Wisdom makes no mistakes; it does not (as was done in Nürnberg in 1803) rack a woman to death in a spiked cradle, and later on find that she was innocent. What Nature, God, exterminates *ought to be exterminated every time.*"[17] Scientists claimed that they were not atheistic discreditors of religion but discoverers of the wondrous ways of the Lord. In time, as America became more secular, notions of evolution came to be part of received knowledge, though there was, and still is, a resistance to the theory by Christian Fundamentalists.

Fielde could accept the Darwinian explanation for the formation of new species, but she rejected the materialist idea that the creation of life was a chance affair, the accidental consequence of blind chemical and physical forces acting on inert matter over vast periods of time. To her, life had come about through the effort of a Creator, and once upon Earth, new species, including man, evolved through an evolutionary process according to discoverable natural law, which operated under God's guidance. Her beliefs were held by many if not most scientists at that time.

While Fielde's outlook on the natural world had changed through her research, reading, and discussion, her views on man's role in nature remained unaltered, reflecting her own burning sense of mission. Since some evolutionists found it difficult to accept the harsh and directionless nature of the "survival of the fittest" ethos, alternatives to Darwin's theory were concocted. NeoLamarckians felt compelled to incorporate a humane element into the process; changes, brought about by the human will, could be transmitted to the next generation, providing a cumulative mechanism for the betterment of humanity. The idea was consistent with notions of progress, and of constant improvement, to which Americans were so addicted.

Fielde placed the human in a separate category, superior to all other forms of life. The fate of humans was to conquer and control nature, but the privilege carried with it a moral obligation: to be concerned with the welfare of all others, to love the whole world. Ruthlessness might apply to different forms of life in the fight for survival, but humans, bound by a moral code, must look after each other. Instead of raw competition, humans should look after the weak and the less fit. A human was to be judged by his or her willingness to care for other humans; her moto was *consideration for others.*[18]

Fielde distinguished between three levels of living beings, a moral law of nature applying to each. At the bottom were those forms of life such as invertebrates, usually with enormous numbers of progeny, where survival was the *only* operative (Self-preservation, the first moral law). Higher on the scale were animals such as the snake or bird, which, while occupied with survival, selflessly look after their young, and even die for them (Love of Offspring, the second moral law). To the human, and to some extent higher animals, applies the third moral law, Love of Man and of the Whole World. Adele Fielde lived by this law, and her impressive capacity for self-sacrifice followed on from this.

Four years after her return to China, she wrote an article on a Chinese theory of evolution, and cosmogony which she had learned from her teacher, Mr. Khu, an erudite Chinese intellectual who had never been exposed to Western thought. She considered him a "treasure-trove" who could provide her with a 4000-year-old version of creation untainted by Western notions, and to her surprise, she found that Eastern and Western versions resembled each other in some respects. According to Mr. Khu, over the ages a dual power, one male and the other female – father heaven and mother earth – produced all that there is out of diffuse, undifferentiated material. "Originally the mountains rose to the firmament, and the seas covered the mountains to their tops. At that time there was, in the divine body, no life beyond the divine life." Gradually the waters receded, with small forms of life appearing, and in time "greater creatures" developed out of "lesser creatures – small herbs developed into shrubs and trees, beetles became tortoises, earthworms became serpents, and insects became birds. The praying mantis was transformed . . . into an ape, and some of the apes became hairless." These created fire which enabled them to cook, and because they were able to eat warm food "grew large, strong, and knowing, and were changed into men." This story speaks of an interdependency of nature and nurture, the inseparability of the organism and its environment. Man is in part responsible for his own creation and improvement, a view which reflects Fielde's thought that humans are unique, the highest of living forms who look after each other, and by so doing they define themselves as human and superior.

According to Mr. Khu, in the early days humans lived in a paradise but they mistreated their gods, and they have paid the consequences ever since. Because man showed disrespect for the divine body (the natural world), the life of man has been difficult; man has destroyed his environment. Every stone, tree, or field is associated with a god, and if a stone is removed from its natural site, its god weeps until the stone is replaced in its former position. One must not remove metals from the earth or cultivate the earth too deeply without offering propitiatory gifts to the local divinity. While Fielde appreciated the story of creation, she criticized a pantheistic system that hobbled the human's capacity to exploit nature in order to thrive. They held to a "false theory. . . . Affecting daily the welfare of hundreds of millions of persons, it well illustrates the practical evil of false doctrine, and by contrast, shows the great economic value of truth."[19]

Lecturing on China, its culture, religions, and the foreign missionary movement, she had made many new friends in eastern American cities, some of whom were wealthy and influential. She was offered the presidency of Vassar College, but she declined, for she wanted to return to her Bible-women. She held most dearly her association with the wizened-faced women she had trained – humble souls who were willing to make sacrifices equal to her own. While scientific investigation and her Philadelphia associations were precious to her, Fielde did not hesitate to leave them. She was a woman with a mission, and for her there was more to life than leading a safe, pleasurable existence.

7 Last years in the Far East

Travel across the Pacific Ocean in the nineteenth century was a perilous venture. Adele Fielde's first crossing had been a nightmare that ended in tragedy, and she fared no better on her second crossing. She sailed from San Francisco on September 19, 1885 on the steamship *City of Peking*, the carrier of over 1200 Chinese herded together in its fore- and midsections, while fifty Westerners occupied the afterpart. Unfortunately, when the wind was just right, it blew the foul air vented from the crowded Chinese section over the saloon and deck occupied by Fielde and the Westerners. Fielde complained that she could hardly breathe, and that the miasmic air, "supersaturated with the effluvia of present and past generations of Chinese," gave her "malarial fever."

When they left San Francisco the weather had been pleasant, but on the twentieth day, when they were only a few days out of Yokahama, they encountered the first of two typhoons. Waves as high as the smokestack crashed down upon them, inflicting great damage. Though there were no casualties, apart from the loss of a horse, passengers spent a night of terror, guarding against sudden, bone-breaking lurches of their ship. The second typhoon, much worse than the first, struck *en route* to Hong Kong from Japan.

> Our captain who had been forty years at sea, said he had never seen worse. The bulwark were broken, the boats all carried away and the decks washed free of cargo and living freight. Eighteen sheep and lambs went bleeting overboard, with other animals, to sink in the surges. There were many hours when we seemed at foundering point, at a time when the slightest misunderstanding of an order, an instant's hesitation in carrying out a command, or a second's inattention on the part of an officer, would have determined for us an adverse fate. But we came at last to the haven where we would be.

Fielde was so ill when they docked in Hong Kong that she was confined to her berth on ship for four days before proceeding to Swatow on the local steamer. The voyage of over eleven thousand miles was one she would not repeat for "thousands of dollars."[1]

Swatow had survived without her. Arriving there in a weakened state, she found the Ashmores and Partridges, Ms. Norwood and a newcomer, Ms. Minnie A. Buzzell, fully occupied in the affairs of the mission, but she was struck by the sallowness of these displaced Westerners. The "bright eyes and rosy tints" of the people back home were missing. "The strain of the physical, mental struggle for existence is almost always visible in the face of the foreign dweller in the Far East." As Fielde looked into the faces of her colleagues, as if into a mirror, she must have realized that she too was paying a high price for returning to her Bible-women. Nevertheless, she was glad to resume foreign missionary work, which she took up in a determined manner despite the discomfort and danger, and at times, suffocating loneliness. After her recent American experience, new worlds had been opened up that distracted her, and perturbed the steady focus required of the missionary.

She had returned to Swatow with new knowledge that was immediately put into use; Bible-women were instructed in obstetrical techniques both in the classroom and at the bedsides. Accompanied by her students, she attended women in the villages surrounding Swatow, a time-consuming task that made exceptional demands on her. Cholera epidemics were common, and as new Western medicines reached China to combat the scourge, Bible-women distributed them, and instructed natives in their use. Fielde was traveling much of the time, and spending nights away from home, a hardship of which she complained.[2]

In an age of remarkable advances in the understanding and treatment of disease, foreign missionaries, and certainly Adele Fielde among them, felt that newly discovered treatments would be greatly appreciated by the Chinese. Indeed, the hospital was a magnet that attracted them, and after the miracles of Western medicine were demonstrated, prospective converts would be more inclined to listen to the Message of Christ. Fielde was particularly anxious that female doctors join the missionary staff, for they could work with Chinese women as no man could. In letters and articles, she urged various Protestant missions to hire young women doctors, and she outlined how they might best be trained to handle the problems they would surely encounter. Though they were slow to appear, once in the missions, medical missionaries in up-to-date hospitals were enormously popular.[3] Still, Ashmore, the leader of their mission, was not that clear "about the extent to which medical work can be profitable for evangelization."[4]

Fielde sometimes found herself in great danger because she was perceived as a threat to the ignorant and superstitious who could not understand what she was up to. The Chinese tended to be xenophobic, a potential threat to Westerners as much as to natives from other parts of the country. In one encounter, Fielde and a companion were surrounded by a frenzied, armed mob, whose head man held a menacing spear, poised to kill. Fielde's response in this critical situation was to advance toward the leader with her arm raised, and with a strong voice she called for peace and silence. The man was taken aback, for a woman who does such a thing must be protected by some hidden power that should not be tested or challenged. In this brief, hesitant moment Fielde took charge, soothing the crowd with quotations from Confucius, and convincing them that she meant no harm, that in fact she was there for their good. Completely won over, they eagerly provided this wondrous woman with good accommodation and a place to preach. Faith, brazen courage, oratory, and diplomacy were Fielde's weapons – all used in a day's work.

Fielde, ailing and overworked, was now the senior woman in the Swatow mission who exercised an authority that subordinates sometimes found intolerable. Unquestionably, Fielde, a strong personality, could be difficult and overbearing. To compound her troubles, she could no longer abide her cramped accommodation. She continued to demand a house of her own, which Partridge claimed would be wasteful, and would upset the harmony of the mission, and she was particularly galled that at one point, funds to build her a house were suddenly cut off by the Committee in Boston. However, they seemed to relent, for within a year of her return, a new "cozy and comfortable" house was built for her, and the old house she had lived in was renovated to accommodate two young female missionaries who would take their meals with Fielde in her house. Newcomers came and went, one married, another developed tuberculosis. For many years she had urged the Board of the American Baptist Missionary Union (and other Protestant missions) to hire woman physicians, and now that one was on site she quarreled with her, and tried to attract others without the Board's authorization. Always complaining to the Executive Secretary about delays in the publication of her articles, and the misplacement of her manuscripts by the editors and printers, she kept the mission in constant turmoil, as she ignored the wishes and suggestions of her colleagues. Fielde developed an antipathy for Partridge's new, second wife who she believed had turned him against her.

Ashmore, the senior missionary, could have controlled the ongoing conflicts because he was respected by all, including Fielde, but he was in America for medical treatment, and to add to Fielde's woes, Eliza, Ashmore's wife, who was her only intimate friend, had been seriously ill for years with a progressive, debilitating disease, and had accompanied him. For several years after her return, their home had been a warm refuge for Fielde, and now she was without friends. Fielde was wearied with conflict, by her own loneliness, and deteriorating health.

Her major source of pleasure was her correspondence with Edward J. Nolan in Philadelphia. She had developed an intimacy with this bachelor which permitted her to write: "the way in which you administer to my wants, when you do not share them, makes me consider you angelic." Their letters were filled with discussion of scientific subjects, and gossip about mutual friends. From time to time he edited and saw to the publication of her scientific papers. She devoured the contents of the *Philadelphia Ledger* he sent, a link to the world she loved, and she looked forward to the news and happenings in Philadelphia. Announcement of concerts and opera, especially

Wagner, made her feel "homesick." When he tried to cheer her up, she replied: "It is all very well for you to believe that the differences between Cathay and England, Swatow and Philadelphia is not great – *You are in Philadelphia*."[5]

Fielde described her humdrum life in Swatow, her visits to outlying stations with her new assistant, Miss Hess, the games of lawn tennis, but she confessed "there is no salient points to sparkle. . . . I entertain frivolity on expectation of leaving here for Europe about the end of 1890. . . . Ah me! How often I wish I were there dissecting a crustacean, and that said crustacean was being preserved from insipidity by a little of your attic salt."[6] Later she wrote: "I count the months to '91. I should count the weeks if they were not so discouragingly many. I wonder if my native land will be so Paradaisical as it now appears! Meantime I am very content in dear, dull Swatow."[7]

She collected samples of rocks, molluscan shells, conifers, and insects for members of the Academy, and she provided Nolan with Chinese stamps for which she had no interest or feeling – "Stamps are to me no more than a gorgeous sunset to a blind man." She felt that stamp collecting was a harmless pastime that "is a much better occupation than reading Schopenhauer, who evidently plunges you into depths of gloom." In her blunt and outspoken (not to say insensitive) manner, she told Nolan, a devout Catholic, of her distress upon learning that a Miss Cox, who she had urged to become a physician, attended an osteopathic college instead, and had given up this career to marry a Catholic! "She has put her fine intellect under bonds to the 'tradition of the elders,' and has forever hampered her reason by the fine subtle meshes of a theology which is perpetually declaring to all 'Go no farther.'" To Fielde, her criticism of the Church was purely academic, for she concluded her onslaught by deploring "that prejudice which nearly all Protestants feel toward all Roman Catholics."[8]

One can only imagine the consternation of the missionary community when, at this time, Fielde published a detailed account of smoking hashish (on three occasions) when she had lived in Bangkok two decades before.[9] Presented as an experiment in psychopharmacology in the *Therapeutic Gazette*, she spoke of induced states of dual and multiple states of existence, "the marvellous thoughts that came to me while under this intoxication. . . . My mind was exalted by an indescribable increase of consciousness." Imagining herself a stringed, musical instrument, she described experiences of orgasmic intensity. This was no way for a Baptist to speak – certainly not a female evangelist. The act could only be a deliberately provocative challenge, a reckless defiance of an authority she could no longer tolerate. Clearly she was on the way out, saying what she pleased, yet she did make the claim that she never smoked again, and in fact she later "thought with increasing horror of the danger I then incurred." She ends by pontificating: "During many years thereafter, drudgery and monotony always made me, unwisely, meditate on this beatification, and then, wisely, on its accompanying perdition." The last remarks were not meant to mollify her superiors. They were addressed to medical practitioners and the public, as a warning.

The stifling heat of Swatow's long summers had always been acutely uncomfortable, unhealthy, with a seasonal upsurge of cholera. The inescapable heat was endured by the Baptist missionaries almost as a penance, but it was also the consequence of a lack of funds, and an unwillingness of the Board of Baptist Missions to provide relief for their workers in the field. By contrast, the neighboring Presbyterian mission had built a sanitorium, really a resort, on Double Island in Swatow Bay where the sea breezes reduced the temperature by 10 degrees. Only if there was room, or if the medical need was great, were non-Presbyterians invited to stay. Fielde had frequently complained about this distressing situation, and finally, in the winter of 1888 to 1889, she did something about it. She asked her American friends to provide funds for a rest house by the sea next to the Presbyterian establishment. Fielde supervised the building, and as much as she insisted that the building be named after its donor Mrs. Cauldwell of New York, the patron prevailed, and the escape became known as Fielde Lodge ("one cannot quarrel with one's guardian angels").[10]

The summer of 1888 had been notable for its heat, for a particularly virulent and persistent epidemic of cholera that killed at least 500 people in the Swatow area, and a plague of caterpillars that stripped the countryside of pine trees, leaving bare and blackened remains. The caterpillars "crawl into our houses, and perpetual sweeping and burning alone keeps them from swarming in our inmost rooms if we did not keep men sweeping them out. All through July they were a sickening horror." In July, she came down with quincy, a painful infection of the throat and tonsils, followed by a low-grade fever that persisted for several months. For more than a year she had noticed a deterioration in her health, and was "physically unequal to the amount of work which I used to do here when I was younger." A physician, Dr. Alexander Lyall, examined her, and reported to Murdock that Fielde had had a "severe attack of oedema of the legs due evidently to a weakened condition of the heart." He discovered that she had had other symptoms of cardiac involvement for several years – breathlessness on slight exertion, and a sense of oppression in the chest, all the more severe in recent times. Upon examination he found a systolic aortic murmur, and other abnormalities, as well as "probably," an enlargement of her heart. Since returning to Swatow Fielde had become "unhealthily stout," an agrevating factor. Lyall felt that her condition had been brought on by the unhealthy heart of Swatow, and that it was reversible, provided she take herself to a cool climate where she could recover and live for many years. In a letter to a friend she wrote "my long residence in the tropics has produced muscular weakness of the heart, which is great enough to prevent my safely continuing the work."[11]

She seemed almost grateful that medical authority was banishing her from Swatow. Though she had told her superiors that she was returning to Swatow for only five years (until 1890), she seemed to be playing a game of making no move, while at the same time implying that her departure was imminent, but her heart had taken the matter out of her hands. "There is a certain satisfaction of having this decision made by circumstances, else I should not be wholly sure that I had no further duty in behalf of the Chinese women, for whom I have so long worked, and for the Bible-women who have such a hold on my affections. As it is, I have no doubts what I ought to do; and so I close my labors here with a peaceful mind." Since Fielde lived vigorously for a further twenty-eight years, she had been well advised to leave Swatow. Fielde was a victim of a series of diseases (infection of the eyes and throat, malaria) in an unhealthy climate, but it may very well be that heart disease was not really the problem at all, since clinical cardiology at that time was in a rather primitive state, and incorrect diagnosis was not uncommon.

Dr. Lyall, listening sympathetically to an articulate and persuasive patient, may have felt he could legitimately remove her from an unhappy situation, and without qualm he could invoke a diagnosis of heart trouble that would legitimize any prescription for treatment, in this case departure from a stressful life in an unhealthy climate. A murmur of the heart, which might have been quite benign, would certainly add weight to a medical opinion. Vague infirmities were often used to remove oneself from unpleasant situations, or to escape from social or family pressures. At the time it was called "American nervousness," afflicting those hard-driving, overambitious individuals who worked themselves into a state of exhaustion. Only as innocent victims of a physical malady could they rest – invalidism was the way out of the dilemma.[12] The James children, William, Henry and Alice, were constantly visiting European spas seeking cures for their weakened conditions, and in this way, for some years they evaded the urging of their family to settle on some profession, earn a living, and become productive citizens.[13]

The summer of 1888 was spent on Double Island taking "heart tonics," and making a rapid recovery. Surrounded by disease in this "land of microbes," she nursed a fellow missionary Mrs. Partridge, gravely ill with "stomach inflammation." For several weeks Fielde's ministrations were intense and demanding, and characteristically she lavished her attention on this woman whom she detested because she felt she was such a disruptive and corrosive force in the mission.

After almost three decades in China, her missionary days were coming to a close. Reasons of health were given for her retirement, but there was also an unspoken matter of principle underlying her separation. Fielde could no longer accept several of the tenets of the Baptist Church, and she was uncomfortable in continuing to evangelize under their auspices. With her tendency to look at the numbers, and analyze the many years of records of the missionary effort, Fielde concluded that the goal of converting a significant number of "heathen" Chinese was a hopeless task; at the present rate of conversion (ten per day), the task would take forever.

Fielde had not only been exposed to the world of science, she had also studied the religions of the East. Though certainly not an adherent of Eastern creeds, she could appreciate their virtues, and while her faith in God, in self-sacrifice, and the moral truths of the Bible were undiminished, her broad tolerance for other systems of belief ran counter to the beliefs of the Baptists. There never was a loss of faith on her part however, nor did she ever become an enemy of religion. Perhaps, after so many years of wrangling with the Board, and with fellow missionaries, who ignored her urgent woman's voice, she had reached an end-point. Indeed, a surprising amount of the communication between several missionaries in Swatow and the home office in Boston was taken up with personal disputes and dissatisfactions that demanded to be rectified, and exhausted the patience and diplomatic skills of Ashmore and Murdock.[14] The sensitivities and private frustrations of those doing God's work were no less than those involved in mundane secular pursuits.

Fielde must have been discouraged by the criticisms of her fellows, some of whom had considered her monumental dictionary as a minor contribution to their great cause, and the two years she spent pursuing her interest in obstetrics and science a terrible waste. Murdock regarded natural history and science as "something dangerous," while Ashmore felt that the mission should confine itself to preaching the Word of the Bible, and "paying but little regard to the science of the West" (especially Darwinian notions of how species, including man, originated). While Fielde's missionary colleagues were repelled by the theory of Evolution, she was attracted to it. They could not comprehend or abide Fielde's willful, perverse fall from virtue, and they yearned for the earlier Fielde "in a state of grace," who had performed great works. But she had had enough, and now it was time to be on her own, free to believe as she pleased, and to profess as she believed. She wanted to dance once more.

The resentment of male control throughout her entire career was unquestionably a decisive element in shaping Fielde's decision. She planned to be a free agent, released from gender discrimination. Her annual salary was now $720, while that of Partridge, her male colleague at Swatow, was $1440.[15] Grossly inadequate compensation for missionary services was always a sore point for Fielde – "Missionaries show neither manful nor womanly respect for themselves nor just regard for others."[16]

Though Fielde was no longer young or healthy, and had almost no savings, she seemed confident of her future, almost defiant. In May of 1889 she wrote a letter of resignation to the Board, really a manifesto, which, beginning "Dear Brethren," outlined her medical problem that required she move to a cool climate where she would ". . . live long, usefully and joyously."[17] Fielde proposed a settlement – that she be given $300 for travel home via Europe, and that the American Baptist Missionary Union invest $1507.90 (approximately two years' salary) in the Mutual Life Insurance Company of New York to give her (a 51-year-old female) an annuity of $100 a year for the rest of her life, and she would make no further financial demands on the Union. She reminded the Union that her missionary activity had prevented her from making provision for her old age. When she had begun, her missionary salary was one-third that of a teacher, doing much less work in the U.S.A., and "now, I am old and can't take up any lucrative occupation." The Committee awarded her $300 for travel, and $1000 as their final settlement, in addition to $1500 which they had paid her previously – an unusually generous settlement.

She insisted however, that no demands of any kind be made that she speak at meetings after she returned to America. " If you knew the terror I suffer when I think of going to missionary meetings, you would remember the nervous breakdown that followed my former experiences in that direction and would wonder less at the apprehension which sometimes impels me to remain forever an exile from my native land. I suppose a nerve once snapped, is forever painful." She was referring to her first return to the U.S.A. in 1883, when she had met the incessant demands of ABMU organizers that she speak to groups of ladies. Now, in her weakened condition, she was certainly unable to satisfy their demands. She wanted a divorce, and by doing so she reluctantly gave up her "children," her Bible-women. The rupture was to be total, and would remain so. "I don't want to be deprived of all the advantages of obscurity without gaining any of the emoluments of fame."

Her letter of resignation ended on a plaintive note:

> As my work for the ABMU is soon to end, I take this occasion to thank you, its representatives, that I have received so much of kindness from it; that it has never hindered me in the carrying out of any of my many special enterprises in mission work; that it has always helped me so far as its duties to others permitted; that it has by word and deed expressed much of regard for me; and that ever since the time when, twenty three years ago, I found myself in appalling desolation alone on the shore of Asia, it has tried to be a kind husband to me.

The words come from the heart, and her final farewell reflected a blending of humility and self-confidence.

Fielde's second tour of China had lasted four years, troubled because she would not satisfy the expectations of her superiors, and because her failing health had made her even more outspoken and disagreeable. Fielde had returned to Swatow after an absence of three years, during which time entirely new systems of thought and behavior had been revealed to her, and these were often in conflict with her earlier, limited range of experience. She had embraced the enlightenment of science, and had exulted in unrestricted, wide-ranging discussion. Now, her criterion for friendly association was that persons be intelligent, honorable and interesting; religious belief did not enter in the selection. The company she sought included Catholics, atheists, and agnostics, and not necessarily pious Baptists. During her two years in the U.S.A., her superiors in Swatow and in Boston were uneasy about just what she was up to, for she did not keep them informed, and even when she had returned to Swatow, Executive Secretary Murdock was frequently complaining to Fielde that he had not heard from her in too long a time. While she was in the U.S.A., they learned about her through newspaper reports of her lectures, often on topics unrelated to missionary work. They took no satisfaction from her New York lecture at the World Congress of Science on "the conception and knowledge of science among the Chinese."[18] She was indeed a discomfiting companion of the devout Baptist.

Her illustrious career as a missionary was coming to a sad end because she had changed, a missionary paying the price for intellectual, secular growth. As she continued to do biological research and read scientific literature, Darwin's evolutionary theory made increasing sense to her, while it was anathema to her Baptist brethren. A restless, assertive person, she had always been difficult to contain, and if authority was challenged, so be it. The validity of rules and systems of thought were, with few exceptions, to be tested against experience, and this was intolerable to the devout, with their rigid orthodoxy. Fielde came to realize that she had to go – the price she must pay to follow her interests, which assured a departure from dogma.

As vulnerable to male dictates as she was, Fielde's strong sense of self enabled her to continue operating without the approval of her colleagues. Though she had placed herself in financial jeopardy, she was a survivor – well organized and not easily flustered. Her arguments against gender bias were based upon fact; they were presented with force and passion but were rarely strident. She never talked about failure, but she was not boastful, never took personal credit, nor did she trumpet her considerable accomplishments.[19]

Fielde had many friends in America, some wealthy and influential, and she had reason to believe that she could make a living as a lecturer and a writer. Precipitate separation initiated by Fielde was an affront to the Board of Baptist Missionaries, and in an instant she ceased to exist in the official Baptist world – without an obituary when she died in 1916. Although she has been discussed in glowing terms by writers, female colleagues, and academics dealing with pioneering foreign missionary and scientific activity of the late nineteenth century, it is probable that Adele Fielde has enjoyed less than her proper share of fame because she was dropped from the Baptist rolls. It is surprising how often she is *not* mentioned in missionary publications or *not* referred to in a conscientious account of women missionaries in China (for example, in Hunter's *The Gospel of Gentility* in which she certainly deserved some prominence). This tough, determined woman would not have lost sleep over such neglect.[20]

Fielde left the Swatow mission when it was in a pitiful, understaffed state. Ashmore and his wife had been absent for extended periods, and when Fielde's closest friend Eliza Ashmore died, Fielde was devastated. The senior man of the mission, Partridge, had sent several desperate letters to the Executive Committee pleading with them to send reinforcements, but few had come. A few days before she left, Fielde wrote a confidential letter to Murdock outlining the problem as she saw it. The problem was Mrs. Partridge (the second), a dominating woman who had "almost extinguished" her husband's personality, and has tried to control all who came under her authority. Fielde was particularly critical of the unwise manner in which she dealt with Chinese. "She confers . . . with . . . juniors among the Chinese" – not with Americans. "She permits the Chinese to rule . . . with the plain design of gaining favor among the Chinese, and without regard to the discipline which should be maintained in mission work."[21] The problem may have been that a strong, domineering woman like Fielde could not abide another with the same characteristics. Beyond that, it would seem that as much as Fielde appreciated the Chinese and loved her Bible-women, she was unable to see Chinese as free, competent agents. She could not tolerate control passing out of the hands of whites in general, and herself in particular, despite the fact that she had written that the only hope of a viable Christianity in China was for the Chinese to build, maintain, and run their own churches, and that the aim of foreign missions was to help them achieve this goal. Perhaps, at face value, with all of Fielde's knowledge of China and her good intentions and benevolence, her statements reveal a deeply buried conviction of Western superiority over the Chinese – us against them – based on skin color, size, culture, social and economic class, educational level, nationality, and an assumption of moral superiority that revealed itself particularly in periods of stress. According to critics, there was a pervasive and damaging ethnocentricity underlying the missionary movement. Scripture proclaimed that the human had complete dominion over (inferior) animals, which had been created to serve humans and satisfy their needs. For white Europeans or Americans with their remarkable record of achievement there was no difficulty going one step further to assume that certain groups of humans were primitive and inferior, justifying their exploitation. Since people of this sort (such as Native Americans) did not fully exploit the land and resources available to them, white people were justified in taking over their land to realize its full potential.[22]

Leaving her school for Bible-women in the hands of a young woman missionary, Fielde set a course for home, westward via India and Europe, because she could not endure another crossing of the treacherous Pacific Ocean and the long, slow, exhausting trek across America. At various times in her career in China, Fielde had been either optimistic or pessimistic about the triumph of Evangelism. When she departed for the last time, she realized, sadly, that with all the efforts of heroic, dedicated souls, little headway had in fact been made in the immensity of China – conversion of large numbers of Chinese was unlikely, and the intolerable misery of Chinese womankind was as great as ever. As reported in the *London and China Telegraph*:[23]

STAGNATION IN CHINA – Notwithstanding the long intercourse China has had with the more progressive nations, writes the *Chinese Times*, and the many mechanical appliances pertaining to civilization she has of late years adopted, one cannot help remarking, with some degree of surprise, how little change has been effected in her national life. Her dalliance with the skill and science of the West is rather a species of coquetry than honest wooing. The truth is that powers less tangible and material, yet far more potent than railways, telegraphs, balloons, or phonographs, must be invoked before any deep or lasting impression upon this slumbering mass of stagnant life can be expected. Spiritual forces cannot be conquered with material weapons. It is China's ignorance that is her weakness, and only enlightenment can produce change. Not that the Chinese people can be called an ignorant people. Many a people far more ignorant has proved itself capable of rapid reform. But China, great as her wisdom is in some things, is densely ignorant of everything that makes for progress. Few may match her in knowledge of the past, but the prophetic spirit that discerns the future is lost to her, and every step she takes forward is taken tremblingly, for it is a step in the dark. The schoolmaster, or, rather, many schoolmasters of many kinds, must be the reformers. And light, once given, will ensure progress with the inevitableness of mathematical law.

8 The voyage home[1]

Adele Fielde's departure from Swatow was a searing experience, an amalgam of anxiety, exhilaration, and pain. Confident and optimistic by nature, she looked forward to a bright future, but an income was no longer assured, and so much that she cherished was being left behind – a troubled world that had taught her how much humans can suffer. She was bringing to a close the defining period of her life – twenty-five vivid years – not a particularly good preparation for a 50-year-old single woman to make her way in America. This Orientalist would never again walk "heathen" streets bustling with potential Christians, nor would she see again her precious Bible-women who had been the major concern of her life for so many years.

Cheerful, and not given to depression, she quickly turned her attention to the delicious prospect of a lengthy stay in Europe to be followed by a new life of freedom in America. Quite deliberately, her travel agenda was determined by the temperature of her destinations – the cooler and healthier, the more desirable. Swatow's stifling heat was demonized, responsible not only for her own afflictions, but for all the intolerable diseases of her flock, and now sailing toward cooler climates, she vowed, "I will take care of my little heart, and encourage it to go on throbbing and loving as long as it can."[2] Adele Fielde was truly on her own, without connection to the ardent missionary establishment that had nurtured and restrained her for so many years. Despite the battles she had fought, and the annoyances that were born of close quarters, missionaries were her family – a remarkable group of brothers and sisters.

Pearl Buck, who grew up in China, the daughter of Presbyterian missionaries, spoke with unquestioned authority about missionaries and the missionary movement. Her father had been so singularly dedicated to converting the Chinese, so blindly zealous in his evangelical calling, that he was barely in touch with the real world, and, compared to him, William Dean, Sylvester Partridge, and William Ashmore were backsliders. Consequently, his admirable, long-suffering wife and his children – those few that survived – led intolerable lives.[3] Pearl Buck experienced intimately the narrowness, insensitivity, and arrogance of some missionaries firsthand, and yet she wrote:

> Among the missionaries are some men and women whose names you probably would not know if I spoke them. But they stand to me as the greatest people I have ever known. Simple, sincere, humble, learning before they teach, sensitive before any soul, appreciative of every human life, of keen mind and profound learning, these have lived their lives out of this world where you live, but mighty in the world you do not know. It is a revealing thing that these great lived much alone in their work, apart from their own kind who often called them unorthodox and non-cooperative, or a score of other names which little men do call those who are greater than they.[4]

She might well have had Adele Fielde in mind, though it is probable that she had little or no knowledge of her. Buck, who decided not to become a missionary, and had many disparaging, if not harsh things to say about the movement, felt, like Adele Fielde, that it was doomed to failure. What Christianity had to offer the Chinese did not, and could not, meet their needs. The success of evangelism required the dedicated efforts of very superior Americans, and there were too few who were interested in the task.

Fielde was a conscientious tourist, eager to learn all she could, and unusually responsive to new experiences, perhaps a reaction to her constricted life in China. One so energetic and determined probably wore out her companions. After sailing around the Malay Peninsula in December 1889, she arrived in Calcutta, India, where she spent three months in its dry and cold northern parts. Fielde was unimpressed by India and the Indians who she felt were an "indolent, dreamy, improvident people." In contrast to her own vigor and activism, she judged them to be hopelessly mired in inactivity, resistant to anything new; the notion of progress was utterly foreign to them, and she regarded Hindus as "shiftless." While the land was fully capable of supporting a large population, people were dying of starvation, a tragedy that the living regarded with indifference. The countryside was the abode of predatory animals, and poisonous snakes that took their toll in human lives every year, a remediable situation, but one that the natives did nothing to prevent because the victims were only children. She found their sanitation deplorable, and their social customs "abhorrent." Western science and medicine were unknown to them, and whatever healing practice they exercised was "primitive." Her general dislike (the Ugly American, nineteenth-century style) extended to their religion and philosophy, which she found fetishistic, and dependent on charms and the mysticism of signs and symbols. She could find nothing good in their well-known occult power and occult wisdom, which she regarded as "imaginary." Their fakirs and yogis were sometimes of great interest, but their powers she explained away as operating through hypnotism – on themselves and others. Fielde, an activist, could not make half-hearted judgments about such matters, and she found the lethargic, fatalistic attitude, and indifference to human suffering of Indians, incomprehensible and unacceptable.

However, it was not all bleak in the subcontinent. She admired the textiles and jewelry, and was ecstatic about the Taj Mahal:

> In no one day in my life have I ever seen so much magnificence in architecture as today. Seeing Notre Dame of Paris, St. Peter's in Rome, St. Mark's in Venice, the Ming Tombs, and the House of the Prophets has been but a preparation for due appreciation of the Taj. . . . The architecture here is worth a journey around the world to see. Not only the Taj, but the magnificent Pearl Mosque, the Audience Hall of Akbar, grandson of the first Mogul emperor, and other structures are the finest I have ever seen.

The Taj worked its magic on Fielde. "I saw the Taj blush roseate at sunrise; gleam white as eternal snows at noonday; and glimmer like 'a house not made with hands' through the moonlight. It is unspeakably beautiful in all its aspects; but most impressive when, under the full moon, it appears as a spiritual creation." One evening she and her friends heard singing:

> A whole choir of angels seemed to be hidden in the dome, and to join in the dirge. A musical instrument, carried with us uttered a single note, and gave the key to an invisible orchestra, that continued to play a heavenly symphony long after the ruder sound had sunk into silence. Music infinitely sweet, clear, and soul-touching, was sent."[5]

The next stopover in her grand tour was Egypt, where she traveled up the Nile to the first cataract, and visited Karnak and Thebes. In the Cairo Museum, she was deeply moved by looking into the eyes of mummified kings who had gazed upon Moses. Leaving Alexandria, she sailed for the Holy Land, and what promised to be an inspired sojourn in the heart of Christendom ended in great disappointment, for she found Jerusalem desolate, not fit for habitation by civilized people. The city had been decaying for 2000 years; it was unsanitary, inhabited by "primitive and degenerate" people "too indolent to wrest a livelihood from the soil and too stupid to escape from the country." Jerusalem's only hope was that it be placed in the care of "some Christian nation," and be subject to the "forces of Christian enlightenment and Christian civilization." This judgment, worthy of Colonel Blimp, reveals Fielde's outspoken, deep-seated ethnocentricity; it stands out embarrassingly, and by present-day standards would not be tolerated.

In Victorian times, organized tours of the Holy Land were very popular. Eager pilgrims in a pious haze wandered about from one biblical site to another awed by their very names, their antiquity, and their relevance to Jesus and the Bible. Fielde was among a group of eleven Westerners that included five Americans, fully taken care of by nineteen Syrians with thirty-two beasts of burden carrying seven tents and all the necessities. They were on the way to Beirut where Fielde was to board the ship *Gironde* for

Constantinople. "We have traveled in the paths trodden by the prophets; we have viewed from the hilltops the land traversed by the apostles; we are among people who wear the same attire and have the same characteristics as did the neighbors of Jesus. Oh, the wildflowers of Palestine! Great fields and hillsides are aglow with them." The week-long trip made by this cardiac invalid was "severe" but "healthful," made no less strenuous by cantering on a horse for four hours a day. Fielde was so taken with magnificent monuments and religious objects, she feared that "real fetish-worship as in China" was possible, and that physical artifacts might become too important and diverting, heralding idolatry and paganism, while Christianity's moral emphasis might decline. The ruins of Ephesus, with the tomb of Luke, and the stones of the Temple of Diana she found impressive, while Tarsus, the birthplace of Paul, was found to be "a dull and dirty little town." The Parthenon and the great temples of Athens were her next destinations, where again she was, as we might expect, responsive to the echoes of the ancient Mediterranean world.

Travel suited Fielde's adventurous nature, and stirred her passion for learning. Frequent changes of scenery buoyed her spirit, and by the time Constantinople had been reached, she was considerably healthier than when she had begun her trip home. She had shed much weight – "adipose" – and had acquired a tan in the sunny trek from Jerusalem to Beirut. Fielde, always the conscientious tourist, read voraciously, studied the history, culture, and architecture of the places she visited, and incorporated her learning and personal experiences into informative lectures that she later gave in America (one such was entitled "Modern and Ancient Greece, its Past and Present Government").

After Athens and Greece, the next stop on the tour was Karlsbad, a charming spa filled with German and Austrian invalids, where she hoped to complete her cure of all the ills visited upon her in China. Arriving in June of 1890, she placed herself in the care of a Doctor Kraus, who after careful examination proclaimed that there was nothing wrong with Fielde except that she was overweight. "Dr. Kraus tells me that I have no organic disease, that my internal organs are all sound, and that the fault of circulation is caused by too much adipose tissue solely. . . . In fact I am really very well now, but I thought it wise to take the treatment for adiposis." She was placed on a fairly rigorous diet, and encouraged to drink the curative springwater. Dr. Kraus prescribed four hours of exercise each day, and since she ate all her meals at restaurants, a time-consuming process, her days were fully taken up with treatment.

Fielde was grateful to Karlsbad for her rapid recovery, and her reduced waistline, and after a few months of a health regimen she made her way to Dresden, a city she came to adore for its beauty and its sublime art. The *Madonna* in the Dresden Art Gallery was "the most perfect in the world," so perfect she could "cut off the ears" of anyone who dared criticize it. The music of Germany she considered the finest in the world, and living near the

Hoftheatre she heard everything that was offered – *Tannhäuser*, *Oberon*, *Carmen*, *Aïda*, the whole of Wagner's cycle of the Nibelungen Ring, and the Passion Play at Oberammergau.

By October 1890, Fielde, an unabashed Germanophile, was settled in Berlin where she resided for nine months, mastering the language, studying German and Swiss forms of government, and indulging in ordinary tourism. Catching sight of the Emperor Bismarck and von Moltke, passing by in their carriages as the crowds cheered, thrilled her. A three-month course in the German language at the Berlitz College of Languages enabled her to read and write the language, but she reconciled herself to the certain knowledge that she would never be an articulate speaker because the grammar was so "fiendish." Recognizing her defect, she wittily wrote to a friend: "German is spoken exclusively at the evening meal; I do not talk while eating dinner." She attended a course on ancient Egypt, spent much time studying the antiquities of Egypt in the Royal Library, and she haunted the museums and libraries of Berlin:

> The museums here are numerous and surpassingly fine, and one should not hasten through them. . . . You see, I have not that "familiarity which breeds contempt" with either museums or libraries. In fact one of the compensations for the outlay of my years in dull old China is that I am not a bit *blasée* in anything, and I bring to all my occupations in Europe a freshness of interest that one who has always lived in the enlightened world can scarcely understand.[6]

What she learned and saw in Germany was the subject of later lectures and writings after she had returned to the U.S.A.

In the 1890s, young American students and those making their grand European tour flocked to Germany rather than to France or England.[7] Whatever drew them to Germany also attracted Fielde; study in Germany was a crucial part of her never-ending education. While she admired the thrift, economy, and efficiency of the Germans, she also recognized serious flaws in them which engendered great social inequities, a consequence of their ready and willing submission to an overbearing government. Yet she found much that was worthwhile in the German form of government, which though autocratic and inferior to a democracy, allowed the people to develop a superior social system: "the strength of the German government lies in the fact that it exacts the most rigid requirements of self-sacrifice, self-effacement, and self-negation from the individual in exchange for social protection." At a time of political ferment, she did not believe socialism to be "the panacea for the ills of German autocracy" because it promised "greatly increased benefits from society without any well-defined reciprocal obligation on the part of the individual," and it was also alien and incompatible with a democratic form of government. Contrasting the two modes of governance, she pointed out that "German paternalism makes society responsible for the well-being of the individual; while American democracy holds the individual responsible for the well-being of society."

Fielde's keen power of observation and analysis, and her feminist sensibility are revealed in her correspondence:

> Germans are perennially interesting. They are more like my Chinese than any other Aryan people – but they are unlike them in being frugal without being sordid and unlike them in possessing a wonderful ideality along with their frank earthliness. The German women, on the whole, offer a convincing argument against the theory that when women have nothing else to do except to make a home, they will do that well. German housekeeping is bad; and the numerous bowlegged and weakboned children are each an argument for coeducation. There is also an impressive difference in the physical development of members of different classes of Germans that is unlike anything I have seen in any other country. I wonder if when we Americans get a population of fifty millions into a space four times as large as the state of New York, and when the struggle for life becomes such as it is in Germany, classes will be as distinctly separate as they are here – and the highest will be fair, trig and spiritual, while the lowest will be stunted, flabby and unimaginative.[8]

However enlightened, analytic, and perceptive Fielde was, she still harbored many unexamined prejudices. Fielde's letter continues: "But Germany is safer than the United States, for she increases her population with something like a million of native citizens every year, whereas we Americans are unprolific, and the worthless scraps of European nations come in to possess the land." This lament had been uttered by citizens since before her beloved Republic was born, and all were oblivious of the original possessors of the land. What Fielde espoused was derived from received knowledge in an America with prevalent racist, anti-foreign sentiment bolstered by the writings of some of its leading scientists, some of whom were Fielde's heroes.

In her travels through the Middle East, Fielde had made many friends, among whom was an American, a Mrs. Davis, "a true lady," whose two sisters had married Mr. Harper and Mr. Dalton, both prominent publishers. The two women traveled, and resided together in adjoining rooms in Dresden and Berlin. While Fielde was occupied with her studies, Mrs. Davis had visited Paris, and upon her return to Berlin, developed pneumonia and died within a week. Fielde, who had tended to her sick-bed night and day, was shaken by the loss of such a close friend with whom she had planned a spring and summer tour of Russia and Scandinavia. Now that Mrs. Davis had taken a trip from which there was no return, Fielde seemed to lose interest in her – "winter's occupations, studies, duties and pleasures." Within a few days she left for Russia.

Fielde arrived in Moscow on May 14, 1891 to find a pogrom in progress, one that had been orchestrated in many parts of the Russian Empire following a new Imperial edict of Alexander III expelling Jews from anywhere within the bounds of Great Russia. Despite denials both by Russians and the U.S.A. Minister to Russia of oppression of Jews, persecution had been going on for a decade, and had now been officially sanctioned by the Czar himself. Fielde was horrified by what she saw – feeble old people, women and children herded together in cattle pens in the cold outdoors, lying on bare ground, sick and too weak to stand, without sanitary facilities or food, waiting for days to be transported to unknown destinations. Without pity or humanity, "Christian" soldiers, officers and men were guarding these prisoners, summarily accused and convicted of activities against the state religion, though no trial had taken place. Rather than continue with tourism, Fielde remained in Moscow for a month to investigate this deplorable situation.

Despite heavy censorship, word had leaked out about the ongoing barbarities – Germany knew of the situation because Jewish refugees had been transported to the border, dumped on the German side, and were flooding Berlin.[9] Fielde must have been aware of the situation while in Berlin before she left for Russia, which suggests that she deliberately went to Russia to see what was going on, and what she witnessed probably came as no surprise. On the other hand, she may have heard vague stories of persecution, possibly exaggerated, and had never given them enough thought to allow them to interfere with her travel plans. Whatever the circumstances, Fielde, an innocent-looking, middle-aged American Baptist missionary woman became an investigative reporter working under the nose of the Russian authorities, observing, digging out facts, and interviewing victims. Since her reports would have disappeared if she had sent them by mail or telegraph, she waited until she reached Sweden to send home a full account of the situation, and she dispatched many articles to newspapers and magazines to publicize czarist barbarity.

Articles had sporadically appeared in the *New York Times* about Jewish persecution in Russia. On May 28, Baron Hirsch in Paris described some of the cruelties, and suggested that the brutality was perpetrated by "lower officials of the Russian Empire who terribly abuse the power vested in them in order to misinterpret the czar's intentions." If Jews were to be expelled, it should be done humanely. Only the Czar could put a stop to the "pitiless persecution."[10] Three days later a *Times* correspondent reported that Berlin was being "overwhelmed by the advance wave of the fleeing Jews, driven on a day's notice from their homes and swarming westward without money, friends or any knowledge of where they are or where they are going. . . . Europe is literally aghast at what is being thus brutally wrought before its eyes." He went on to speak of "wild primitive hates and passions," and "This strange creature, Alexander III, finds that even Peter the Great was too civilized," and has swung back "to the blood-stained barbarism of Rurik and

Ivan the Terrible . . . a mad revival of the dark ages."[11] On June 14, another report appeared in the *New York Times*, stating that the German government had protested the expulsion of Jews into Germany, but could not prevent it because the border was too extensive. The correspondent stated that it was impossible for the Czar not to know what was going on.[12]

Adele Fielde's detailed report of events was published in the *New York Times* two days later.[13] It carried special weight because it came from an impartial reporter who could not be accused of being a Jewish agent. The eyewitness was a lady missionary, a tourist in Moscow who set down on paper all that she saw. Fielde had sent her Moscow report to a Baptist minister who passed it on to Rabbi Gottheil, chairman of the Thirteenth Convention of the Jewish Ministers' Association of America, being held in New York, and he read the report to an assembly of twenty-five rabbis. The proceedings, the report itself, and the outcome of deliberations was incorporated into an article in the *New York Times*.

> Late in the winter, before the imperial edict of the 9th of March was issued, it was known that the Jews were to be expelled from Great Russia, and the police began their usual visitations to Jewish dwellings. . . . The father of the present Czar permitted Jews who were competent artisans, Jews who had attained a certain degree of scholarship in the Russian schools, the children of Jewish soldiers who had served twenty-five years in the Russian army, and also some other peculiarly serviceable classes to dwell in Great Russia. . . . So intelligently had the Jews taken advantage of the political opportunity for education and for the exercise of handicrafts that they had become leaders in Russian progress. Their present persecution does not originate among the common people, who live very amicably with the Jews, but is incited by the government. . . . There are in fact, today no less than 635 laws directed especially against the Jews, and besides these, are several thousand regulations affecting this people adversely. While they are deprived of the privileges, they must perform the duties of Russian subjects, and must serve in the army, pay taxes, and remain in Russia. Even to advise a Jew to emigrate is itself a punishable political offense. Under the Russian autocracy, everything and anything is criminal, according to the mood of the Czar, expressed through the omniscient and omnipotent police. During the last few weeks the expulsion of the Jews from Moscow has been carried on with cruelty. Houses where Jews are supposed to lodge, are between midnight and dawn, surrounded, and rooms where women and children are sleeping are entered and carefully searched. Every Jew, of either sex and of any age, who is unable to show an official written permit to live in Moscow is hauled away in fetters . . . and now even those who have permission papers of recent date are often warned to leave the city within a day. This forces the Jews to depart with business unsettled and debts uncollected, and often unscrupulous Russians take

advantage of the opportunity to get the property of the victims at a fraction of its value. About half of the Jewish residents of Moscow have been expelled within six weeks.

The most moving part of Fielde's account was a series of seven case studies of individuals chosen at random, who had suffered appallingly at the hands of the authorities.

A committee was set up to raise money for relief of victims, and a letter was written appealing to President Benjamin Harrison, and the people of the U.S.A., "asking that a protest be sent in the name of humanity to the Russian Government against its merciless persecution of those whose only crime is their religion." The public in general, and American Jews in particular, learned the truth and were aroused by reliable reports such as Fielde's. President Benjamin Harrison was prevailed upon to use his influence to stop the persecution, and, shamed by the protests of the U.S.A. and other nations, the President received the personal assurance of the Czar that Jews would henceforth be treated like all other Russian citizens. Though pogroms were not officially instigated or sanctioned thereafter, they still took place sporadically but regularly. Oddly, while Fielde was observing events in Moscow, angry and deadly riots against foreigners erupted in the China she had recently left.

Having done her bit, she continued her itinerary through the Scandinavian countries and Holland. Six weeks were passed in Zurich and Berne in Switzerland studying the Swiss form of democracy, and Fielde concluded that their government was the most advanced and democratic in the world. Years later when living in Seattle, her detailed study of Switzerland's method of direct legislation helped Fielde convince the citizens of the state of Washington to vote for an Initiative, Referendum, and Recall Bill that would enable them to participate directly in the governing process, thereby countering big-money interests and the corrupt political machine.

A month was allotted for Paris, where she lived in a *pension*, and wrote charming descriptions of her fellows in residence:

The clientele of course, is constantly changing; but of those who are older inhabitants than I, there is an ancient French countess with the charming manners of the old noblesse, a great variety of lace caps and the prettiest mode of salutation in Paris. She is the author of a volume of sad poems, a staunch Catholic, and a Royalist. She bears her fallen fortunes and the loss of all her kin with a fortitude that makes her nobility seem very real. Then there is a Persian general, brother of the Shah's ambassador to the court of St. James, Prince Kahn. In spite of his hairless pate, red nose, stony black eyes, and the ever hidden probability that he owns a harem in Teheran, he is a very agreeable and courteous fellow-border. We also have a youngish child of Israel, born of a German father and French mother, in America, and possessing the advantage of

> being able to speak three languages like a native of three countries. He is chatty and right-hearted and when he comes down to breakfast all perfumed, he is the sweetest smelling of his tribe."

There was hardly a play, concert, opera, or lecture that she did not attend.[14] "Paris is inexhaustible in its resources for pleasure and instruction. The grave as well as the gay may invest months here with profit. The winter weather has been unvaryingly bad. The best I can say of it is that there has been neither an earthquake nor a typhoon." Fielde must have eaten many wonderful meals, and yet, in all her travels, she never mentioned food except for her diet in Karlsbad.

In Paris, Fielde's new companion was Miss Florence Keen, daughter of the famous Philadelphia surgeon, William W. Keen.[15] Together they had seen all the sites, and now they planned a trip that would take them to Italy, Spain, and Portugal. Granada enchanted her, but she was unimpressed by the great Escorial:

> a vast granite edifice built by Phillip II . . . that moody monarch, who chose for his Patron-saint the canonized Lawrence, who ended his days by being fried on a gridiron after he had fried tens of thousands of other saints because they differed with him in theology. There is the sternly simple room where he received ambassadors, the chairs on which he rested his gouty legs, the oratorio, where he expired while hearing High Mass, his coffin and the tombs of his four wives. There are here most interesting portraits of that terrible trio, Phillip, Torqemada and the Duke of Alva, who form together so salient a point in the history of ecclesiastical bigotry.

Then it was back to Paris after satiating themselves with French, Italian, and Central European cities. Fielde and her companion had exposed themselves to many of the jewels of Western civilization, stopping a few days here, a few weeks there, to see "everything" worth seeing. These serious, dedicated gawkers, attempting to do the impossible, came away with a remarkable amount of knowledge, and some insight, firmly convinced that they had seen the ultimate in art. The anonymity of the Greek and Roman sculptors prompted her to write:

> Their lives; their histories; their hopes; their sorrows; all that they had; has passed into oblivion. But who can truly say that they do not still live in this world? They stir emotions; they win affection and admiration; they convey ideas; they are powers that influence human weal. Their souls are immortal among men.[16]

The brilliance and charm of Paris enchanted Fielde, and it was here that she spent the summer of 1892, her last in Europe. Her global travel ended by crossing the gray Atlantic for New York, where she arrived on October 12.

Extensive travel between the Orient and the U.S.A. by Fielde, a skilled observer and published writer, held promise of an autobiographical travelog. She wrote carefully organized travel diaries illustrated with vivid and colorful accounts, but they were no more than a mere outline of a book, and unfortunately she never gave them further shape or polish to ready them for publication. Perhaps she felt that there was too much of herself in them, too much autobiography, and that it would be unseemly if the saga was told with her always in the foreground. She was forceful and ambitious for her work but not for herself, and though a mighty laborer, she would never thrust herself into the limelight. Fielde chose to be a writer of impersonal manuals, guides, and dictionaries – a cipher, the teller of tales of the daily life of others – and in doing so she had become an invisible link between the Chinese and Westerners.

9 New York

A determined, free spirit, obligated to no one, Fielde had roamed about Asia and Europe, carefully doling out her travel allowance and terminal pay (her alimony), provided by the Baptist Foreign Missionary Society; now she was back in New York. Returned to a country where she had close ties in several cities, and free to settle wherever she wanted, she chose New York with its extraordinary cultural offerings; at heart she was an urban sophisticate. The absence in China of Western performing arts had whetted an appetite for drama, music, and lectures which she had developed during her two-year stay in Philadelphia. To her confidant Nolan, she wrote: "New York continues to be very interesting to me. My native land has for me the charm of novelty combined with the sweetness of familiarity. I am studying it."[1]

Still, it seemed undeniable to her that American artistic creation could not compare to that of Europe, and especially to that of Germany:

> I hope the Statue of Liberty won't fall upon and crush me if I speak the truth, and say that I do not care one scrap for American music. After one has supped on nectar and ambrosia, he does not want lobster salad. A full feast of Wagner in Germany interpreted as only the idealistic Germans can interpret, and set forth complete and perfect – as at Dresden, Munich and Beyreuth: Ah! until one has starved till he is very hungry indeed, he cannot go from that to the scraps he gets here. . . . And I have heard the Arion Society sing! That made me homesick for the Vaterland.

On another occasion she wrote: "American life is interesting, and there is a certain practical comfort in dealing with one's own – but for the things that enchain the taste and enchant the spirit – well, *they* are in Europe!" These feelings were further reinforced by the ineptness she found in New York illustrators of her book whose work could not compare to that of the Europeans.

Fielde's view of European achievement as towering over that of her native land was widely held by elitist Americans. On the one hand, they were proud of their country, its vastness, its promise and pioneering spirit, its boundless future, and on the other, they were conscious of the vulgarity and ignorance of the masses (as described by European visitors such as Charles Dickens and Mrs. Frances Trollope),[2] and the inadequacy of American education. In cultural and theoretical matters, creative Americans, lacking the confidence to be daring, looked to Europe for approval and inspiration. What sustained them was their belief in their country's inherent exceptionalism, and the certain knowledge that the future belonged to America with all its energy, genius for invention, and growing wealth and power which ultimately thrust it on to the world stage.

Fielde was taken with the calm, more leisurely pace of life in Europe, and she resolved that she would never let herself fall prey to "the *Rush* that characterizes American life." But she was a rusher, and, perhaps conscious of her true nature, she was trying to save herself from her inclinations. She had intended to live an unhurried life in New York, to "sip all the juice in my oranges before I tossed down their rind," but her plans were shredded by her enthusiasms and her insatiable drive, and within a year she was complaining about the lack of hours to attend to correspondence and meet with friends. This was hardly surprising, since in addition to lecturing on her travels two to three times each week, she became deeply involved in the suffragist movement, and carried out biological research on ants in her home, and at the Marine Biological Station at Woods Hole on Cape Cod during summers. Judging from her litany of evening activities, almost every new play and opera had to be seen, every concert heard, every lecture or discussion group attended.

When Fielde returned to the U.S.A., the country was immersed in the 1882 presidential election that turned out Benjamin Harrison, the incumbent big business president, and replaced him with Grover Cleveland. As manufacturing and mighty industries grew, and robber barons prospered, labor unions organized as well, and so the time was marked by great labor unrest. Fielde observed a marked deterioration in the political life of the country since she first left America. In her view, the vote, which had been the sacred trust of responsible citizens, had become a means for attaining power and wealth at public expense. The corrupted political process was now under the control of "predatory and parasitic elements," largely those of "foreign birth, unaffected by American traditions, often contemptuous of the people and laws of the United States." Their only interest in the Republic was to exploit for public gain. The threat to the "Puritan heritage and Anglo-Saxon traditions" could best be prevented by restricting foreigners from entering the country, or at least to becoming highly selective about who was to be allowed in. But Fielde was also troubled by the rot from within, for "many of our foremost citizens of Puritan ancestry and Colonial descent were equally reprehensible" having picked up bad habits during the Civil War.[3]

In May 1892, responding to a perceived "yellow peril," the Senate passed the Chinese Exclusion Bill, one which Fielde and many, if not most, of the educated elite deemed beneficial for the U.S.A. Despite her love for certain Chinese, she was in favor of excluding Chinese and other Easterners (as well as eastern and southern Europeans) who by her standards were either physically, mentally, or culturally defective. Newcomers would dilute the vigor of the existing American population with reduction in the "efficiency of the nation." Anti-immigrant sentiments had been especially strong in the mid-nineteenth century giving rise to a "Know Nothing" political party, and numerous organizations dedicated to the exclusion of immigrants from American shores. Laboring classes wanted an end to immigration to protect their jobs, and anti-Catholic prejudice was also an important factor since most of the "undesirables" were Catholic.

By the 1890s when Fielde returned, a new wave of immigration was in full flood, many newcomers settling in the New York area where they subsisted under the most intolerable conditions, and under Fielde's nose. Anti-immigrant feelings were stirred up once again as natives gazed upon masses of undersized, impoverished, ignorant people crowded together in hovels. How could these people compete with "real" Americans, and contribute to the nation? Whatever her liberal, humane convictions were, Fielde was strongly influenced by the widely held scientific arguments of the day concerning natural selection and survival of the fittest – legitimate scientific principles that were used to justify ancient fears and xenophobic prejudices.

The eugenic movement, which arose to improve "the inborn qualities of the human race," or at least to halt its deterioration, came to life in America at about the century's end.[4] Eugenics, formulated and named in 1883 by Francis Galton, a cousin of Charles Darwin, appealed to enlightened people because it was based on new knowledge of heredity and genetics – intellectual triumphs at a time of progress when great scientific, medical, and technological advances were astounding the world, Edison was inventing the miraculous light bulb and phonograph, and Luther Burbank was creating new and improved forms of wheat and other plants by the application of the laws of heredity. It was felt that the benefit of *positive* selective breeding was beyond question when one considered the superior Darwin–Galton–Wedgewood and Bach families, and the degenerate Kallikak family, was a convincing argument for *negative* selection.[5] In increasingly secular times, people were no longer prepared to accept the Will of God as inevitable, or to let nature take its course according to the social Darwinism of Herbert Spencer. Rather they became actors who could manipulate the forces of nature for their own benefit as they applied new knowledge and ideas provided by Mendelian genetics to human problems. Eugenics was regarded as a milestone in the advance of civilization, for humankind had reached a point where it was now able to actively participate in the evolutionary process. Darwin's natural selection would be replaced by artificial selection – selective breeding of the superior, sterilization of the defective, and even destruction of inferior humans, which could lead only to the improvement of the breed. In this way, it was agreed that the superman and the super race could be created, as advocated by such luminaries as Frederich Nietzsche, Francis Galton, G.B. Shaw, and Herbert Spencer.[6] However, Fielde was concerned only with arresting the deterioration of the existing, predominantly Anglo-Saxon, American stock.

Although Fielde's New York in the Golden Nineties was a lively, cultured city, it was also a city rampant with crime, prostitution, and alcoholism, teeming with immigrants, arriving at the rate of eighteen thousand per month. Almost no organization or facilities existed to accommodate these wretched people who lived and worked in the most crowded and inhuman conditions. Social services, public health measures, and schooling were grossly inadequate. Fielde and her contemporaries saw the country being overrun by impossible numbers of people who were, by obvious standards, their inferiors, without education, skills, or any redeeming qualities. Despite the fact that Fielde's U.S.A. was a nation of immigrants, often the wretched and downtrodden of Europe and Asia, Fielde and virtually all of her American contemporaries, born into a privileged Victorian society, manufactured a self-serving account of their past that was incomplete and lacked historic perspective. Because of deep-seated assumptions of natural superiority, and a defective sense of history, they could not comprehend how "less desirable human beings," and in time their descendants, could rise to the high level of propriety and achievement of native-born Americans. To them the entire problem of deterioration was preventable by fiat that would restrict the entry of foreigners with their inferior hereditary material – the anti-immigration movement was really an arm of eugenics. Still, there was a serious contradiction in Fielde's thinking about these matters, for she herself had seen how the "lowest" of Chinese peasant women (those who would certainly be excluded from American shores) could demonstrate surprising intelligence, qualities of leadership, and, with encouragement, become literate – seemingly an argument for the possibility of social Lamarckian evolution that evaded the tyranny and iron restriction of genetic-based Darwinian evolution on which eugenic theory was based. Despite the fact that Fielde had witnessed in her Bible-women the capacity for self-improvement – how much humans could change and grow – she was unwilling to acknowledge that they could or would do so on her home soil. All she could do was admire and approve of a few, select individuals for what they were, regardless of their creed or race.

Some theorists were concerned about allowing large numbers of immigrants into the country because, in America, severe environmental and social conditions that had kept the numbers of these people down in their native lands would be removed, and without these challenges they would outbreed native stocks with the consequent deterioration of the overall endowment of the people. Lamarckians predicted that with the removal of age-old challenges to which immigrant people were accustomed (which improved their ability to survive, traits that could be inherited by the next generation), there would be degeneration of their inherited qualities. Thus, both materialist, Darwinian evolutionists and Lamarckians had their reasons for keeping foreigners out of their country.[7]

Apart from the profound ethical problems involved in carrying out a broad eugenics program, in time, analysis showed that the scientific basis for the notion of eugenics was seriously flawed because of the heterogeneous nature of the human, ignorance of the true genetic nature of humans, and the gross underestimation of the influence of environment on the development of the individual. To Fielde and her contemporaries, the idea seemed a good one, and they should not be judged by late twentieth-century standards, and the consequent nightmare of Nazi depredations. Today, the field is utterly discredited, and can now be looked upon as an example of the horrendous consequences that can follow the inappropriate application to humans of a popular but unexamined theory that carries the imprimatur of scientific authority but is really the mantra of amoral zealots.

During the years Fielde had lived in the East, from the time of the Civil War to the 1890s, American wealth, achievement, and influence had grown beyond anyone's expectations. But historians have also considered it a "a vast gray zone of American history, monotonous and inconclusive, an era of evasion, avoidance and postponement, glazed over with a mix of flamboyant rhetoric and sterile purposes."[8] In a time of rapid economic change, blacks and the poor seem to have been forgotten, and the Native American terribly abused. The main business of government was to facilitate the exploitation of the land, not to redress any imbalance between the rich and the poor, not to interfere with those who were making fortunes. In a country where social injustice was so appalling, reformers like Henry George, Theodore Roosevelt, and Alfred E. Smith became potent, effective voices, and vigorous reform movements were founded – especially in New York City in the 1890s.

The cultural authority of the Church and Protestant sectarianism were no longer as dominant as they were when Fielde had departed for Bangkok many years before. Moral and intellectual authority had become secular, and the social sciences, formulated by secular thinkers, were increasingly accepted, and considered relevant. Though Fielde had been in far-off China, changes in her beliefs and attitudes seemed to reflect what was going on back home.

The management of her adopted city was an important concern to Fielde, who must have been troubled by the pervasive corruption of its government. She was probably aware of civic corruption in America when she lived in Philadelphia, and she certainly knew of it in China, but thievery in New York brought the practice to a new high (or low). Piracy, looting of the public treasury, and rigged bidding for government contracts were an accepted part of American political life, not only in New York but especially in a raw, new town like Seattle where Fielde lived after she left New York. Vice and dirty politics in the remote village where Fielde grew up were almost unknown, and so the contrast with her urban experience was stunning. A fast learner and a realist, she quickly came to understand the facts of New York City politics. The city was afflicted with a corrupt and brutal police force and dishonest politicians, whose primary aim was to fill their pockets while maintaining enough order to weaken efforts for reform.

Richard Croker, the successor of Honest John Kelly, boss of the Tammany Hall machine, oversaw the distribution of the spoils ("honest graft") which he did equitably among his cronies.[9] Large amounts of money came from clients who wanted lucrative government contracts, but he boasted that it was never taken from the public coffers, which he considered sacrosanct, the people's money, and he was proud that he was never the direct recipient of "dirty money" from prostitution and gambling. An affable but thoroughly corrupt man, he pleased the wealthy with whom he identified and whose interests he protected, and yet, like Robin Hood, he was admired by the common people who thought he was working for their benefit. He became immensely wealthy and lived ostentatiously – in a style befitting royalty, with no less than seven homes and at least one estate in England. His greatest moment arrived when his horse won the Derby, though his elation was dampened by the cold treatment meted out to this grubby American upstart by British blue-bloods. Croker was despised by muckrakers like Lincoln Steffens and William Allen White. As the boss of Tammany, a political machine whose motto was "to hell with reform," he dreaded any change that would result in reduced patronage and graft. A master political manipulator, for many years he and his cronies vanquished such reform-minded political candidates in New York as Theodore Roosevelt and Henry George, whom he regarded as troublemakers.

Soon after Fielde arrived in New York, she found herself among reformers of all kinds who were hammering at the gates of this glamorous but impious city. Reformers and liberals had spawned numerous organizations and movements that promised to cure society's ailments – those dealing with government reform, world peace, veterans, medical and legal affairs, labor unions, universities, and temperance, to name but a few. Movement for the reform and strengthening of the central government by establishing a stable civil service and eliminating the spoils system had been going on for several years. If this was revolution, the revolutionaries were largely well-to-do, middle- and upper-class elitists with great respect for private property, and only a secondary interest in extending privilege to the underclasses.

Since Fielde's visit to her home country in the early 1870s and mid-1880s there had been an explosive growth in the women's reform movement. Numerous women's organizations such as the YWCA (1871), Women's Christian Temperance Union (1874), the Women's Educational and Industrial Union (1877), and other groups advocating temperance, pacifism, and women's equality had come into existence, enthusiastically supported by middle- and upper-class women, while working women organized under the banner of the "Knights of Labor," and later the Women's Trade Union League, led by Harriot Stanton Blach and Charlotte Perkins Gilman.[10] The leading spirits of the entire effort were Elizabeth Cady Stanton and Susan B. Anthony who had founded the National Women's Suffrage Association (1869) with many branch offices, one in New York. Stanton and Anthony realized that reform leading to equal rights for women would come about through the exercise of political power, which meant that women must obtain the vote and wrest power from political bosses. The resolution of another dreadful "moral" problem, alcoholism, so harmful to women and destructive to family life, could only be political. To a large degree, American society deemed women unfit to participate in public affairs, to be looked after by males, a view affirmed by law, both religious and secular, written by men. Women were invited to participate in the abolitionist movement, but not to speak out.[11]

Stanton, Anthony, Lucretia Mott, and Victoria Woodhull directed their energy into organizing all women's groups around the suffragist cause which they thought was not only just, but that the woman's vote would also be an antidote to male, political corruption.[12] Machine politicians were uninterested in female suffrage; indeed they feared it because women would inject a moral, issue-oriented element into politics that was not in their interest, and so they fended off importuning women's groups by humoring, ignoring, or confounding them. In the elections of 1872 women had been duped by Republican promises, and they were embittered by the passage of the 14th and 15th amendments to the Constitution which enfranchised black males but not black or white females; abolitionists and radical Republicans had considered female suffrage to be of little importance.[13] American women representatives were stunned (and galvanized into action) when they were unable to participate in an international abolitionist congress in London because of their gender. Feminist leaders concluded that feminist and abolitionist struggles were two different creatures, and that women had to fight their own battles without dependence on men. A suffragist victory was paramount because it would provide women with the vote, a weapon to defend themselves. There were many pressing issues demanding attention such as the rights of black people, divorce, temperance, education, child welfare, and the conditions of working women, each with vigorous advocates, but Stanton, Anthony, and Lucy Stone deemed them secondary to the suffragist struggle, thereby creating dissension and controversy within the feminist, reform movement. A significant number of women were not convinced of the primacy of the suffragist goal, and the linking of trade unionism with the feminist cause was damaging and divisive because it was considered radical, and distasteful to the influential conservative, middle- and upper-class members.[14]

Adele Fielde probably chose New York to be her home because here, as a writer and lecturer without institutional affiliation, she could best spend her time as an advocate of desperately needed reform. Realizing that the city and the state set the pace in reformist thinking for the rest of the country, she wanted to be at the center of the ferment. Elizabeth Cady Stanton and Susan B. Anthony, the prime movers and towering leaders of the fight for women's suffrage and equal rights for women, resided in New York State, and Anthony was then organizing the effort to attain the vote for women at the New York State Constitutional Convention of 1894; the very fact that the convention was to take place was in itself a victory for reformers.[15]

It may be no accident that Fielde, who had for many years been studying the structure and functioning of governments in preparing for her lectures, became a reformer after leaving China and wandering about Europe. She chose to spend the next part of her life in the thick of American social controversy as teacher and polemicist, her guiding principle being that ignorance of civil rights was at the basis of American moral and political failure. Fielde had witnessed dreadful events both in China and New York, and yet she retained her idealism and her belief in the power of the rational mind. Once people knew the facts (and believed in God's love, regardless of religious affiliation), they would do the right thing, and she intended to spend her life teaching her fellow citizens the facts.

She hurled herself into the suffragist cause in America, but she came to the battle late in life. When she had left for the East where the problems of women were different (and worse), she was a young woman, and when she returned to America to stay a quarter of a century later, the American feminist movement was fully formed with able leaders and effective strategies. Earlier, on her two visits to the U.S.A., she had spent her time defending her behavior abroad, then in her scientific pursuits, and finally in her full-time career lecturing about China. She had never mentioned any involvement with feminist causes or their leaders. When she finally settled in New York, Fielde was an extremely able reinforcement in the ongoing battle, an inspired field officer rather than a field marshal, who is rarely mentioned in accounts of the feminist, suffragist struggle.

New York offered her another striking advantage – it abounded in intelligent women of wealth who wanted to be of use to society through charities and church work, and who realized that their yearnings could be satisfied through a person such as Adele Fielde. She was a magnet for women of social position who viewed her as a humane and sympathetic individual, brilliant, articulate, and fearless. She had a kind of star quality, a world traveler with something of an exotic past that attracted women who saw in her everything that they would like to be. Mrs. E.M. Cauldwell of Manhattan was just such a woman. She and Fielde had met at the First Baptist Church of New York where Fielde lectured in 1870, and she became Fielde's closest, dearest friend, someone who had supported her financially in China, who remained her stalwart friend despite Fielde's drift away from Baptist orthodoxy. Fielde became one of the family, living with the Cauldwells on visits to New York, and she dedicated her book *A Corner of Cathay* to Mrs. Cauldwell.

Mrs. Cauldwell was Fielde's entrée into wealthy New York circles, and together they plotted Fielde's future. Since Fielde's resources were minimal, it was necessary for her to earn a living to supplement a small and inadequate annuity, the meager fruit of years of savings. Together, they decided that she should make her way by lecturing rather than writing for newspapers and magazines, although she was well versed in writing. On her previous visit Fielde had been enormously successful lecturing under the auspices of the Baptist Foreign Missionary Society, and had raised large amounts of money for the missionary cause. Now she would do the same for her own benefit, and rather than lecture in churches she would speak in private homes, or hired halls, and instead of waiting for offerings, a fixed admission would be charged at the door.

Mrs. Cauldwell initiated Fielde's new career of drawing-room lectures in January 1893 by inviting 600 people to her home for a discourse on China. Speaking with complete authority, embellishing her story with anecdotes, sometimes humorous, discussing religion, and the suffering of helpless women, her talk was an explosive success, so much so that women crowded around Fielde offering their homes for future speaking engagements. Following this introduction, with Mrs. Cauldwell as manager, she was kept lecturing three times a week for three months, and for the next thirteen years, while residing in New York, she was in great demand. At first she addressed the wealthy society women of New York in drawing-rooms, but in time those who came to listen and learn were of mixed social background – the general public. Fielde lectured at colleges, theaters, institutional and church halls, to scientists, religious people and scholars, and political and civic groups, on an impressive range of subjects of timely interest, based upon newspaper reports and articles in journals. Soon she exhausted the topics she knew intimately – China, the Chinese, and missionary work. She herself probably tired of them after innumerable variations and repetitions, especially when her firsthand experience with the Orient had come to an end, and there was little new information to freshen presentations. Once finished with lectures based upon her missionary experience, those that followed were almost entirely of a secular nature, switching from religion to politics, science, and social problems – a vast, global smorgasbord. She never had trouble finding subjects for her talks, always overflowing with ideas, free moving, and never stagnant.

Competent journalists can tackle most subjects by reading, interviewing relevant individuals, formulating opinions, and then assembling the information into a credible article without being particularly authoritative. With her strong journalistic bent, Fielde could do the same, fashioning interesting lectures from her reading and study, but many of her lectures derived from her scholarly research in science, notes made in foreign libraries during her travels, and her experiences in China. Helen Stevens, Fielde's friend and early biographer, states that she kept scrap-books filled with reports of her lectures.[16] As a professional lecturer, her diaries listed at least fifty titles on an astonishing range of the social and political problems of many countries that were in the news. She also spoke on problems of race, the "Negro question," "the spread of the white race in Africa," pygmies, Australian aborigines, policy on immigration from China and Japan, and the status of Asians in the U.S.A. Fielde's active involvement in biological research at this time is reflected in the subject of some of her lectures – airships and the law of gravitation, the new theory of the origin of the species, what animals think, ant life, the memory of ants, evidence for life on Mars, the new theory of matter, and worldwide tuberculosis.

For a woman who had experienced gender discrimination, who had devoted much of her life to improving the lot of abused Chinese women, and was presently involved in the suffragist movement and in political reform, her public lectures, at least from their titles, seem relatively free of any explicit feminist slant, nor did she ever write any substantial feminist tracts. Indeed some of her pronouncements would be strongly condemned by feminists. Equality of opportunity and equal rights, whose origins derived from her personal experience, underlay Fielde's argument, but contrary to what might be expected, she believed that women were most fulfilled as wives and mothers, and she urged budding young professional women to forget their ambitions, meet a young man, marry, and have children – not the view of the modern feminist, rather that of a conventional Victorian. Women could make their choice but Fielde knew what was best, for after all: "only women could have babies."

When working for the League for Political Education, she wrote to a friend:

> Each day I teach civil government, parliamentary usage and statute law to a hundred and fifty women. I am not utterly devoted to my work, doubtful if I am pointing out to my pupils their highest spheres of usefulness. True, they are bright and winsome women; but, sometimes when I look into the sweet, eager and tired faces of that class I silently say – "Oh, you dear, aspiring, strenuous souls! I wish that every one of you was the mother of seven children or the grandmother of twelve; and that you had your lives and time full of honest, healthy, calm domesticity."[17]

How could she advise young women, she thought, to spurn the consummate life of marriage and motherhood? Urging these women to have babies was not without its eugenic element – their offspring would be the salvation of America! Consistent with this notion was her criticism of American women who married Europeans, an opinion which was eccentric, jingoistic, and almost perverse:

> American men are the finest in the world. Their chivalry and generosity and true heartedness has made American women the finest in the world. No American woman who fails to recognize the reason for her own superiority, nor who fails to feel due appreciation of that reason, deserves the best.[18]

In 1904, President Theodore Roosevelt proclaimed in his message to the American people that the duty of the man is to work, and the duty of the woman is to be a housewife and mother. This declaration, and another such remark – "The woman who flinches from childbirth stands on a par with the soldier who drops his rifle and runs in battle" – incensed many women. To control the damage inflicted by these inflammatory statements, Roosevelt's alert staff had the popular and admired Adele Fielde interviewed on the subject of women's place in modern American life, for they knew that both the President and Fielde shared an exalted view of motherhood. The report in the *New York Times* bannered "*Miss Adele M. Fielde Indorses President Roosevelt*" covered five columns, in which she was quoted as saying:

> The woman who goes down into the Valley of the Shadow of Death three or four times, perhaps in the course of her existence, and each time returns bringing with her a new life, does more for humanity than the woman engaged in any kind of intellectual activity. She is a far more important member of the community than the writer of books, the opera singer, the woman scientist, or any other of those engaged in the pursuits which to-day lie open to the American woman and in which she has often made a name and fame for herself . . . the professional woman and the business woman undoubtedly have their place in our life. But it is not the highest place."[19]

Fielde's declaration must have pleased Roosevelt immensely.

Significantly, several of the areas of achievement by women listed were those in which Fielde had excelled, so that she was speaking of the life she might have wanted for herself. As for the opera singer, she was passionate about opera (and theater), and idolized the leading male and female singers of the day. Fielde's surprising inconsistency was not unique. One has only to look at another contemporary such as Mary Cassatt, an ambitious, unmarried painter whose sole creations were warm, intimate portraits of mothers with their small children.[20]

Fielde scoffed at the argument that having children only creates more humans who will suffer disappointment and hardship in "the struggle of life." This might be true in China, but not in America: "It does not matter here whether one be born in a tenement or in a mansion, there is an unlimited opportunity for happiness." Clearly, Fielde was drawing upon her own history of impoverishment – she had worked her way through college and had made something of herself, and she expected others to do so as well with determination and hard work. She was addressing middle-class women who were not compelled to earn their living, who could afford to make a home and raise a family, not the vast numbers of young women, married and single, whose income was dependent upon their own earning power which would be disastrously curtailed by pregnancy and childcare, urgent issues taken up by Margaret Sanger in her advocacy of birth control.[21]

Fielde was exhorting the "right type" of women to assume the responsibility, the duty, of having babies to overcome "a constant addition in the number of children born of illiterate parents." Imbued with Darwinian notions, and heeding the grim warnings of the eugenicists so popular at the time, she felt that if these women did not have children, "the race would soon lose its best characteristics." She ended the *Times* interview by stating: "I am convinced that the truest joys in life come to the woman who devotes her life to the best realization of the term 'a good wife and mother'. That is a career that calls for the highest order of intelligence."

Feminists involved in the battle for the vote for women saw no conflict between the eugenic and suffragist causes. If women could vote, the world would be a more enlightened place for mothers to better raise their children whose greater potentials would be realized – an avowed goal of eugenics. Still, if there was true gender equality, with real opportunity for women to fulfill their hopes, many women would choose to work in well-paid jobs outside the home. Clearly they would have fewer or even no children if there was no eugenics-inspired state help, quite the opposite of what Fielde and the eugenics advocates desired.[22]

Her naive outlook was an amalgam of early experiences with a feminist overlay derived from her encounters in a male-dominated society. Despite her extensive travel and interactions with people all over the world, she was disturbingly ethnocentric in her consideration of people in the abstract, as were most people of her class. The views of this vigorous, aggressive professional on the aspirations of women were certainly at odds with her own behavior and ambitions. Although her advice to young women seemed to spring from nowhere, it may have had its origin in the electrifying trauma of the loss of her fiancé Cyrus Chilcott whom she idolized, and with whom she had hoped to make a home filled with children. Never again did she consider another man as a possible partner in marriage. She might have advised young women to create a family because she herself may have felt condemned to a lonely struggle while yearning for her saint and the children she would never have – dreams untainted by real life, and the actual stresses and strains of family living.

Although she never shrank from expressing an opinion on any subject, she seemed to have made a distinction between her passionately held causes (temperance, women's suffrage, civic education, clean, efficient politics) and her public lectures by which she earned a living. Always the analytical scholar, never the rabid reformer, she would not tolerate violence or confrontation. At no time in her writing and speeches did she advocate civil disobedience as did Susan B. Anthony. Her immediate backers were usually well-to-do women with conservative husbands, but fully sympathetic with Fielde's irreproachable concerns. She had begun as a schoolteacher in New York State, had been a teacher and missionary in China, and now, back in America, she continued to teach what she knew well, a secular missionary in her native land. Newly arrived in America, she was unsure of her knowledge of the country's economy, and so she did not teach the subject, nor express opinions until she was sure of her material. She confided to a friend: "I keep my views to myself, conscious that I may presently read something that will change them! Alas! I am almost a stranger in this dear land of mine."[23]

As well as her lecture circuit, she gave intensive courses on the Orient (on at least one occasion lecturing every night for ten nights), and for this she received $1000, a not inconsiderable amount of money. However, her basic income came from public lectures which she gave two to four times every week. Despite an ample income, her savings grew very slowly because she was exceedingly generous in responding to urgent appeals to support many causes. She was a good business person, and was confident of her ability to handle money, but she had no qualms about parting with her savings – getting rich was not her goal. The story is told that in her later years in Seattle, Washington, she was asked to donate money to support the Prohibition campaign, one of Fielde's earnestly felt causes that had originated in her experience with the ravages of alcohol among the Chinese. After a quick calculation to estimate how much she could spare, she responded jokingly: "If I limit myself to one new gown this year and to a few other lesser economies, I will be able to give fifteen hundred dollars without any very embarrassing deprivations."[24] This was a remarkably generous gift for a woman of her means.

Her income was sufficient to rent rooms in an agreeable boarding house at 130 West 43rd Street with "a large south window, a spacious room, two clothes-rooms, running water, and comfort: in a perfectly *still* environment." Upon moving to her quarters, "my new nest had to be lined with my feathers, which I plucked out of my trunk." Her landlady was a college classmate at Albany, now a widow, who rented rooms to twenty-five boarders. Though not clearly stated, Fielde does not appear to have cooked for herself. She probably took her meals in the house, or ate in restaurants, a living arrangement that pleased her.[25] Fielde had sampled many cuisines on her travels, but no food ever impressed her enough to describe or praise it. In keeping with her pro-European bias in cultural matters, she spoke disparagingly about lobsters, clambakes, roasted clams, and watermelon.[26]

Fielde was ravenous for information, much of it for use in her lectures. Soon after her arrival in New York, she was busy with "Single tax, Nationalism, and other political eonomical studies relating to the welfare of my America."[27] She had access to numerous libraries, not only for their books, and "prowling the current literature," but for providing a place to meet and discuss ideas with other women. At the Mercantile Library she joined a Social Economic Reading Circle of five "bright Ladies," for now that she was retired, she had time for such invigorating activities. While reading in the Astor Library, assuaging her "hunger for fresh books," she met many interesting women, authors and literati, including "Virginia Penny . . . a wrinkled wisp of a woman, in black. She is the author of a thick book 'How Women Can Make Money,' and she lives in the Home for Indigent Authors!" Another author was "a pink dumpling of a woman." Although Fielde was an earnest person dedicated to good works, her irrepressible sense of humor made her an attractive advocate of serious issues that were no laughing matter.

Quite simply, no matter how weighty the issues at hand, the welfare of others was always foremost in Fielde's mind, and the extent to which one sacrificed oneself for that was, for her, the measure of a person. Without fuss or self-aggrandizement she left a trail of good deeds behind her, helping in any way she could. For instance, she assisted a friend in building a library in a small town in New York, writing letters asking experts about books, about the construction and the arrangement of shelves. She spent a considerable part of each summer looking after old and feeble elderly people, often the relatives of friends.

Edward Nolan, a bachelor, was Fielde's dear, gentle friend in whom she confided until her death. They seemed to have an intimate brother–sister relationship rather than a romantic liaison, for he was seven years younger than Fielde, and a Catholic. For many years, Nolan had been the companion of a Mrs. Gilbert, a consumptive who was separated from her abusive husband. Incredibly solicitous of Mrs. Gilbert, she also became the constant concern of Fielde, giving rise to innumerable discussions about her health and care. When Mrs. Gilbert returned to her husband, Fielde was surprised, and wrote to Nolan: "I also know the queerness and 'cussedness' of women's ways."

To cure Nolan's mental depression she urged him not to underestimate his own worth. She confessed that there were "only about three men in the world in whose absolute loyalty a woman [Fielde] might at all times safely trust – and you are one of the three. That makes you very valuable." Her beloved Cyrus Chilcott must have been the second in whom she had absolute trust, but there is no clue about the third. The evidence suggests that after Chilcott, Fielde had no passionate relationships with men (or women), and if there were bad times when this strong person had to lean on someone, there were always dear, loyal women friends. She sought her satisfactions elsewhere to become a fully realized person with a very successful professional career.

Fielde advised Nolan to pursue a new, interesting occupation because he was not fully appreciated at the Academy of Natural Sciences of Philadelphia, and to find and marry a "dear, bright, sweet little Catholic woman with money enough to pay her expenses. . . . Equality in economic fundamentals is surely conducive to good fellowship – which is conducive to enduring affection."[28] A Protestant would not do, for it would be an "error of judgment" for a Catholic to marry a Protestant woman. "As to converts, I do not approve of them anyway." Then she asked: "what is the use in your not getting out of life all its possibilities of joy?" Fielde heaped praise on Nolan, a timid man, and frequently expressed concern about his failing health, and his welfare. She exhorted him to take a European vacation, and to follow a detailed itinerary that she provided. Nolan's complaint that he was not interested in politics and reform, and had no desire to change things, was incomprehensible to Fielde, evidence to her that he was not well, and was unable to take care of himself: "I am absolutely luxuriating in all that you abhor."[29]

Not unexpectedly, when Fielde settled in New York and had been taken up by the women of the city and their causes, she became active in the suffragist movement. The struggle was not new, having been led since the 1840s by Susan B. Anthony, Elizabeth Cady Stanton, Lucretia Mott, and later by Carrie Chapman Catt, and Anna Howard Shaw, polemicists who had struggled relentlessly to convince the male-dominated legislatures that women had the right to vote.[30] Fielde was on friendly terms with all of them. While these women were prominent leaders of the national movement, there were numerous state and local suffrage organizations, New York's being the most publicized and important because success here would be the key to winning the vote for women at the national level.

In the spring of 1894, Fielde and her colleagues were furiously involved in preparations for the Constitutional Convention of the New York State Legislature to be held in Albany, where there was an opportunity to amend the state Constitution to enfranchise women. If suffragists were victorious here, a similar amendment in the federal Constitution would be sure to follow: "committee-meetings, drawing-room debates, interviews with reporters, preparation of public documents, construction of plans . . . distribution of literature, giving out of petitions, etc., succeed each other so fast that fifteen hours a day is the least time in which I can compass the portion of the campaign that falls to my share." Fielde, and many other women, went to Albany, speeches were made, mass meetings organized, politicians importuned, and a petition signed by 600,000 people was presented to the committee. However, there were other women, some socially prominent, who opposed the suffragist amendment because they believed that politics and governance were best left to men; they managed to get their petition signed by fewer than 20,000 supporters. However, the numbers were disregarded, the petitions were considered as equally persuasive, the arguments of both sides were duly acknowledged by a supposedly neutral legislative committee which, not unexpectedly, decided against inclusion of a suffrage amendment – a repetition of events at a similar state convention in 1867.[31] The public was not interested, and in fact, politicians knew that those who made suffrage an issue faired poorly at the polls. At the end of the battle, Fielde spoke of "the hope of enfranchisement for my sex in the Empire State, a hope that bubbles, and scintillates and *rages*, withdraws silently into some remote recess to bide its time." She had worked so hard and for so long that her studies and her friends had been neglected, something she declared would never happen again.

A disappointed and exhausted Fielde recovered her strength at the Marine Biological Laboratory in Woods Hole where she attended a summer course in Marine Botany – "a tonic." Recovery began when she traveled overnight by steamer from a dock at the foot of Murray Street on the East River, to Fall River, Massachusetts, and then boarded a train to New Bedford where a steamer crossed Buzzards Bay to Woods Hole, a leisurely trip that included a good meal on board, sleeping on the deck under blankets, and a cup of hot milk in the morning. Three months were spent at Woods Hole, learning, doing research, swimming, and visiting her friends, the Sharps at Nantucket. September was passed at the Mohunk Mountain House Hotel in New York State, with her friends, the Cauldwells,[32] and by fall she was back in the race, lecturing four times a week.

Despite the pressure and her self-imposed burdens, Fielde was a buoyant, happy person. At a clambake with other scientists at Woods Hole, "The little circle of mine in which I sat was dignified, and I was the only member who descended to badinage. One cannot be sportive all by one's lonely self; so I gave it up and talked Botany . . . I felt much bored when I got home." She complained of two starchy professors, both women. "I believe the element that made social ebulition impossible was little, stiff, firm, learned Dr. Randolph, she of Bryn Mawr."[33]

In 1895, attempting to coax Edward Nolan out of a bout of depression, she wrote:

> you are now, and always to struggle for life – a joyous life. Just consider *me*. Five years ago now [1890, when a serious cardiac problem was (incorrectly) diagnosed], I knew that any day might easily be my last. But I decided that I would live and I would have a deal of interesting and happy experience. I have lived well, and have had much that it would have been a pity to have missed in living, and I propose having lots more of good times, and having them several tens of years yet if I can.[34]

Fielde was convinced that Nolan's condition could be alleviated by her pep talk, a change in environment, and travel.

The unsuccessful effort in Albany had been led by six women which included Adele Fielde, and five women of wealth and social standing – Mrs. H.M. Sanders, Mrs. Robert Abbe, Mrs. Ben Ali Haggin, Mrs. C.A. Runkle, and Dr. Mary Putnam-Jacobi. Disappointed but not disheartened, meetings continued to be held to discuss the defeat, and to outline a plan for the next round of the battle. They concluded that the main weakness in their cause was an insufficiently informed citizenry – too few men and women were aware of the issues at stake. To correct this defect, they established The League for Political Education, really a replacement of the New York Voluntary Association of Equal Suffragists that had been active during the Convention. The League came into being in January 1895, with Mrs. Sanders as president and Adele Fielde as recording secretary. Though she had charismatic appeal – a quick thinker, a fine writer and speaker – she never craved attention, and was willing to remain in the background, the work-horse of an organization dedicated to a cause she believed in, the consolidator of the group. Perhaps for this reason she was not as widely known nor as prominent as other women, but those who interacted with her were greatly impressed. Whether she was awed by the famous suffragists, national spokespersons, is not known. The League proved to be a stable, respected institution that was still very active at the time of the passage of the 19th amendment to the federal Constitution which assured women the right to vote (1920). No longer a female preserve, the League created a national forum, sponsoring lectures by many luminaries including Theodore Roosevelt and Woodrow Wilson.

Though Fielde was an active scientist at this time, as will be seen, the League was the central focus of her life for the next thirteen years, dedicated to enlightening the citizenry about politics, the workings of government, and civic rights and responsibilities. The headquarters were at the Berkeley Lyceum, 23 West 44th Street, where Fielde served as a receptionist, answered questions, and handed out literature. Interviewed by the *World*, she was precise in her speech, the model of restraint and reason with an element of pedantry:

> As to the question whether women ought to vote, that depends, in my opinion, on the answer to the question whether the innate tendencies of women, acquired or natural, are going to complicate or assist in the solution of the pressing industrial problems which at this moment imperil our safety as a people. Many women are themselves the strongest possible arguments against woman suffrage. My own view is that all native-born, self-supporting women should be enfranchised. This however is not a suffrage league, although the majority of the members thus far are suffragists, and the officers of the league are the same women who comprised the Voluntary Committee of the suffrage campaign of last spring before and during the session of the New York State Constitutional Convention. The League is distinctly for political education, and is ready to help women of all beliefs and conditions so far as it can.[35]

The League established women's clubs with instructors who gave courses on political education which involved study, and carefully chosen readings. Annual membership of the League cost almost nothing, and tuition for the courses was only a few dollars. Though the groups were open to men, few joined. Mrs. Runkle instructed one group on the history and growth of American civil government, and Adele Fielde lectured on "the powers and duties of New York officials." According to Fielde, they did "not teach theories, simply facts," advocating "no particular form of government." All they wanted was good government, and she hinted that the parties in power would soon learn that they would lose their strength unless they came to appreciate the inevitable enfranchisement of women. By disregarding the will of many thousands of women, politicians aroused "intelligent womanhood to a knowledge of what government is and how it should be administered."

There were special courses given by Fielde for which the student paid, providing her with an income. She lectured on political economy, civil government, and parliamentary procedure, and from the latter came her book *Parliamentary Procedure* of 1899, a literate work that went through two editions, the first in New York, and a second in 1914 in Seattle. Fielde also gave a weekly lecture without charge, on current events, municipal affairs and business relations. For many years she organized and led a program "Educational Excursions," in which the class would visit city departments (fire, police, docks), and institutions (stock exchange, Bellevue Hospital, the Post Office, Immigrant Clearing House, Navy Yard); papers were then prepared for presentation to the class.[36]

In 1897 Fielde published *A Political Primer of New York State and City* – basically an outline of the course she had been teaching – systematically discussing the responsibilities of officers of all the boards and departments of the city and state government. There were sections on elections, naturalization, and citizenship, the judicial system, the court system and its personnel, and the function of various departments – finance, fire, health, parks, railroads. There was an abundance of statistics, salaries of officials, and numerous maps of the state and the city outlining counties, Senate, congressional and judicial districts, and boroughs. Ever the teacher, much of the book is taken up with instruction in the form of examination questions and their answers. Overall, the work was a remarkably comprehensive outline of civic and state government that could be understood by any reasonably intelligent person. It was a portable primer of 104 pages that "left no one in the dark as to the essential features of the new government of the great city."[37] Fielde gave the copyright to the League which derived a considerable profit from sales, since it went through four editions of 5000 copies each, and was still being used during the First World War, twenty years after it first appeared.

Fielde also wrote pamphlets and short essays that promoted the teaching of the League. To instruct her students on proper behavior in discussion and debate, she wrote *Fourteen Rules for Polite Conversation*, which was a regular part of the course of instruction, another popular work sold by the League. Fielde insisted on polite behavior in discussion, for not only did she think rudeness was offensive, but also that it rendered a person less effective in argument. She continued to write magazine and newspaper articles, and assembled several of these in a book, *A Corner of Cathay*, in 1894. That year she also published *The Stray Arrow or Chinese Nights' Entertainments*, a collection of forty Chinese tales gleaned from illiterate story-tellers in Swatow. Some were romantic, dealing with match-making and marriage, some had a moral, others illustrated a proverb, while still others ended with an O. Henry twist of fate. Although she considered these "frivolous folklore," she wanted them read, and urged her friend Edward Nolan to write about the book in Philadelphia newspapers where he had connections.[38] As a teacher she was not shy or diffident, and she passionately believed that the public should be informed about issues and causes, and about other cultures.

A Corner of Cathay was a popular, illustrated volume that received favorable reviews when it appeared in 1894 ("a rather exquisite volume"). In addition to presenting Chinese stories and legends, she described Chinese life and culture with great understanding and accuracy that could only have come from her years of intimate experience. The sixteen chapters of the book, replete with Chinese sayings and aphorisms, cover such disparate topics as farm life, marriage, mortuary customs, children's games, schools, legal matters, superstitions, the Chinese conception of evolution, fabulous animals, Confucianism, Taoism, and Chinese. Her discussion often captivates us, as does the charming, didactic opening of "Measures of time:"

> Time is the one good of which all men have the same amount. Other valuable possessions are unequally distributed; but the hours are of like length to us all. The use of time is ultimately a matter of free will, and constitutes the main difference between the weak and the wise. One who is so conscientious as to hold in careful regard other people's time, is evidently on the road to perfection. The Australian savage who notes only day and night, and the European who habitually carries a watch marking the seconds of which he heeds the flight, are at the two extremes of human culture. The Chinese are midway between. They have gone as far in civilization as any men who have no clocks . . .
>
> [The dissertation ends:] the masses of the people have no time-pieces. As a consequence, appointments are made with a broad margin for waiting, and he who meets one within an hour or two of the time fixed, is thought to practice that punctuality which is the politeness of princes.[39]

Fluent in the language, and trusted by the people, Fielde had studied and recorded whatever she happened upon. Over time, she had interviewed the Chinese on many subjects, penetrated the seeming impassive facades, and had learned much that few Westerners knew, and in so doing, she had bestowed on them, especially the women, individuality and dignity, touching upon the fanciful and more delicate side of their nature, their enthrallment by superstitions, and their penchant for preposterous stories. A careful observer, Fielde wrote gracefully, simply and clearly, and by so doing she removed the half-knowledge that had obscured a true appreciation of China. Despite her own wit and sense of humor, there seemed to be little humor in her stories about the Chinese, perhaps because there was so little to laugh about in their hard life.

A distant China was in the daily news as a participant in war with Japan, and in conflict with greedy Western imperial powers.[40] In both instances, a lumbering, inept, corrupt giant was savaged.

10 Religion, science, and the occult

Growing up in a very small town in northern New York State, and under close observance, Fielde was brought up in a traditional way, soaking up the beliefs and attitudes of her parents and her community, but, even then, after thoughtful analysis of some subject, when she came to a different conclusion from her peers, she did not yield to the pressure to conform. As an independent teenager, she switched her allegiance from the Baptist creed of her family to a more tolerant Universalist denomination, based no doubt on a close comparison of the two sects. Fielde remained an eager advocate of the basic principles of Christianity, but it is not surprising that in her later years her views came to differ from those of most ordinary churchgoers. Surely Fielde's vision of a merciful God of Love in a land of grinding poverty and injustice (which she had grimly experienced for a quarter of a century) would differ from that held by an American, coddled in a benign environment of plenty, whose lofty theological convictions had never been put to the test. Her move away from the dogmatic, male-dominated, and authoritarian tradition of Calvin (and of the Reverend Dean of Bangkok) to a more humanistic religion was, in fact, part of a general drift by many Americans who were abandoning the narrow doctrinal beliefs of their elders, and spending their leisure time reading romantic novels rather than the Bible.[1]

Her freethinking ways became evident when she was a missionary. On a social level, in Bangkok and in China, she would not be confined to the community of missionaries with their strict, fundamentalist beliefs. She was a most conscientious worker, but at the end of the working day, to seek relief from boredom and stress, she consorted with others outside her religious community. Since the missionary movement would not countenance a challenge to the literal Truth of the Bible, nor could missionaries appreciate the inherent value of science, her Western friends – government representatives, professional and business people with their families – were not particularly religious, and were skeptical of biblical truth, and this no doubt gave rise to lively debate. Living in China, she was immersed in a civilization with its own system of beliefs and a cosmology older than her own which she had to respect, however much they might conflict with her sacred God-given truths.

Although in her early missionary days she professed that salvation of the heathen through the Word, with all its mystery, was the single most important aim of the missionary, she was inevitably drawn to the social and ethical problems of the societies in which she lived. Eventually her plea to the heathen became: Accept Christ and His teachings, not the Church – an appeal that was unacceptable to the Baptist missionary organization, and the reason for her leaving missionary work. It was in the realms of teaching and secular enlightenment that she was most comfortable as her religious beliefs became more private and interiorized. The essence of her religion came to lie in the immediate relation between oneself and God that would give rise to a moral evolution, striving to improve the spiritual and material welfare of all mankind; salvation could not come about through the dictates of a church. The surest way of attaining an ideal, heavenly state on Earth was through social beneficence, so that she came to see the greatest service to which the missionary enterprise could aspire was as a kind of Peace Corp, and over time this function has become increasingly important, if not dominant. At the level of the individual, Fielde surprises us in advocating marriage and motherhood as offering "greater facilities for self-sacrifice, self-abnegation, and devotion to others – the only true culture."[2]

As a missionary in Swatow, Fielde took it upon herself to translate the Book of Genesis into Chinese, to be used in the religious education of her Bible-women. Dissecting the text word by word, she re-examined the story of the Creation, its titanic cosmology which she had learned in childhood, and believed was at the very foundation of human existence. With this as the starting point, augmented by all she had seen and learned – for she had been exposed to the widely discussed notions of Charles Darwin, and was aware of the latest findings in geology and paleontology – she began to realize that there were different ways of interpreting the overarching problems of Creation and existence – the origin of Earth and life upon it, and the wondrous diversification of living forms. Fielde was by nature a critical thinker with an inquisitive mind, and it was natural for her to proceed from questioning the absolute truth of one chapter of the Bible to examining all others. In time, she departed from orthodoxy, adopting a religion that loosely fused religious and scientific belief. She might be able to approach and understand her God through science. To some extent her faith resembled Unitarianism, with a decline of denominational concerns, and an emphasis on the moral and rational elements of religion. She had returned to China in 1885, her last tour of duty as a Christian missionary, heavy with a sense of purpose, but her message was increasingly that of a secular teacher rather than of an evangelist. Despite the temptations to stay in America, "the wrinkled faces of the dear women always glimmered in the air between me and any turning that led away from them." They were her family in need.

Upon her return to America, Fielde chose to be a biologist, living and working in a community of scientists in Philadelphia, and in Woods Hole throughout the summer, where the development of invertebrates, adaptive evolution, and selection of heritable variation were topics of concern. In this environment her religious views changed rapidly. It is not known how much a lowly student took part in discussions with the finest American biological scientists of the time who taught there – F.R. Lillie, Jacques Loeb, Charles O. Whitman, E.G. Conklin, T.H. Morgan, and William M. Wheeler, among others – all formidable men who may have awed Fielde. Wheeler, a difficult man, was much impressed by Fielde – her intelligence and original, inquiring mind.[3] She also met several women biologists who were deeply involved in research – Cornelia M. Clapp and Helen Dean King, among others – and as class photographs indicate, she came in contact with many female students. Indeed, there were so many young women in those classes, one wonders whatever happened to them, and why we have heard nothing more about them. In the male world of science, none of these talented women scientists, including Fielde, ever received their just recognition. On the whole, neglect and frustration was their fate over the next half-century.

An account of Fielde's religious convictions which she held after she had left the Baptist missionary movement, so far removed from the rather orthodox views of her youth, were summarized by her biographer Helen Stevens.[4] Fielde came to believe that Scripture was fallible in its scientific accuracy and in its chronology – a damnable belief to her Baptist colleagues. To maintain that some biblical accounts were scientifically acceptable was to her absurd, and, like many, she held that the Bible was a compilation of imaginative, poetic accounts of the experience of a primitive people, and not to be believed in the literal sense – "great wisdom but imperfect knowledge." She admired the Old Testament as a remarkable document for its time, but she deplored the fact that it was so negative. Fielde would replace all the "thou shalt not" commands with "something more positive, something that will point out the way of duty, something that will instruct us in what we shall do."

According to Fielde, the New Testament was a precious but flawed document, its imperfections arising over the ages by the additions and revisions of various authors which could be readily identified; even so, there was some inconsistency in her belief. While she considered the New Testament to be true in all essential details, it was not to be taken as literal truth. She was groping for an acceptable, reasonable position to provide a rational foundation for many of the biblical miracles and happenings. She believed in the miracles which Christ had performed but she played down the magical aura others associated with them, and she did not believe that He had supernatural powers or could call upon heavenly forces to assist him. She was of the opinion that a hypnotic state on the part of viewers might explain His turning water into wine, walking on the waters, and feeding the multitudes with a few loaves of bread and some fish. Christ might have possessed "abnormal psychic powers" which would explain his bringing the dead to life, and of healing the sick and the blind. Other miracles such as the calming of stormy waters might be the result of coincidence. Her *ad hoc* attempts to downplay the supernatural, and to flatten out a book of miracles to sound like a perfectly reasonable, materialistic account of a life, were not convincing. The power of her faith was such that it had permitted her to explain marvels through accurate observation and contemporary scientific theory – a personal religion indeed.

Christ was central to her religious belief, not because He was capable of performing extraordinary feats, but because He was truly a moral and beneficent man who preached the love of mankind. His teachings were at the heart of all true religion, which humans craved. One senses that when she speaks so admiringly of Christ the man, she conflates Him with another ideal, Cyrus Chilcott, the husband she never had, who, over the years, was increasingly idealized in her memory. She had become a missionary because of him, had followed him to the Orient, and by the cruelest turn of fate, he had been snatched from her. She yearned for Christ and Chilcott, but they were both beyond her reach in this world. There seems to be a sexual element in her worship of Christ:

> The person who has lived in this world who seems to me the one that I should like above all others to be permanently near, is Christ. I am utterly unorthodox, taking the creed of any church, Protestant, Catholic or Greek, as a standard. I do not highly esteem churches of any faith. But when I pass out of this life I expect to immediately inquire for the Man of Nazareth. . . . I have no doubt that Confucius and Buddha, both of whom were honest truth-seekers . . . will be in fellowship with Him.

In time, Fielde had begun to appreciate the virtues of non-Christian creeds, and to see that Christians had no monopoly on wisdom and righteousness: "Cogent reasons for all good works, abundant stimulus towards being our best selves, infinite argument against evil, lie outside theology and creed. I can see that a man may be utterly an agnostic, and yet have reasons for being completely good in all the relations of life, and earnestly devoted to such works as being an earthly immortelle." Formal religion can be separated from the properly lived, moral life: "If I believed in no future life, no heaven, no hell, no God beyond Nature and no religion but the Law of Duty, I do not think I should in my outward self be markedly different from what I am." These are statements that a self-respecting Baptist would never make.

She believed in two kinds of immortality: that which arises from the creations of philosophers and artists which move men's souls long after the creators are gone: "who can truly say that they do not still live in this world?" These people "are immortal among men." There was a second kind of immortality: eternal life in Heaven, which she fervently hoped and believed would be her reward. There she would find all the people she admired and liked, and those whom she wanted to be her friends in Heaven were the ones who had received her highest stamp of approval. In contrast to her sophisticated and reasoned approach to religious life, there is something simplistic and naive about these fairyland wishes of her theology. In Heaven, after a life of struggle and imperfection, all her wishes are fulfilled; Heaven seems to be reduced to a gigantic, never-ending cocktail party to which the "best" people were invited.

After breaking with the Baptist Missionary Union, and shedding the certainties of sectarian Christianity, she never again joined any religious organizations, though, while shunning them, she founded or joined many secular groups. When living in Seattle in 1915, she was invited to join a "group of one hundred," headed by a Congregational minister, whose members proposed to dedicate themselves to make the Sermon on the Mount their guide in their daily lives. She politely declined, giving a somewhat frivolous, dismissive excuse that she lacked the time for such a program, and that she was too involved in other causes. However, she refused to join for more complex reasons: "I have . . . just read again, very thoughtfully, the Sermon on the Mount. I have never been able to live up to my own interpretation of the Sermon. It is probable that I shall fail in the future as I have in the past." She goes on:

> The precept of the Chinese, the Hindu, the Greek, the Persian, the Moorish teachers have entered into my ethical creed without conflict with its Hebrew elements. In a blundering way, I follow the Parsee mandate for the morning – "This day will I speak, think and do only that which promotes the true life." Almost every day, there comes to me a clearer conception of the true life. At present that conception does not impel me to unite with any organization whatsoever.

However polite the refusal, it was a blunt declaration of independence, one that paraded her erudition, her refusal to be constricted by the dictates of organized (male-dominated) religion. Her own convictions, which transcended the boundaries of conventional Christian observance, and were formulated on the basis of personal experience and study, suited her better. On a trivial level, she disapproved of the ritual of present-giving at Christmas. On December 20th, 1893 she sent presents to Dr. Nolan which were to be delivered to a mutual friend. She emphasized: "These are *not* Christmas gifts. I have decided not to send my friends any sort of Christmas token hereafter because I dislike having stated times for exchanging gifts, and think that such exact and fixed arrangements unreasonable." She went on to say that she would send gifts at any time but December 25th.[5]

Darwin's *Origin of Species by Means of Natural Selection* (1859), and his later work on the origins of humans, which were vigorously debated in America after the Civil War, presented a direct challenge to the biblical version of Genesis, and tore apart the complacency of the Victorian world. If laymen had not been able to appreciate the potential utility of science, and were suspicious about where science would lead, they now had real cause for alarm, for, according to the new thinking, nature neither followed orderly rules dictated from above, nor was it benign. Abhorring open warfare, as had occurred between Thomas Huxley and Bishop Wilberforce at the meeting of the British Association for the Advancement of Science in 1860,[6] liberal theologians and religious scientists, and the majority of intellectuals, came to an accommodation they could live with – evolution, and the disappearance of whole species, was considered part of the divine plan. According to Fielde, nature was not an "irresponsible force. . . . The laws of Nature are, to my thinking those of God, who, acting under a sense of responsibility, chooses to exterminate evil. Infinite Wisdom makes no mistakes. . . . What Nature, God exterminates *ought to be exterminated every time*." Fundamentalists however were utterly opposed to such a godless, materialist notion as natural selection, and this group included many of Fielde's fellow missionaries who dismissed the theory of evolution by natural selection as pure drivel.

Fielde could not accept the idea held by atheists and agnostics that life arose by chance, by a fortuitous combination of chemical components in a hospitable environment. To her, the ever-present Creator was the originator of life itself. However, once created, living matter functioned according to natural laws, also of divine origin, that man could reveal through scientific research. However, she had to accommodate the notion that the Creator seemed always to be elsewhere, and had done His great work at another time.

Intriguing accounts of Darwinian thinking provided her with facts and opinions consistent with her experience, that a reasonable person (which she considered herself to be) must think about. Seemingly contradictory explanations, requiring further study, initiated her entry into science. She wanted to understand the mechanisms God had devised in nature, and the general laws by which God's grand design could be comprehended by humans. Though these matters were both troublesome and threatening to her superiors, they presented no problems for Fielde, whose belief in God as the Creator of all things was unshakable.

Nor was there discontinuity or rejection in her religious life, as she distanced herself from ritual, intolerance, and narrow sectarian belief – rather she learned to appreciate the virtues of the religions and creeds she had encountered in the East. She rejoiced in her evolving, eclectic theology: "I have really come to enjoy religion. I have a creed I can heartily believe in all its details; one that offends neither my intellect, nor my heart nor my common-sense."

The welfare of man was at the heart of her creed, and in accordance with the Book of Genesis, she believed that humans had dominion over all animals – the "culture and conquest of nature was man's mission on earth." Fielde insisted that religion and science be discussed without restraint, and was aggrieved by the comments of a learned doctor about a prospective minister who sought a position – "to have anything to do with the teaching of the doctrine of evolution might compromise him with his congregation." She condemned the doctor for his remark, which "places him in the position of a charlatan and vitiates his claim to be either a true scientist or a true Christian. Let us have truth though the heavens fall!"

Fielde most certainly understood the social and religious implications of evolution and natural selection, which postulated a biological world of murderous, relentless competition – a far cry from an ordered world presided over by a loving God. She accepted the idea of a gradual change of living forms to produce new species, as opposed to *de novo*, separate, and ongoing creation of every species. However, many deemed unacceptable the proposed mechanism by which gradual change was brought about – natural selection – for it was cruel, random, and without moral values, especially as it pertained to man. It was not possible for such a process to operate in the Christian universe of God's great design. From this anti-Darwinian position sprang the Neo-Lamarckism of Edward Drinker Cope and Alpheus Hyatt, both of whom Fielde was likely to have encountered in Philadelphia and Woods Hole. Fielde's version of their complex theory, incomprehensible to Darwin but taken up by many, was that mankind had a special destiny in the order of nature. God created man and all living things, but man had a special relationship to God because he was created in God's image, he was blessed with a spiritual nature, he could think, and he had an inherent moral sense. She believed then that this sense was underdeveloped, but could be improved through use to lead to the betterment of society through a cumulative process over generations – through inheritance of an acquired moral sensibility. She and many others expected that the stunning developments in science and invention would be accompanied by a concomitant progress in moral enlightenment, naively optimistic that the world was already improving at a rapid pace in every way, albeit with minor setbacks such as small wars, massacres and famines here and there, but that ultimately the Christian ideal would prevail, brought about gradually through an evolutionary mechanism. Fielde did not live long enough to fully comprehend the catastrophe of the First World War, or the unimaginable horrors of the mid-twentieth century.

The products of scientific endeavor – knowledge or theory – can be exploited for good or evil. Along with the profound insights provided by Darwin, his theory of how evolution worked – by a process of selection – gave rise to the Eugenics movement which advocated improvement in the quality of the human population by selective breeding, the destruction of defective humans, and, as played out in the U.S.A., a nation of immigrants, the exclusion of people with undesirable traits. Eugenics was very popular in Fielde's time, based as it seemed to be on science and rational thought, and Fielde, like many other native-born Americans, subscribed to this "scientific" theory, which is now completely discredited as bad science, and immoral social practice.

According to Fielde, the rule of natural selection applied to man was radically different from the rule pertaining to all other forms of life, resulting in a set of bizarre, fanciful ideas, frequently confounded by her own experience. Animals might kill each other in accordance with the law of survival of the fittest, but love and cooperation would prevail in humans, who would look after one another so that "the fittest might survive in some higher form of existence." Humans could control their destiny. She believed that the "higher" and more complex the form of life, the more regard individuals have for each other. Clams live according to the first law of moral nature – self-preservation alone. Higher organisms such as the snake obey the law of "love of offspring" as well as the law of self-preservation, and the more the organism approaches the level of man, the more selfless care is taken of the young. Finally, at the top is the human, who is "capable of loving the whole world."

Complex, theoretical systems of belief, and the mediation of a particular Christian creed, were not necessary to advance the human race from the Kingdom of the Earth to the "Kingdom to Come," and for man to gain entry to the Kingdom of Heaven. Transcendence would be based on moral evolution rather than on "religious covenant." The various sects within the Church, each with its own rules and rituals, were not of any consequence in her thinking, and indeed she came to be almost contemptuous of these denominations each with its own peculiar set of beliefs.

Despite the fact that she had many lifelong friends in the Roman Catholic faith, she made no effort to conceal her anti-Catholic views, and her criticisms, apparently, did not offend them. Exposure to the world had rid her of the traditional anti-Catholic prejudice, a part of her provincial Protestant upbringing, but it found new expression as she developed her own religious system, and confronted the intolerance and rigid dogma of the Church. However, most Catholics would not have appreciated her anti-Catholic utterances, whatever their nature and origins. While touring Europe she wrote to her close friend Edward Nolan, a Catholic, that the sole objective of a church, "a purely human organization," is to promote religion among the people. It has no right to punish anyone, especially for what they believe. She was appalled by the Spanish Inquisition:

> And may I just here gently observe, that Spain, the country where Roman Catholicity prevails everywhere, and has everything its own way, the land that has been for hundreds of years orthodox, the country in which there are even now but 6000 Protestants, the country where Torquemada, Phillip II, Alba and a host of the like ilk have held sway, is as utterly heathen as is China. . . . If Spain be an example of the beneficial results of pure Catholicity, may the good Lord prevent the spread of the creed. . . . Had I started in life as a Roman Catholic, I think what I have seen in southern Ireland, Italy and Spain would have made me Protestant.[7]

To the orthodox, the questioning and redefining of the boundaries of Christian doctrine were blasphemous at worst, confused, carping and quixotic at best. Yet Fielde had not the slightest hesitation in proclaiming that Christianity was the best of all possible religions, for "the noblest human beings I have known have been Christian . . . the highest order of character is to be found where Christianity has influenced its development." She judged a religion by the quality of its finest human products, not by the behavior of the bulk of its adherents – certainly an unusual and incomplete criterion for assessing the quality of a specific set of religious beliefs.

Fielde's religious views changed to accommodate her interest in science in a dynamic, interactive way. Curiously, a third element in her thinking was occultism, and the possible existence of forces that could not be accounted for by natural science. She read extensively works on several forms of spirituality – Christian Science, theosophy, and Eastern and African occultism. While in New York she continued to read authors who might provide her with insight and contribute to her understanding of the subject – Swedenborg, Mary Baker Eddy, William James and others – authors interested in psychical research. Although she had a continuing interest in the subject, she remained unclear in her understanding of occultism and spiritism. Fielde usually wrote at length about subjects of interest to her, but we find virtually nothing about abnormal psychology and the occult. However, she did report on the smoking of hashish in an investigation of "alternate states of mind" in which she experienced not dual, but multiple existences.[8]

Paradoxically, Fielde may have become more receptive to the ideas of the East and the insubstantial world after returning to New York where an American style of spiritualism had been flourishing for half a century despite the thunderings against this heresy from ministers in their pulpits.[9] Hosts of Americans seemed to be susceptible to the siren calls of occult mysteries – mesmerism from Europe, phrenology, animal magnetism, hydropathy, and on a more mundane level, vegetarianism and the fads for wholesale panaceas such as wholemeal bread and Graham crackers. Men, women, and children endowed with profitable psychic powers were not uncommon, and there were over a million followers of all classes in the U.S.A. forming a shocking list of adherents that included Harriet Beecher Stowe, Robert Dale Owen, judges, professors, writers, and statesmen. A thriving National Association of Spiritualists had attracted much attention, and newspapers were filled with accounts of their activities. Learned tomes were written about them, and how they communicated with the world beyond by rapping, tipping, speaking, singing, or writing. Fielde and her friends were undoubtedly exposed to those inclined toward spiritualism, and may have believed there could be something to it. Being a born experimentalist, Fielde's reaction was to put spiritualism to the test. To many, spiritualism fulfilled a religious need, but to Fielde it had little to do with Christianity which she interpreted in the most pragmatic way. Spiritualism flourished among the bereaved desperate to contact their lost loved ones, especially after the Civil War; it was a kind of necromancy. Perhaps Fielde toyed with spiritualism hoping she might be able to communicate with her lost lover, Cyrus Chilcott.

At one point, she and her friends attempted to determine whether there was something in the claim that the living could converse with the dead. More in fun than serious, Fielde and her friends wrote secret messages that no one saw except the writer of the message, and these were securely stored, with the understanding that whoever died first would attempt to convey to the surviving member the message on the paper; not surprisingly, messages were never received from the afterworld. For such a determined person, her probings of the occult, though persistent, were half-hearted, and yet so many of her friends were spiritualists – one was president of the Seattle spiritualist organization.

In 1897 and 1898, while living in New York and lecturing on political systems and parliamentary procedures for the League for Political Education, Fielde, ever interested in the comparative study of religions, attended a series of twenty-one lectures given by Mr. Virchand R. Gandhi of Bombay, an ascetic Jain, on "The Significance of Man and the Universe from an Oriental Standpoint." Mr. Gandhi, an intelligent, articulate man, came as the representative of the International Society for the Education of Women of India to the World's Parliament of Religions, a group that was of particular interest to Fielde. Gandhi, deemed a "profound thinker, scholar and philosopher," was sponsored by women's organizations which organized lecture tours around the U.S.A., attempting to familiarize Americans with Eastern ideas – "the development of the interior spiritual consciousness latent within every one and the intelligent recognition of the finer forces in human nature and how to use them." Fielde attended all his lectures in New York (admission $2 for six lectures), and took detailed notes which she rewrote and organized. The whole, complete with diagrams, comprised 140 pages – almost an entire book detailing the principles of Hindu and Jain philosophy, and Buddhism.[10]

Mr. Gandhi's aim was to provide the listener with a guide to the "pure" living of one's life, not only for the operations of the mind – meditation, control (right knowledge, right belief, right practice), and the attainment of a "superconscious state" – but also for proper physiological function. In effect he was providing a complete manual for the living of a pure life, with detailed instructions for proper breathing (to control the "vital force"), the best diet, the best exercises, and the best sex. Allotments of time for each activity throughout the day were prescribed. The physiological principles espoused bore little resemblance to those of the Western world. Advocating mastery over worldly desires, and a simple life of contentment with little, he frowned upon sensual gratification of any sort.

Gandhi covered such matters as the "concentration of the mind" ("day-dreaming is an immorality"), the control of one's mind through yoga, the nature of the soul ("the immortal ego" which "has a past without beginning and has a future without end"), and reincarnation. Spirituality meant the possession of "a power by which you may elevate a living soul to a higher plane of existence."

Mr. Gandhi included in his talks subjects of more current, social interest. He spoke of the curse of the caste system, the invasion of the "Mohammedans" who invaded India and "forced their religion upon the people, the Koran in one hand, the sword in the other. . . . The Christians also came with the Bible in one hand and the bayonet in the other. However, during the famine they gave food – and that was a truly Christian act." He did not fear to offend, for he continued: "Some of the missionaries wrote home 'The famine has been a blessing to the Hindus. Many have become Christians thereby'. . . . Every convert in India has cost you $1000, and while one was being made 183 new Hindus have been born." The arrogance of the "priestly class" which "keeps people in ignorance, and degrades them," enraged the Swami. "Whenever any *class* of people claim the sole right of teaching religion, they soon believe themselves to be the sole possessors of religious knowledge." His views must have struck a particularly sensitive chord in Fielde.

Mr. Gandhi's discourse was remarkable, and, to Western ears, novel. His words rang with wisdom and common sense, for a large part of his talk was a practical guide to living, filled with rules and codifications, copiously endowed with simplistic illustrative anecdotes that were impressive but in fact would crumble upon analysis. According to the Swami's teaching there were three different classes of mind, three things and three steps were essential for "transforming the lower into the higher" class of mind, and eight stages to reach a state of "superconsciousness." These were mystic notions, and strange, Eastern theoretical systems that Westerners could not easily digest or accept – vital forces which are purified by a system of breathing, leakage of "energy," and the transformative power of vibrations produced by the spirit. There were precepts, moral rules that Westerners would find familiar and comforting – "Do not injure any living being by thought, word or act . . . speak no untruth . . . practice virtue for the sake of virtue. . . . We must understand morality, purity, chastity. . . . Humility with a desire to serve humanity."

What Fielde made of the Eastern canon is difficult to guess, though there is little question that she was an attentive and receptive student. Here and there, the Swami's words were echoed in Fielde's writings and speeches, and Hindu and Buddhist holy people were added to her pantheon of the elect, fitting companions of Christ, though always at a lower level. In later years there seemed to be a philosophic calm, a sense of "right living" in her manner, and though a determined advocate, she was not strident – perhaps the consequence of Eastern influences. This had not always been the case, for she had, on a trip to India, contemptuously dismissed Indian mystics, and had been openly skeptical of the spiritual experiences of Chinese women.

11 Ants

Two years in Philadelphia (1883–1884) had broadened Fielde's horizons. She returned to China with up-to-date knowledge of obstetrics, basic training in biological research, and a view of the origins and workings of the world that was frequently in conflict with a dogma she had not previously questioned with any seriousness. Her new knowledge of modern obstetrical practice was inserted into the curriculum of the Bible-women school. Since midwifery in China was in such a primitive state, proper information about hygiene and the delivery process, imparted by Chinese women to their Chinese sisters, could only result in the sparing of pain and the saving of lives – a boon for the disabused women in a harsh land.

In the remoteness of China, Fielde's scientific work was driven by her intense curiosity and her desire for knowledge. It was a diversion to relieve monotony and boredom, and to escape from the pressing, insoluble problems of proselytizing the impoverished, ignorant multitudes. In her solitary pursuits, with magnifying glass and microscope, she studied insects and their larvae in pools of water, the habitation of moth larvae near her home, and the silk glands of insects. Following the work of one of her Philadelphia mentors, Joseph Leidy, she looked at trematodes, small worm-like creatures that were potentially hazardous to health, and she reported on fresh-water, microscopic organisms in all their magic variety.[1] Accounts of her work on a scattershot array of subjects were sent to the Academy in Philadelphia where they were read at meetings, and published in their *Proceedings*.[2] Fielde, who was a free agent, seemed to be casting about, trying to decide on which part of the natural world she would devote her precious hours.

Fielde's well-written scientific papers reveal that she was a careful, patient investigator, and a dynamic experimentalist at a time when most scientists and naturalists were purely descriptive, or concerned with problems of taxonomy. She had the makings of a first-rate, perhaps a great scientist, but she was already in her mid-forties with an inadequate scientific background, and too many other interests and responsibilities to allow her to become a prolific author of scientific papers and a major force in science. While her publications reveal an abundance of curiosity and drive, in some there is evidence of a deficiency in professional training. In one publication she failed to include the name of an insect larva – the object of the entire study. In another publication, she reveals that she did not know how to convert degrees of temperature from the Fahrenheit to the Celsius scale, a routine calculation that would not trouble any trained scientist.[3] To succeed in experimental science she needed blocks of undisturbed, unhurried time, something scarce in Swatow. Nevertheless, she continued to describe the natural world precisely, quantifying as much as possible, doing small experiments requiring the use of the microscope. A decade or so later, when she returned to America permanently in busy retirement, she was able to apply herself more fully to experimental research, but she never entertained the idea of confining herself to science alone nor of seeking a paying position to support her research. By choice, she remained a self-taught amateur, a woman of such breadth of interest that science could not contain her – perhaps not typical of other women aspirants who suffered because of their sex.

Scientific investigation in America had begun in the eighteenth and early nineteenth centuries by people who might be considered amateurs. They were not educated in science and natural history because colleges and universities did not deem these subjects sufficiently important compared to classical learning. Those who indulged their interests in the natural world did not make their living doing so, nor were they supported by institutions; rather they were gentlemen of means, physicians, lawyers, businessmen, and clergymen with curiosity, and time on their hands. By the 1820s paid professional scientists began to appear, and, as the nineteenth century progressed, they increased in number, earned their living as scientists in government and universities, and took command of the scientific enterprise, but none of these professionals were women.[4] Until the latter part of the nineteenth century, women were unable to become professional scientists because training institutions would not accept them, and if they persisted in their interests they had to do so as amateurs, unaffiliated with institutions, sometimes helping their husbands. Opportunity for the training of women opened up long before they were hired as professionals, and they still lagged behind well into the twentieth century. Women's colleges such as Vassar, Mount Holyoke, Smith, and Bryn Mawr were few in number. Not only did they train women for science, they hired them to teach and do research – but only if they remained unmarried.[5]

It should come as no surprise that the historical record (until recent years) is remarkable for the apparent absence of women participating in science and natural history. For instance, in *The Origin of Natural Science in America* by George Brown Goode, an authoritative survey of American scientific achievement published in 1901, many hundreds of men are mentioned, some discussed in detail, while only four women are referred to in passing. One of these, Miss Jane Colden, "the first lady in America to become proficient in plants," is discussed as an addendum to an account of her father, Cadwallader Colden.[6] However, modern scholarship has revealed that throughout American history there have always been productive, imaginative women scientists and natural historians operating as amateurs, supporting themselves through private wealth or family, some assisting their husbands in their scientific work. They did not receive their deserved credit for they worked in the shadows, isolated and often at great disadvantage.[7]

The formal training of biological scientists in America in the 1880s was in a rather haphazard state. Most biologists were graduates of medical schools, and few were educated to do research. Americans were just beginning to establish a system of higher learning based upon the German system, in which a Ph.D. degree rivaling those of European universities was conferred for presenting a thesis based on original research. Adele Fielde was fortunate that she could acquire scientific instruction, albeit in an *ad hoc* manner, since there was no established system for training women. Her plight was acknowledged by authorities at the University of Pennsylvania, and had accelerated the founding of its School of Biology, in part to satisfy the growing demand of women to be educated and to carry out research. To this end, Mrs. Bloomfield Moore, a wealthy Philadelphia socialite and a friend of Fielde, generously endowed the new school, and provided support for young women.[8]

Fifteen years after her initial scientific training, and permanently settled in America, Fielde chose to concentrate her efforts on the study of ants, their physiology and their behavior, and to abandon scattered studies on disparate subjects. Her decision to focus on ants was a wise one, not only because of the ant's intrinsic fascination and endless possibilities for study, but because a concentration of effort would result in higher productivity and a greater visibility and recognition by her scientific peers. She was drawn to the study of ants at the Marine Biological Laboratory in Woods Hole, perhaps because there was never a shortage of material, and they were more conveniently studied than other social insects like bees. Most important of all, one of the world's great ant biologists, the scholar William Morton Wheeler, spent his summers teaching and carrying out research there. Sensing that her scientific training was incomplete, Fielde seized the opportunity to get the best, most concentrated instruction available in America by enrolling in summer courses at the Marine Biological Laboratory, which accepted women as students. Here, elite investigators of biological research from the U.S.A. and Europe ran courses, as they do today.

In 1893, Fielde, an elderly student, studied botany, and attended an intensive embryology course directed by F.R. Lillie of the University of Chicago, one of the great founders of the Marine Biological Laboratory, and in July 1895 she immersed herself in the world of invertebrate zoology. Courses were exceedingly intensive involving lectures and laboratory work each and every day, from morning to night. Pointedly, she did not take vertebrate zoology, offered during August, because she hated dissecting cats, or even fish – anything with a backbone that brought the object of dissection and study uncomfortably close to the human: "last summer I smelled shark in my nightmares, for weeks after the Course was finished."[9] For whatever reason, she found herself to be an entomologist, studying ants. The study of small creatures without backbones has always been less popular among scientists than animals of human size. Fielde was unusual, not only because she decided to devote much of her time to science, but because she chose to study small creatures: ants. Even more unusual, she was not so much a gatherer, classifier or describer as an experimentalist, interested in mechanisms – in how things worked. Although they were rarely mentioned, women such as Charlotte Taylor and Margaretta Morris were studying insects in a serious way before Adele Fielde was born, and they were followed by others, some of whom by the end of the century were paid professionals affiliated with famous institutions, writing for scientific journals and belonging to scientific societies. Still, they were background figures.[10] Although there were a few woman entomologists active in her time, such as Anna Botsford Comstock, Annie Trumbull Slawson, and Edith Patch, Fielde seems to have had no real, professional contact with them, perhaps because they were fieldworkers, collectors and classifiers, not experimentalists in a big city as was Fielde.

Information and ideas abounded in Woods Hole, an ideal setting for a budding scientist, and between 1893 and 1906 Fielde spent nine summers working there, arriving in May and remaining until October. She became a part of the scientific community, presenting several evening lectures on ants, which were listed in the Annual Reports of the Laboratory, and several of her papers, presumably the texts of her lectures, were published in the *Biological Bulletin*, the house organ of the laboratory. That Fielde was permitted to lecture to a group of men on professional matters showed that some progress had been made in closing the gender gap, for not many decades had passed since women were not permitted to address an assembly of male scientists.

Always craving cool weather, Fielde escaped the terrible summer heat of the city to work by the sea. With characteristic humor, she taunted her friend Nolan in Philadelphia, left behind in the stifling city: "I am miserable in being so comfortable here when the newspapers tell me of the awful heat, and my reason urges upon my imagination the fact that my friends are being broiled alive in New York, Philadelphia and Pan-Ting-Fu."[11] Having a great capacity for making and keeping friends, she took time off to visit them throughout the summer in the Adirondacks and on Nantucket Island. In September, after most investigators had departed, the laboratory became an "intellectual banquet hall deserted" which she found enchanting. The air was cool, but she could still swim and run about the beach to warm up. It was a restful place with its "luscious air . . . its abundance of wildflowers and brilliant sunsets." Aware of the fact that she was overweight, she began a "Karlsbad diet" to eliminate "adipose." Much to Fielde's delight, Woods Hole had the power to restore both spirit and health.

The study of social insects, bees, and ants reaches back to antiquity whose testament – literature and folklore – is rich in astounding stories of their

Figure 11.1 Adele Fielde, a student at the Marine Biological Laboratory, Woods Hole, MA, summer 1893. Fielde is in the back row, third from the right

prowess. In Greek mythology, a son of Zeus who was king of the ants turned himself into an ant, and coupled with Eurymedusa, mother of the Graces. Some of their offspring, Myrmedones, became followers of Achilles – ferocious fighters without mercy called Myrmidons. Pliny was impressed by the ant's capacity for work, and man has always drawn lessons from ants as models of cleanliness – licking themselves and each other. Fielde relates how ants kept their young "scrupulously clean."

> I have seen an ant, when she wanted to be specially well groomed, catch hold of another ant by the leg and make her lick her back, which she could not reach herself. . . . When their young get soiled, they will pick them up, as much as to say, "you naughty boy" and forcibly wipe them clean in the nest. The ants carefully remove all debris of an unclean character from their nurseries.[12]

The Old Testament advised the lazy to look to the ant for inspiration. The autocrats, including King Solomon, were disturbed by the fact that ant society was so organized and well run without an apparent leader in command, an observation that could give rise to the dangerous idea that strong leaders were dispensable. On the other hand, the democrats were not pleased with the inflexibility of the society; each ant was condemned at birth to fulfill its limited role, functioning rigidly like a clock wheel in the telling of time. Yet all ants were of equal status (long before the notion of equality of individual humans crossed men's minds), and all property was communal – an inspiration for monastic life but anathema to the spirit of modern capitalism.[13]

In the past, those who have shown an interest in insects have tended to be overwhelmed by their diversity and number, their varied behavior, and the immensity of the taxonomic problems they presented. When Fielde was studying ants at the beginning of the twentieth century, there were a remarkable 3000 known species of this insect alone, and now, a hundred years later, there are at least 10,000, and the list is growing. The modern era of the systematic study of insects began with de Réamur's *The Natural History of Ants*, one volume in a series of six on insects, written between 1742 and 1743 and published for the first time in 1926. William Morton Wheeler regarded René Antoine Ferchault de Réamur as the greatest entomologist of all time. Wondrously endowed intellectually, he studied the growth of molluscs, and the formation of pearls, and made major contributions in physics (including the development of the thermometer), meteorology, and industry. Among his varied explorations, he discovered how to make steel, and he was also involved in the radical improvement of rope-making, porcelain, and dyes. Thomas Henry Huxley expressed the highest admiration for him: "From the time of Aristotle to the present day I know of but one man who has shown himself Mr. Darwin's equal in one form of research – and that is Réamur. . . . I know of no one who is to be placed in the same rank with him except Réamur."[14]

Though important work on ants was carried out in the early nineteenth century, the modern study of this insect was established by a strange assortment of colorful, "amateur" myrmecologists without formal training or a degree in biology, whose interest was secondary to that of their vocation. All were active in the late nineteenth and early twentieth centuries; Auguste Forel, a professor of psychiatry in Zurich, Eric Wasmann, an anti-evolutionist Jesuit priest from Holland, Carlo Emery, an Italian museum curator in Geneva, Horace Donisthorpe, an English dandy and man about town, and Sir John Lubbock, a Member of Parliament and banker who invented the bank holiday, and later became Lord Avebury. Together with he, Thomas Huxley, John Tyndall, and a few others were for many years an influential inner circle of the Royal Society which oversaw science in Britain. In America, William Morton Wheeler, the only "professional" biologist of the group, was professor of economic entomology at Harvard University, and spent summers at the Marine Biological Laboratory at Woods Hole.

Without doubt, Fielde interacted with the Reverend Henry C. McCook, an enthusiastic entomologist, an authority on spiders and ants, and a pastor of a congregation in Philadelphia. McCook, an active member of the Academy of Natural Sciences of Philadelphia, made a major contribution to the field by first describing the honey ant. The sole function of some of these ants is to take up and store food for the colony, and in doing so they convert themselves into immobile honey-pots. Both Fielde and McCook attended lively biweekly meetings at the Academy over which Joseph Leidy, President of the Academy, presided. The astonishing and revered Leidy, who almost certainly influenced Fielde, discovered trichinella in pork (the cause of trichinosis in humans) and also described the first dinosaur fossils in America, establishing the correct configuration of these extinct beasts as we know them today. For many years he had worked on insects – the anatomy of the honey ant, the mechanism by which insects fold their wings, the sac in the queen bee that stores sperm, the role of the house fly in the spread of disease, the living contents of millipede and termite intestines, and the control of insect infestation in Philadelphia parks. He was such a kindly gentleman that he once ate a cake crawling with ants rather than perturb his hostess about insects in her food.[15]

Fielde probably settled on the study of ants through conversation with McCook, and Wheeler at Woods Hole where he must have instructed her. Wheeler and his wife admired Fielde, became good friends, and maintained a correspondence after she resettled in Seattle. Retired to New York, but abounding in energy and curiosity, Fielde was in a position to follow the old tradition of amateurism so common in the entomology of the time. She had no formal degree in biology, and she was only a part-time worker without institutional affiliation or support; no one paid her to do biological research which she could carry out at home. Apart from summers in Woods Hole, Fielde did not have much scientific company, and almost none was female.

Ants and other social insects have always fascinated people, largely because of the food they provide, and the destruction they visit upon humans and each other. The complex, organized societies they form have been a never-ending source of wonder – how can such small, inconsequential creatures behave so gregariously, so rationally, so like humans, specializing in their labors to become skilled artisans, water carriers, cultivators of fungi, "cattle" tenders, foragers, nursers of the young, soldiers, road-builders, and slave-keepers, all of which tasks require some memory, judgment, and the ability to recognize and communicate with each other? The process of recognition is immensely complex, and is poorly understood, even today.

Confounded similes and anthropomorphisms spring to mind, and human characteristics and emotions are ascribed to these organisms with their miniscule brains. Some ants are fierce and murderous, heroic and selfless, others are timid and peaceful, while others are thieves, greedy and selfish. The harmony of the nest is sometimes disturbed by the ambitious worker who attempts to usurp power, but on the whole there seems to be a balance between the forces of cooperation maintaining the colony, and disruptive individuals. There are political lessons to be learned from ants – cooperation and compromise are desirable, indeed necessary for survival. Observers have described ants exercising, feigning death, indulging in mock combat, and being playful – mounting the backs of other insects and riding them. They have been described as sleeping cuddled up with their legs and antennae folded against their bodies, and when they get up they seem to yawn, though they do not breath through their mouths, and then to make their toilette before they begin their work.

Investigators have furthered their experimental studies and insights not only rationally, but intuitively, asking what a human would do if confronted with the problem created for the ant by the experimenter. Forel, a socialist, drew the sweeping conclusion from observing ants that only in a socialist system can mankind live in peace, and his *magnum opus* was entitled *The Social World of the Ants Compared with that of Man*. Apart from those who disagreed with Forel's politics and philosophy, there were others who felt that however tempting it was to analogize ant and human behavior, to apply such words as communism and fascism to ant societies, and to ascribe moral behavior to the ant was misleading overinterpretation, often incorrect – in science, ants should be described on their own terms.[16] Wheeler, when discussing the communal behavior of ants, said:

> our interest is aroused by an undeniable resemblance to our own condition. Reflection shows that this resemblance cannot be superficial, but must depend on a high degree of adaptability and plasticity common to man and the social insects . . . to live in societies, like those of man and the social insects, implies a shifting of proclivities from the egocentric to the sociocentric plane.[17]

It is difficult to believe that Fielde herself did not draw lessons from her observations on ants that she would apply to humankind. After several years of concentrated ant-watching, Fielde recognized many shades of behavior:

> Individual ants have different temperaments. . . . Ants of some species are as varied in character as human beings, and have different capabilities. . . . Some are irascible, others docile; some have strong maternal instincts, while others dislike the care of the young; some like quiet homelife, while others like to go afield and roam about; some learn more quickly than others the things I wish them to do. . . . It is hard to believe that ants have not some of the emotions of human beings.[18]

Since Fielde's time, the behavior of animal societies, including the human's and the ant's, have been systematically studied, and great advances have been made in elucidating characteristics common to all societies, and in the formulation of predictive rules and laws which go beyond the description and classification of behavioral phenomena of earlier research. To this end Edward O. Wilson, a myrmecologist studying individual ants and ant societies, has formulated the broad discipline of *sociobiology*, which attempts to define and understand the biology that underlies social behavior through knowledge of the social, physiological, and genetic functioning of vertebrates and invertebrates, all within the context of the evolution of social behavior.[19] Through her studies, Fielde made real contributions to the establishment of this edifice by providing information on the structure of ant societies, adaptations of ant societies to change, and the mechanisms by which ants communicate.

Fielde may have been inclined to study the ant because in doing so she created an entire society that she could nurture and control. Perhaps, unconsciously, she recognized similarities between industrious societies of ants and of hard-working Chinese, both vast in number, balanced on the threshold of survival and annihilation. While there was great frustration in the gulf that lay between her expectations for change and the reality of Chinese society, she was the demiurge among the ants, which were totally dependent on her, and under her control. Fielde could effectively manipulate this one to see how it worked, creating colonies, changing conditions here and there, and evaluating the effect of the changes.

Her earliest publication on ants had to do with the construction of a portable ant nest, one that would enable her to establish ant societies and observe them at will. In a sense, she had attempted to do the same with humans when she had a school and dormitory built for Chinese women, and introduced them to new ideas and techniques, hoping to produce changes in them and their society. Upon her return to America, she attempted to alter the political and social nature of her native country, again through women, but the consequence of her manipulation both in China and in the U.S.A. were not so clear, and probably not as intellectually and emotionally gratifying as her controlled probing, and experimental manipulation of ants.

The ant, which arose in the time of the dinosaur and rapidly spread over the globe a hundred million years ago, had a very special appeal to Fielde. After all, this extremely successful insect, lord of the entire Earth's surface, lived in a complex society dominated by nourishing females, their success stemming from their ability to adapt to the environment. Life derived from the queen; female workers were heroic, selfless, clean, and orderly, and did the work, and fought the battles, probably with Fielde's unconscious approval and satisfaction. Not without a breath of scorn, she referred to pathetic, short-lived male ants as "wildly amorous" on warm days, "stupid," "lazy," and "useless." "The kings are not clever, never follow a trail, never take part in the care of the young, and are at all times dependent. . . . [Queens] condone the stupidity of kings of their own lineage, and tolerate from them attentions to which no response is conceded."[20] Here, Fielde was probably engaged in more than objective description.

Ants have relatively few enemies, the worst being, like in human society, members of their own species. Their variability has led over vast periods of time to the emergence of great numbers of species. Above all, they have flourished in extraordinary numbers through their ability to live in an organized, cooperative manner, devoted to the welfare of the colony.[21] The primary allegiance of the individual is to the colony, a fundamental biounit, and the survival of the colony at the expense of the individual is the paramount strategy; ants do not live solitary lives. Based on a kind of group identity (or nationalism) to the exclusion of all others, constant warfare between colonies of ants is the rule of ant life. Cooperative living within the colony to form a kind of "superorganism" involves more than one generation of ants, each with a life span of years (except for males), each with their own specialized functions (warriors, workers, etc.), in a *eusocial* arrangement which has enabled the ant to become an extremely successful, dominant group.[22] Within the ant nest, the eggs and larvae are cared for by adult workers (females), and the adult emerging from the pupal stage is freed from its casing with the help of fellow ants. To a limited extent the young learn from their elders, and they bear the responsibilities they assume for the rest of their lives.

To study ants and their behavior, the colony must be available for observation, and so Fielde's first work in myrmecology, begun in 1899, was to devise an inexpensive, portable case that housed ant nests of her making. Ants could then be viewed freely through the glass ceiling of the nest, and colonies could be transported between her winter residence in New York, and Woods Hole. Since she had no affiliation with a scientific institution other than the Marine Biological Laboratory in Woods Hole during summers, she carried on her ant research in her rooms through long winter evenings, a diversion from her teaching responsibilities. Sometimes she observed ants "day and night," and on more than one occasion recorded a room temperature of 40 degrees Fahrenheit. Occasionally, when visiting friends, she would carry along ant colonies in her portable case – part of her baggage. This kind of research cost almost nothing, and required the simplest of equipment.

Doggedly, by trial and error, Fielde perfected a portable ant nest within a case that proved to be popular, which was quickly adopted by workers in America, Europe, and Africa. Fielde, and presumably others called these "Fielde nests." Wheeler took an interest in the making of the apparatus, advising the use of a special glue for which she thanked him although she felt other glues were just as good. She turned down his suggestion that strips of mica be used to cover the passageways in nests – Fielde felt that celluloid was better. Fielde's choices may have been perfectly valid, but perhaps she was trying to maintain an intellectual independence from the greatest living myrmecologist. However, she did use Petri dishes in which to observe ant colonies, as suggested by Wheeler.

Artificial ant nests and their containers had been devised previously, but they had their disadvantages; they were not portable because they were either too large and cumbersome, or they contained spillable containers of water. After some experimenting, Fielde devised a case with a handle on top, and a hinged door that opened on the side, revealing shelves holding up to six nests of various sizes. The floor of the nests comprised glass sheets sitting on white blotting-paper which facilitated the viewing of ants, the walls of the nest, and the partitions to create rooms were made of glass strips, and the roof of the nest was a sheet of glass, usually covered by a towel which could be removed when viewing ants. Each nest had a chamber for food (sponge-cake with honey or molasses, apple, banana, and mashed walnuts) that was kept clean, dry and light, simulating the outside world, while the chambers for eggs and larvae were kept dark by a cover of blotting-paper, and the air within the chamber moistened by pieces of wet sponge which also provided the ants with drinking-water. To empty an egg chamber (for cleaning), one simply let light in, and eggs would be carried to another, darkened part of the nest. Ants could be maintained in a sleek, healthy state for several years, closely examined through a magnifying glass, in nests that were easy to keep clean because they did not contain earth. All four stages of the ant's life could be observed in the nest – eggs, larvae, pupa (or chrysalis), and adult.

Fielde's involvement with the study of ants seems to be a recapitulation of the history of myrmecology. She began as a naive, independent worker, observing how ants behave, and describing any odd behavior she happened upon. As her knowledge of ants grew, her observations led to questions about ants and the formulation of experiments to answer the questions, and so from being a passive observer she became an increasingly manipulative and intrusive presence in their lives. By the time Fielde began to study ants, a considerable amount was known about these and other social insects, and she must have been reasonably well informed. She refers to several prominent myrmecologists (Forel, Lubbock, Janet, Wheeler, and others), but her references are few, as if her work sprang entirely from her own experience – and in a way, it did – a world she created. Most of her papers have no references at all, and some references are incomplete, perhaps due both to Fielde's inadequate scientific education, and to faulty editorial scrutiny – a pattern that was not uncommon in biological research and publications of that time. On the other hand, Fielde's observations seemed to overlap very little with information in the literature because the work done on the vast empire of ants was so sparse that almost everyone who was involved in their study was a pioneer. References would not be required unless one was steeped in the literature, and inclined to quotation. In one of her twenty-three-page reports of experimental results and discussion, she referred to no other workers in the field except for Wheeler, whom she thanked for identifying the ants with which she was working, and only mentioned Forel's method of marking ants.[23] In a second paper of sixteen pages no reference is made to other myrmecologists.[24] Strong, self-involved, and thoughtful, Fielde looked to nature and not the printed word for her inspiration in science, perhaps motivated by Agassiz's words on the subject ("Study Nature, not Books") emblazoned on the atrial wall of the Marine Biological Laboratory. She was carrying out original research, and her accounts are really personal odysseys, those of a viewer starting from point zero, learning about the behavior of individual members of a society. In so doing she was an authentic pioneer in the study of the individuality of ants, of their learning habits and memory, and of their adaptability to change.

Fielde did not differ from other, contemporary myrmecologists and biologists in the style of presentation of their work. Two of the classic books on ants, by Forel[25] and by Lubbock,[26] are poorly referenced according to modern standards, and the references are often incomplete, and names are mentioned in a general, collegial way without specific credit for specific work. Since dates are often not supplied it is sometimes difficult to credit anyone for being the *first* discoverer of a phenomenon. Fielde is never mentioned by these authors, though they discuss the very function (sense of smell of ants) which Fielde had studied.[27] However, later authorities, including Wheeler and Schierla,[28] are more generous. Further difficulty is encountered in the determination of priority because so much of the literature, especially the early work, is in obscure publications written in Italian, French, and German.

The reports of Forel, Lubbock, and other earlier workers are often personal stories, anecdotal, experimental adventures related in the first-person singular, in the style of a pure nature writer such as the eighteenth-century naturalist Gilbert White. Sometimes the reader is beset with tales in a manner reminiscent of those told to the detained wedding guest in Coleridge's *Rhyme of the Ancient Mariner*. From time to time the reader is taken into the author's confidence with a quaint aside – "Friend reader, this shows you that" – or an apology for experimenting on, and dissecting insects. Forel writes, "I think dear reader, that you will now understand the need for experiments – which are cruel, I admit, but no more cruel than what nature is doing everywhere, at every moment."[29] Fielde's writing was crisp, informative, and objective, but unlike the work of later investigators, modern scientists who presented their heavily referenced, data-ladened, beautifully illustrated reports in an impersonal, third-person voice.

The field of inquiry was relatively confined, the number of investigators small, and so these enthusiasts formed an intimate society where everyone knew everyone, and had a cordial understanding of each others' work. Aggressive display of ego, and assignment of credit for every fact was unseemly, as each related their story, but for newcomers like Fielde, a woman without prestigious scientific credentials and affiliation, and not in the club, there must have been a sense of exclusion as evidenced by a strident note in some of her writing. Repeated, explicit attribution to one's own work, though justified, was not what a newcomer should do.

Watching ants, singly and in groups, day and night, over the course of years, provided Fielde with intimate insights into their lives – their behavior, their temperaments, and how they functioned. She was the author of a thousand small revelations that could only be brought to light by eyewitnesses; she learned that though casual observation might suggest that all worker ants looked and acted alike, they had individual preferences, and capabilities. Some ants were of ugly disposition, others pacific, some had nurturing instincts and preferred to stay home, while others liked to wander about. Ants could adapt to new situations, and had the capacity to learn, and remember an experience for as long as three years. They learned how to run through mazes, and when alternative solutions were presented, ants tended to stay on the path already learned; this study was regarded by Schneirla as "pioneering."[30] Although they are social organisms, ants can live very well in isolation, and can be tamed so that they lose their fear of humans. Fielde recorded in detail how ants build their nests, lay their eggs, and care for their larvae. She observed that if the top of a colony was exposed to light, and protected by glass, ants would scramble to the upper surface of the glass and cover it with earth to prevent light from entering. Both Forel and Lubbock had found that ants reacted to the ultraviolet component of sunlight, but Fielde, delving deeper, cultured ants in chambered glass dishes, each chamber permitting a different color of light to enter; if ants preferred light of a specific wavelength, they would congregate in the area with that light. Ants were not attracted to any light, but they were averse to violet, and indifferent to bright red, green, or blue light. Red and green were like darkness to them, and violet was most luminous.[31] Fielde learned to cover her nests with orange glass through which she could observe ants without disturbing them.

She could describe with authority the effects of nutrition on the development of the egg or larva. Ants would rather starve to death than eat their colony fellows or eggs, but would gladly eat members of another colony.[32] If eggs and larvae were not turned constantly and licked, they became covered with a *penicillium* mold which was removed by licking, serving as a source of food for workers. Fielde measured the timing of progressive stages of egg to larva and pupa, and, though she quantitated her observations, she recorded them in words, not in a convenient tabular form, probably because she was not a well-trained scientist. Her active, vigorous mind can be seen at work as she attempted to correlate the time it takes for a larva to hatch with the size and sex of the adult ant into which it develops. She established the fact that ants are born with complex, instinctive patterns of behavior by showing that when separated from adults at birth, they are still capable of building elaborate nests that are indistinguishable from those made by experienced adults: "*Before an ant is five days old it has all its reflexes established*, and appears to have sprung as from the head of Jove, full grown and completely accoutred, into active existence." But the ant was not a machine that merely reacted to stimuli, capable as it was of learning and remembering.

From the beginning, Fielde was actively experimenting, manipulating ants to garner new knowledge. For instance, she placed ants from two different colonies in one chamber and watched what happened. Each colony established its own nest and looked after its young while some ants of each group (between one and five) fought each other to the death. The following day eighty ants were found slain, and after five days one group had been entirely eliminated, and the young of both groups taken into the care of the victors.[33] This was an epic tale of heartless brutality, perhaps reminding her of the pogrom she had witnessed in Russia; in the case of ants, however, the actors could be controlled, and their activities measured. Some discoveries were really rediscoveries, but to Fielde her innumerable observations seemed fresh and new, the foundation for her version of the ant world.

Fielde's major scientific work was on the sensory systems of ants, and of these the sense of smell interested her the most. That ants have a keen sense of smell was recognized in Chinese folk-tales, and was postulated by a French myrmecologist at the beginning of the nineteenth century. Ants operate in a world of odors, depending on this sense more than they do on the detection of vibrations, or on sight through their compound eyes, which was usually poor. Blinding an ant does not completely incapacitate it. If one antenna (which houses the scent receptors) is removed, the ant still functions well, but remove both and the ant is immobilized, essentially isolated from the world, unable to recognize its young, its friends or enemies despite being able to see.[34] Fielde observed that some antennae-less ants of angry disposition fought friend and foe indiscriminately. If ants in the midst of combat were sprayed with a strong perfume, hostilities ceased, for they could not tell friend from foe, and they walked about aimlessly.

Ants distinguish friend from foe by their odor which is derived from the queen. It is a "specific odor," genetically determined, which does not change and is remembered throughout the ant's life.[35] Two hostile ants, separated for months and then reunited, will sweep their antennae over one another by which they smell each other, determine that their odors are "foreign," and resume fatal hostilities immediately, battling for as long as eighteen hours without respite, with mandibles locked on each other's parts. Fielde showed that ants, reared from eggs removed from the nest immediately after laying, and raised apart, immediately recognized their biological mother (queen), when reintroduced to her among a group of five queens.[36] Ants recognize their nest kin by odor, every colony having its characteristic scent, a mingling of odors derived from the queen and from all members of the colony. Adding to the complexity, Fielde found that the queen produced a second odor which changed with age (progressive odor), different in queens of different lineage and imparted to the worker ant whose own odor changes with age. This change can give rise to feuds within a colony between ants of different ages, deadly excitement growing as the differences between the ages of the contesting ants increased.[37] She reported that ants can recognize others of their own colony even after being frozen and thawed or briefly washed with alcohol. This was in fact an old observation of Lubbock that was not acknowledged by Fielde.

Members of other colonies, even of the same species, have distinct, composite scents, presumably blends, and so they are alien, eliciting a response of fear and hostility which gives rise to deadly feuding between colonies, or the killing of unfortunate strays. The nest odor however can coat very young ants (callows) of other colonies or species, and, if done sufficiently early, render them acceptable to a foreign colony into which they are introduced. Acceptance may be explained by the fact that the inherent odor of the pupa or ants less than three days old is very weak or is even non-existent, and is masked by the constant licking by adults of the colony so that they are coated with the nest odor by which they are recognized as friends. Fielde maintained "mixed nests" containing several different subfamilies of such ants living together amicably for over a year, an experimental feat considered remarkable by myrmecologists. The loyalty of the ants was to the colony, for they would attack ants of any of their own subfamily introduced from outside.[38] Wheeler, an exacting critic, was deeply impressed by the author, her work, her acuity, and her experimental facility.[39]

Fielde also distinguished an odor deposited on the feet by which ants can create and follow their own trail and be guided in their return journey to the nest, though they cannot follow the track of a foe. It is still not known whether this odor, first described a century before by Bonnet, is different from the nest odor. Another investigator, Bethe, postulated that the scent of the track was "polarized," enabling ants to orient themselves, and determine their direction of travel, to or away from their nest.[40] However, this popular and attractive theory was disproven by Fielde, sufficiently confident of herself to cross swords with a European savant.[41] Fielde did not hold to Bethe's notion that ants were reflex machines, reacting to stimuli, and without memory. In her opinion, experience affected their response, and she had data to support her belief.

Fielde experimented with ants bearing elongated antennae consisting of a series of twelve segments, the first attached to the head, and the twelfth outermost and terminal. When cut away, even after months, there was no regeneration.[42] Fielde became an adept ant surgeon, perhaps the first who, rather than wrenching away the entire antennae, skillfully removed segments of the antenna one by one, and then determined the functional consequences of the deficiency. The experiments were ingenious, and her findings were astonishing – so astonishing that some of her colleagues were skeptical about the entire enterprise, and to this day the validity of her results has not been unequivocally established. Indeed, some of her conclusions are unclear, or appear to contradict the results of previous studies. Carefully removing the terminal unit (the twelfth), and permitting the patient to regain its health, she found that the ant had lost its ability to detect complex nest odors which diffuse through the air. When ants with just the terminal segment removed were placed in an alien colony, they evinced no alarm reaction, could no longer grasp that they were in hostile territory, and fatally, made no defensive moves to preserve themselves. Removal of two terminal segments of the antennae enabled ants from different colonies to live together in peace. Apparently the eleventh was a sensory unit that also detected nest odor by physical contact with other ants. When the tenth segment was removed, the ant became befuddled because it could no longer detect a scented trail and so could not find its way home. After removal of the next two segments (the eighth and ninth), the (worker) ant could no longer discern the odor of the queen-mother nor of the very young to which it was formerly devoted so that it became neglectful of its responsibilities, and lost all interest in the community.[43] Elimination of the next two segments (sixth and seventh) enabled ants of different species to live together. With ants deprived of the terminal seven or eight segments, Fielde created a colony containing five different genera living together in harmony, regurgitating food to one another, the ultimate gesture of amicability.[44]

Wheeler, in his classic text of 1910, discussed the antennae experiments at some length, expressing skepticism about Fielde's results. His conclusion that confirmation of the work was needed was elaborated upon by a government entomologist who, in fact, did not believe that the antenna had anything at all to do with olfaction, a patently incorrect assertion. A year later (1915), a testy Fielde replied in the *Proceedings of the Academy of Natural Sciences of Philadelphia*, a journal to which she had ready access through her friend, Edward Nolan:

> Dr. N.E. McIndoo quotes Dr. W.M. Wheeler's objection to my discovery that "the olfactory organs of an animal may exhibit 'regional differentiation.'" This objection, unsupported as it is by physiological tests applied to the ant, should influence no investigator. If there be error in the process of experimentation or flaw in the logic of the deduction, the critic should indicate the point of departure from a correct course. It is true that my statements are "unsupported by other observers," but lack of support by other observers is a misfortune that necessarily befalls the research worker who makes the earliest observation."[45]

Though she had ceased doing research for almost a decade, she was still interested, and she was protective enough of her work to respond in a literate and aggressive manner. It is probable that others were unsuccessful in repeating Fielde's experiments, and rather than publish the negative results to her embarrassment, they simply let the work die in silence. The fact that, to this day, such remarkable results are not part of the working knowledge of entomologists would suggest that this is what happened, although there are probably some realities waiting to be confirmed, lurking among her fascinating results. Perhaps, dominated by her enthusiasm, and her great powers of rationalization, Fielde tended to overinterpret her results and explain away those that ran counter to her brilliant conception. Her critical faculties may have been clouded by the allure of an attractive hypothesis – another instance where a non-existent order is superimposed on a scatter of data. However, her work shows that beyond describing, she had a strong experimental bent, and beyond this she was striving to generalize and theorize.

In 1904, Fielde published a paper with George H. Parker of Harvard University on the response of the ant to vibrations, a work done in Woods Hole, and Fielde's only scientific publication that bears the name of a second author.[46] In agreement with earlier work, they found that the ant does not detect sound vibrations through air, and in rigorous experiments they demonstrated that ants do not respond to a wide range of sounds produced by a piano, violin, or whistle. However, they found that ants, like moles, react to vibrations in the solid surface beneath their feet – a tactile sense that would be useful to ants whose mode of living is subterranean.

Spending so much time observing ants, Fielde could hardly help witnessing odd events that revealed secret faculties, and peculiarities of ant behavior. Some ants she marked at birth, and then tracked throughout their lives. She showed that ants that had never seen a body of water could be induced to swim. A colony of ants on a board were accidentally isolated on a small "island" separated from a "mainland" by a channel of water, and, to Fielde's astonishment, the ants transported the pupae and very young ants of the colony across the water to the "mainland" and established a new nest.[47] In another instance, Fielde placed a yellow ant in the midst of a colony of small black ants; she expected the foreigner to be rapidly destroyed, but to her amazement the black ants froze, as if hypnotized.[48] She was amazed at the ant's tenacity for life, witnessing a headless ant that walked about for days, ants without abdomens that continued to live and eat, and severed heads that moved their antennae for many hours.[49] Fielde had become familiar with an entire world of ant life from which she derived insights into the physiological basis of their social behavior. The salient points of the work described above barely suggest the enormity of her effort and the vast treasure of data she had amassed alone, tending her creatures by herself. The work attracted attention, and her supply of reprints of articles requested by her colleagues was soon exhausted; new batches of a hundred each were needed.[50] She had published twenty-two papers with original data on ants beginning in 1900 and ending in 1907, her last summer at Woods Hole, and the year she moved to Seattle. Her publications, listed in the *Royal Society Catalogue of Scientific Papers*, have become part of the living literature of myrmecology, and at the end of the twentieth century, she is still referred to by workers in the field. Between 1965 and 1994, more than half a century after publication, she was quoted ninety times in scientific journals.[51] As an active scientist she belonged to several scientific organizations, which included the Academy of Natural Science of Philadelphia, the American Association for the Advancement of Science, and the Philadelphia Geographical Society.

With Fielde's move to the West, her research on ants came to an abrupt end, and her interest in science, though never entirely lost, was not what it had been in the East. From time to time an analysis of some unusual event was reported in the *Proceedings of the Academy of Natural Sciences of Philadelphia*. Most probably the communications were simply parts of letters from Fielde to Edward Nolan, the Academy's secretary, which Nolan must have regarded as interesting enough to warrant publication. In 1911–1912, Fielde spent four winter months in Tuscon, Arizona, living in one house and taking her meals at another a few blocks away. She reported that to her annoyance, many dogs along the way barked at her, but over time they ceased to be aroused. Contact was never made nor were there any conciliatory gestures proffered. Since the dogs did not bark when she walked in the dark, though they were aware of her presence, she felt that they had initially responded to a new scent she had laid down to which they had become familiar and which no longer triggered them to bark. The analogy to the role of olfaction in the behavior of ants is apparent.[52] In another communication, still concerned with the function of the antennae in olfaction, Fielde speculated on the possible role of olfactory receptors in the attraction of male butterflies and moths to females, and the role of the memory of odors in determining where the female lays its eggs. How does the female decide she should lay her eggs on material which the adult does not eat but serves as an excellent food for the developing larvae? Does the adult remember the desirable odor of its early life as a larva?[53] Questions were raised but no attempt was made to answer them; this would be left to others. Her brief publications seem to be the reflections of a retired person with an active mind, in her mid-seventies, looking for something to do and drawn to peculiar phenomena. Fielde had given up systematic, intensive experimentation years before, but her curiosity never faltered as she applied her considerable expertise and acuity to fathom puzzling wonders in her everyday life.

Fielde had entered the scientific arena because she was intensely inquisitive, and had experienced the exhilaration of discovery. When she moved to Seattle she seemed to abandon both her life in New York and her systematic scientific studies. Whether there was a link between these two great, sudden shifts is not known. Possibly a sense of passing years or of failing health influenced her, but the energy with which she attacked new problems in Seattle would belie this. As a person of such astonishing energy and drive, she may have felt that she was settling into a life of fixed habit, humdrum and predictable, and was impelled to make a clean break with the past, and start a new life. There seems to be no convincing explanation for her radical move.

Although in Fielde's day women in science acquired their training with difficulty and were not afforded the professional opportunities available to men, Fielde never suffered because of this gender discrimination. Her interests were too broad to consider becoming an institutional-based professional scientist. At all times she regarded science as an avocation, entering and leaving without financial consideration. As an alert individual she could see that bright young women were not given opportunities that were rightfully theirs. In her years as a summer student at Woods Hole the majority of students were women, yet they were rarely heard of again professionally, for appointments for women in American universities were rare. As a missionary she had suffered gender discrimination, and had railed against injustice, and perhaps she saw that if she entered the scientific field she would have another battle on her hands; she declined to enter the ring because there were other attractive paths to follow.

12 Seattle[1]

> I am determined to live joyfully. So I seek the new. I will stay in Seattle a while at least, and grow up with the country.

Popular and much admired, and with many friends, Fielde had been leading an agreeable life in New York City for fifteen years. Taking full advantage of the theater, concerts, and museums, working on ants, spending summers in Woods Hole, involved with the suffragist movement, and conducting courses on government, her days were overflowing with activities that were dear to her. Lecturing to the public on China and on foreign affairs, and sheltered by adoring women of wealth and social position, her more than adequate income enabled her to live well, free of financial worry. It would seem that she had everything one could wish for, yet, in a puzzling way, this 68-year-old woman was not content to spend the rest of her days without change and new challenges. At a time when caution and prudence might be expected, Fielde decided to uproot herself, make a complete break with her settled, comfortable life, and go off to a place distant and different from what she had known, where she would settle among strangers in a frontier city – and reinvent herself. As will become apparent, her new life followed the same pattern as that established in New York. Why she chose to live in Seattle, a city she had never visited, is not known. If she was to transplant herself and become an exile, why not choose a more attractive, civilized center like San Francisco, a city where she had lectured and which she knew? Perhaps the raw, unfinished quality of a relatively small city like Seattle attracted her, where her efforts would count for more than they did in New York, as one among any number of talented, influential people. The decision was not made on impulse, although it seemed so to her friends who had no hint of her private deliberations over several months, and they were at a loss to explain why she should want to leave New York. She had sufficient capital to assure a commodious life, and she felt confident that she could always make a living writing and giving public lectures on China and the various countries in which she had lived and studied; China, a land unknown to most Americans, was irresistible, exotic, and of particular interest to those on the Pacific coast.

One of the reasons she gave for leaving was her declining health. Years before, beset with conflict and a growing sense of boredom, she had left the "unhealthy" climate of China due to what seemed to be a serious heart condition that inexplicably disappeared while she was in Europe, on her way home to America. In New York she suffered from chronic bronchitis, undoubtedly brought on by the climate and the bad city air, and she thought it best to remove herself to healthier, more open spaces. What prompted her to flee to the cool Pacific north-west may have been the intolerable heat that periodically afflicted New York and the eastern seaboard. These excuses were not very convincing however; she probably moved because she became restless, settled in one place for too long. She enjoyed adventure and travel, but she had no desire to be perpetually on the move. A compromise that satisfied her was to live somewhere like Berlin or Paris for a period of several months, immersing herself in the culture, language, and history of these places.

It seemed that a moment would come when Fielde would decide it was time to move – geographically and intellectually – to make an abrupt and radical break after a time of intense involvement, leaving behind a trail of dear friends and admirers. A broadening of her religious beliefs had been a major factor in her separation from the missionary movement and China, but there is no certain explanation for why she stopped doing research and publishing original scientific work. After a decade in the field she had become as successful and admired as any American woman scientist of the time. The work entailed almost no expense, and seemed to fit into her mode of living, but it demanded much of her time, and caring for her ant colonies must have been an enslavement that curtailed all other activities.

She left New York with its attendant pleasures, and its social and political activities, and she left science. Her days of serious scientific investigation were behind her, although in 1914 she was still protective of her work on ants, vigorously answering any criticisms. At times she commented on problems in public health such as the role of insects in diseases, but Seattle, little more than a raw frontier town, lacked scientists and a scientific community, and there was no one who could have helped her with her research. Still, she did not lose her scientific outlook. Of course Fielde was close to 70 years old when she moved to Seattle in 1907, and may have regarded herself as "retired," but this did not stop her busying herself in the local social and political issues of the day, where she showed no lack of energy or focus, selecting activities that would provide her with friends, and wide public acclaim.

Though she had the capacity to live and work alone contentedly, she made friends easily – but carefully – wherever she went. Several people who knew Fielde well have commented that she had little tolerance for fools, and that those she selected as real friends had to be intelligent and interesting. She had a "genius for friendship," and those who were her friends found her affectionate, concerned, and helpful. A single woman traveling alone, she sought out traveling companions, and met new sets of people, so that her list of American and foreign friendships was long, and kept alive by letters. One of her friends, a Mrs. William Pierson Hamilton of New York, remembered:

> She was frequently at the Hamilton home and her influence and inspiration were experienced by the Hamilton children as well as by their mother. They found her as eagerly interested in their lives as they were themselves; and in addition she had the power to make the commonplace world around them as fascinating as fairyland. Ants, for instance, she could turn into human beings with funny little individualities and characteristics of their own. No part of the earth was so remote that she could not make it near and real; and no child could listen to her charming tales of horrifying experiences in China and Siam without being thrilled. When she went West her letters were a constant source of delight . . . and the old ties were never forgotten or neglected.[2]

Of all her friends, Mrs. E.M. Cauldwell was the closest. She became part of the Cauldwell family, an aunt to the five Cauldwell children who adored her, as did their children. When this missionary had visited New York for a second time while they were still young, they had forgotten from the first visit what she was really like, and they had half expected a somber spirit, someone who would insist that they pray for the heathen. To their amazement she arrived in odd-looking clothes made by herself, resembling Mother Hubbard, and insisted that the first thing the family do was to go to the Barnum and Bailey circus, presently in town. Featured was a giant from China whom Fielde happened to know, and their conversation in Chinese drew a crowd. A child was prompted to cry out: "See, mamma, the Fat Lady is talking to the Giant." No one laughed harder than Fielde.[3]

As for her own family, she acted as if she were alone in the world, not communicating with or even mentioning its very few surviving members. As far as is known, she never returned to her place of birth.

Rather than sever her ties abruptly, and say her final farewells to her New York friends, she decided to take a one-year leave during which she would travel to the Pacific north-west. Although there may have been an understanding that this was just a test separation, she had in fact sold or given away her furniture, books, nature specimens, paintings, and plants. She gave her valuable Chinese water-colors, done by the artist Go Leng of Swatow to illustrate some of her books, to the Metropolitan Museum of Art. Fielde did not accumulate things, and so she did not have too much to give away. Other than a few precious books she had collected, she rid herself of anything she did not often use, and she advocated the frequent review of one's inventory, that anything not used in the recent past should be discarded. She gave away books she had read, and destroyed all letters she had received. She did not collect paintings or *objet*, and did not approve of family heirlooms. "In order to live the joyous, simple life, one needs often to struggle successfully against one's inheritance, to dispossess oneself of all that forebears have amassed, even of their convictions."[4] Could this bold conviction have its origins in Fielde's history – the impoverished descendant of illustrious forebears?

Bidding farewell to her friends the Cauldwells, Fielde left New York in June 1907, never to return. She spent several months drifting across the great expanse of the continent, stopping here and there to see the sights, and making a study of anything that interested her. A train took her to Colorado Springs where she spent two weeks. Short visits were made to tourist sites including Pike's peak before she reached Yellowstone National Park where she remained for six days. The grandeur and beauty of the passing landscape was testimony to her that there was a Creator, and that He had indeed blessed this land. Her wandering continued a curious pattern of avoiding direct passage to a destination – getting somewhere was an opportunity to explore, to study, and to make new friends. Fielde's journeys between Asia and America had taken months, even years, to complete. It would seem that, from time to time, the vagrant life satisfied her restless, inquisitive spirit.

By July, she had arrived in Tacoma Washington, where by arrangement she met a Dr. Fisher, an old friend from her days in Swatow, and together they journeyed to Burton, Vashon Island on Puget Sound. Here she peacefully spent the remainder of the summer at Vashon College. Accommodations was comfortable, the weather agreeable, and the scenery magnificent. The great Hemlock trees reminded her of those she had known in her childhood, but she deplored the fact that they were being cut down, that there was a "dreadful waste of wood."

Newly arrived settlers had come from everywhere for a variety of reasons, but for most there was a common desire to start a new life and make a fortune. Fielde found them to be an unlikely mixture which she noted in her diary: "The folks are not assorted; the educated and the untutored mixed in every circle; a curious hodge-podge, as many states represented as there are persons. One accurate in speech, his next neighbor ungrammatical in every sentence. This is not the 'Simple Life'; it is the crude; but the impressive feature is the mixedness of it all."[5] By September, she had had enough of the quiet life in nature, deprived of intellectual stimulation and companionship. She proceeded to Seattle, uncertain whether Seattle would be the city of her choice. She wrote to a friend from Vashon Island:

> I shall probably remain on the Pacific coast for a year or so; moving along, north or south, at my pleasure. I have arranged to omit my classes in New York for next season: I am looking for "the land of heart's desire." Do you know a country this side of Paradise, where there are no earthquakes, no cyclones, no pestilences, and where there is a constant temperature of 70° F?[6]

Arriving in Seattle, she settled temporarily at the Fairfield Hotel close to the bustle of the city center, and close to the public library. One of the first

Figure 12.1 Snapshot of Adele Fielde taken in 1907 shortly after she arrived in Seattle

things Fielde did was to make a study of the climate using records kept by the Weather Bureau for the past seventeen years. The record showed that the city was relatively cool throughout the year, information that she had to know before she committed herself to the region. Having lived in Swatow and New York with their blazing summers, one can understand why she spent the hottest months of each year in the Adirondacks and Woods Hole. Reassured by her study that she would not have to endure intolerable heat, she decided that Seattle was the place for her. She rented a five-room flat, spent a month buying furniture, having the rooms painted, and hiring a Norwegian maid to do the housework – she was now comfortably settled in the west.[7] For Fielde, it really was the end of her life on the East Coast, and her interest in scientific research, despite Wheeler's attempt to urge her to continue with her work on ants. But her research had come to an end, and she bequeathed her ant cases to Wheeler. It was the beginning of a new chapter in her life, and now only social activism was her link to the past.

Seattle, a lively city in 1908, had been pristine forest little more than half a century before – within one's living memory. The hilly site, on the water, resembled Swatow, but the land was far more beautiful and healthy, and the climate much more inviting. In the first decade of the century the city had tripled its population, and by 1910 it was home to over 200,000 people of all ethnic groups. Middle and working classes were coming to the fore, replacing the original settlers as the city became a commercial and manufacturing center linked to the east by a new railroad. Imposing buildings and homes began to appear, and city parks were built, heralding a new sense of civic identity and pride. Fielde described her first impressions of Seattle to Wheeler:

> Seattle is a cross between a vast mining claim and an unbounded lumber camp: the everlasting necessary grading of the streets and the strenuous building operations being always and everywhere in evidence. It is a man's city; remote from the Pacific Grove sort of woman's retreat – where it is "always afternoon." Seattle is intensely secular, wholly self-absorbed, with the crudity of early youth; and a settled habit of self-laudation. But there are very nice people here too, and the glimpses one gets of the glorious mountains, when their gray veil of clouds is lifted, is something ever worth while.[8]

Soon after Fielde had arrived in Seattle she was invited to join a national reformist association, the "Committee of One Hundred," which urged the establishment of a National Department of Health proposed by Senator Owen. For this cause she was enlisted to write and distribute pamphlets extolling the virtues of such an organization. She incorporated parts of the senator's speeches into articles she submitted to newspapers, and she sent letters to thirty-five Congressmen urging them to vote for the Owen Bill. "This is a work of education of the people, and the formation of a public opinion that will move the federal legislatures to right action; and this work will probably need to be continued for some years."[9]

This brand new metropolis was wide open, dominated by powerful special interests, and run by vote-manipulating ward bosses. Since the Civil War, appalling political corruption in a land of booming economic growth could be found everywhere in the west. Seattle, a city of churches, abounded in saloons and other establishments where gambling and prostitution prospered under the benevolent eye of a corrupt police force – all a threat and a challenge to middle-class values. The city was the second most active center of white slavery in the U.S.A.

Adele Fielde arrived in Seattle on September 3, 1908 at a time when there was a pressing need for reform, despite earlier attempts to set matters right. She could not abide what she saw, and so she (and many other "Davids") responded to the call to slay the formidable political machine by forming or enrolling in organizations dedicated to the elevation of the moral tone of the city. Against a legislature controlled by a powerful and effective railroad lobby, frustrated reformers, Democratic and Republican, joined forces with religious leaders, professionals, small business people, trade unionists, and women's groups, to do battle, and slowly, inexorably, improvements began to take effect. Adele Fielde, a self-appointed activist, part of a network of reformers, and member of over twenty organizations, vigorously operated at the local, state, and national level, dedicated to the improvement of the world, specifically in the fields of government reform, public health, social welfare, and in the arts – a remarkable achievement. To Fielde, these issues, along with the problems of child labor, temperance, and world peace were all aspects of one great cause – the improvement of the human condition. Despite her busyness, trying to keep as many balls in the air at the same time, she could handle complexity; her affairs were always kept in order, and her life never descended into chaos.

A woman firmly rooted in middle-class values in a capitalist country facing dreadful social problems, she did not consider fundamental economic reform, or any alternative economic system, as the solution to the questions she confronted, nor did she appear to think in terms of conflict between social and economic classes. She was a secular pragmatist, working within the existing system, concerned with the physical and moral well-being of people. Fielde was a deeply religious woman, but she did not consider that the solution to terrible social problems lay in religion. In the suffragist struggle in the west, obtaining the vote was the most important weapon to attain an end – the betterment of the lives of women and children.

Fielde could recognize what had to be done to solve an immediate problem, expending her enormous energy effecting numerous piecemeal solutions. Some social problems could be solved by private charity – those who had sufficient should help those in need. As for the lower classes, Fielde had no doubt that Americans, however lowly their origins, should be able to pull themselves up by their bootstraps in this land of unlimited opportunity. On a larger scale, she believed in educating citizens about the structure of government, and the nature of the social problems confronting them so that they would know how to organize pressure groups and how to induce the government to do their enlightened bidding, indispensable for the alleviation of many social problems, by legal means.

Fielde never gives the impression that she settled somewhere like New York or Seattle to remedy a local defect. Rather, she knew that wherever she found herself there would be need, and that she could make a difference because she was confident in her ability, expertise, and stamina. Fielde's background was religious, but she never called for prayer, nor were sin or divine intervention invoked in her argument. Though idealistic, there was a strong rational, pragmatic element in her good works. Perhaps she did not become a legendary figure comparable to other great American reformers and suffragists of the nineteenth century – such as Elizabeth Cady Stanton, Susan B. Anthony, Lucretia Mott, and Anna Howard Shaw – because she was too involved in local affairs, forever writing unsigned pamphlets, and books of rules and procedures. She was as brilliant and knowledgable as they were, but she did not manifest the grand sweep, nor the system-building talent of her contemporaries – that last inch – nor was she as defiant or daring. Perhaps her enormous energy was dissipated among too many interests, and in too many places – China, New York, Seattle – and she had spent her best years buried in China.

Fielde took an immediate liking to Seattle, a "big straggling village with a great city in the making." It was a metropolis, overflowing with raw energy and promise, but plagued with political, social, and health problems with which she was familiar. The many churches that dotted the landscape kept company with saloons, gambling houses, and brothels. A large and disorganized population of decent people suffered at the hands of rapacious private interest groups and a corrupt civic government that made the election of reform candidates difficult, if not impossible. Soon after her arrival, she made a study of the city, as she had of Berlin, Switzerland and New York, and within months Fielde was exercising her great organizing and communicative talents, throwing herself into the maelstrom, and mobilizing the women of the city. Those who had no knowledge of her soon became aware that there was a tiger in their midst. Hardly a month had passed since her arrival when the *Seattle Post-Intelligencer* published an article with Fielde's portrait, listing her achievements in China, New York, and Woods Hole, and proudly announcing that Miss Adele Marion Fielde planned to reside in Seattle. The report stated that since her arrival she had been following the work of the Board of Health in combatting an outbreak of the plague. This detailed story was followed by another written by Fielde – the role of the flea in the spread of plague, and methods to stop the spread of the disease.[10]

Her reputation among some women had preceded her, and with her forceful, attractive personality she was immediately taken up by a circle of enlightened women who established an earnest discussion group. Here, Fielde was the first among equals, just as she had been in a similar body in New York that had included women like Mrs. John D. Rockefeller. The Seattle group, dubbed the "Rainy Day Club," consisted of twelve women, and it remained a coherent society for the next eight years, without any change of membership until the death of Fielde. During the rainy season of the year, they met every two weeks at members' homes, where they discussed books, literary trends, and social issues.

Out of idleness no goodness can come, and so when there was something to be done, it was to be done immediately, and with maximum effort. Fielde, ever the woman of action, was enlivened when she had a cause to fight for. Within a month of her arrival in Seattle, dedicated to the idea of social justice with equality between men and women, she was writing tracts in support of the suffragist cause, and hammering out the constitutions of three suffragist organizations.[11] An article, "A Score of Reasons Why Women Should Be Enfranchised," was published in several newspapers and reprinted. Ultimately, over 100,000 copies of this article in pamphlet form blanketed the state, courtesy of the Seattle Suffrage Club, as the battle for equal suffrage gathered momentum. Throughout 1909 and 1910 Fielde engaged herself in grass-roots politics, speaking everywhere, and writing in support of the cause. The enormous organized effort to sway public opinion proved successful, for in 1910 a Constitutional Amendment enfranchising women was passed by the voters, with 40,000 votes to spare. Many groups and individuals had taken part in the struggle to bring American practice into line with American ideals, and Adele Fielde was not the least of these crusaders.

In a letter to Anna Howard Shaw, President of the American Woman Suffrage Association, and a protegée of Susan B. Anthony, Fielde wrote of her active participation in the political fight for woman suffrage. She spoke of standing in the rain in mud outside polling booths with other women, asking people how they would vote, and trying to convince them to support the enfranchisement of women. She shook her head in disbelief as "colored men" (some former slaves), planned to vote against the amendment, as did some trade unionists, foreign-born men recently enfranchised, gamblers, and thieves. She commented on the fact that although they were all courteous to her, such people would determine the fate of women's rights. Interestingly enough, when politicians arrived at the polling booths in automobiles and were asked to support women's suffrage, they offered a deal – they would vote for women's suffrage if women would support their candidates; Fielde's reply was "No thank you." At the end of the day she wrote,

> But when I reached home and sat down to think, I knew that the iron had entered my soul. I, a teacher of government, had been subjected to the humiliation of asking the ignorant, the vicious, the scorner to vote for my enfranchisement, an enfranchisement that should be mine by right of birth, of education, and of good works. I decided that I would

> cease to love my unjust country unless I should hear the news I hoped for within the next few hours.

But the phone soon rang to inform her that the suffrage amendment had passed easily, despite the efforts of some antisuffragists – both male and female – and her dark thoughts lightened:

> I was born in New York, and I have been enfranchised in Washington. It is better to be enfranchised than to be born; because being enfranchised is a certain good, consciously enjoyed, while being born is an unconscious process of uncertain value. I shall stay in the State of Washington, where I am now in reality an American citizen.

To Fielde, voting was a right, not a privilege.

Fielde, an expert in civics and the structure of government, was dismayed by the blatant corruption she found in Seattle and Washington State politics. Although elections were held, the city was dominated by a political machine. Powerful financial interests, working through an army of ward-healers, maintained their power by excluding the rank and file from the nominating process. Special interest groups thrived, and the public treasury was looted. Only party members could vote in the primary to select a candidate who had previously been chosen by party leaders. To counter such an undemocratic arrangement, a State Constitutional Amendment on the Initiative, Referendum and Recall – three cardinal principles of direct legislation – was submitted to the State Legislature for its consideration, with the aim of breaking the hold of special interest groups. If the amendment was passed, legislation could be introduced in the Legislature upon petition by a certain number of voters. If a bill was rejected by the Legislature, a petition signed by a specified number of voters could have the bill voted upon directly by the people. In Recall, a reasonable percentage of voters could petition for a new election to decide whether an elected official should be removed from office.[12]

To promote the amendment, reformers organized a Direct Legislation League which piqued Fielde's interest despite its listless history and lack of leadership. Fielde had already made a detailed study of the beneficial effects of direct legislation in Switzerland, and so to breathe life into the league it was not difficult for her to write an eight-page pamphlet on the subject which was reprinted in newspapers in the state. Fielde also arranged for 25,000 copies to be printed (at her own expense) which were distributed by labor unions, at City Hall and libraries. The tract prompted a group of people (all men, as Fielde notes) to gather at her home to revitalize the Direct Legislation League. Fielde worked mostly with women, but she had no difficulty working with men – as equals. Fielde wrote the by-laws, and officers were elected. The League engaged in publicizing speeches in favor of their cause, and Fielde was pleased that

> All the grangers, all the labor unions, all the Single Taxers, all the Socialists are in favor of direct legislation, as soon as they understand what it is. . . . The great end in view is to bring the power of self-government into the hands of the people. The opposers to this effort are all those who profit by methods of legislation that they can "influence" by personal means. The "special interests" are all on the side of indirect legislation. We shall win, in time.[13]

Fielde was an ardent follower of Henry George, whose Single Tax on land was designed to put a stop to ruinous land speculation by entrepreneurs who would amass vast tracts of land, especially in the west, and pay almost no taxes on them until they could sell at enormous profit.

Now that women had the vote, the next step was to make sure that the Direct Legislation Amendment was passed. Change required that citizens, especially new women voters, be made aware of the deficiencies of their political system, and that they be convinced that direct legislation was desirable. Women had never voted before and were politically ignorant, raising fears that they would not make intelligent use of their new-found right. Large numbers of new voters had to be quickly educated in political matters, and to do so Fielde proposed the founding of the Seattle Civic Forum, an educational organization supervised by a board of prominent, reform-minded citizens, with a constitution and by-laws written by Fielde. With the Forum as a platform, loosely modeled after the League for Political Education from her New York days, she lectured in every corner of the state, bringing to bear her studies of European, Australian, New Zealand, and American forms of government – the advantages and disadvantages of each, and the way to improve the American system by adopting elements from other systems of government. Lectures were not political harangues, but were factual, substantive, and covered a broad range of concerns: *Socialism and Democracy Contrasted; Paternalism vs. Fraternalism; Human Life, the Nation's Most Valuable Asset; The Child Labor Problem; The Eight-hour Law for Women Wage Earners; the Proposed Enactment of a Workman's Compensation Law; State Supervision of Charities*, to name but a few. The Forum lasted four months, from June to September 1911, and in the following year, voters in the State of Washington approved the Constitutional Amendment on Direct Legislation.

The Forum had been a purely educational instrument, and out of it grew, as proposed by Fielde, the Washington Women's Legislative Committee with the same membership also dedicated to active politicizing, as well as instructing the women of the state about legislation of special relevance to them, matters concerning "the home, children, foods, sanitation." The organization appealed to many women, and branches were quickly established throughout the state. Not only did it have an effect in the struggle for the Initiative, Referendum, and Recall amendment during its five years of existence, it also played a major role in the passage of legislation regarding temperance, prostitution, the defense of civil liberties, and minimum wages for women. The Committee was one of a few women's groups of similar, progressive outlook, all working together, each taking the lead in a specific issue, supported by the others.

Soon after the passage of the amendment, a petition was signed for the recall of Mayor Hiram C. Gill of Seattle, a political hack who administered a city rife with corruption – saloons, gambling, and prostitution, and a very tolerant police force. By 1915 Seattle was "dry," and prostitution and gambling were under some control.[14] Eventually, essential services were taken out of the private sector and placed in the hands of government – street railways, sewage, garbage collection, water supply, and electric power.

A boomtown like Seattle suffered serious ups and downs in an unregulated economy dominated by powerful, selfish interests with short-term gains in view. In the depression and panic of early 1908, thousands of people in all parts of the state were thrown out of work, most of whom were drawn to Seattle. Jobless multitudes strained the resources of charitable societies, many run by Fielde's friends, all belonging to an association called "Organized Charities" supervised by a board of which Fielde was a member. Dismayed by this calamity, she formulated a plan in which the state would hire the unemployed, a view that was brought to the public's attention by a leading newspaper – "Woman's Plan for Unemployed."[15] It was Fielde's contention that the state was responsible for providing work for able-bodied men – building roads and clearing land. The state would be enriched, people would benefit, the public would get something for its money, and the strain on charities would be reduced. The proposal had much in common with Roosevelt's National Recovery Act of the 1930s. A bill embodying the plan was introduced in the Legislature but was defeated. Fielde continued to fight for this cause, publicizing her plan in several newspapers, also presenting her argument entitled "A Scheme for Labor Colonies Under State Board of Charities and Corrections" at the State Conference of Charities. So exercised was she that at her own expense she arranged for 10,000 copies of her newspaper article to be reprinted and distributed throughout Washington and Oregon. In a letter to a friend she commented that her plan was favorably received, especially by charitable organizations, "but there is, and always will be, secret and powerful opposition to the plan, from employers of labor, who wish to have the demand for work far exceed the supply."[16]

In a relatively new city which was in some disarray, Fielde was especially concerned with problems of water supply, sanitation, and the prevention and treatment of disease, not unlike those threats she had confronted in Swatow. The need for improvement in public health came to be her first concern, and within weeks of her arrival in Seattle she had decided to do something about it. After studying statistics on health in Seattle over the preceding three years, she concluded that the city was in need of an isolation hospital for those afflicted with the bubonic plague, typhoid, and other infectious diseases. She wrote a data-filled report, showing the need for a hospital, and submitted it to the Mayor for presentation to the Board of Health and the City Council whose eighteen members she importuned, and with her informed and persuasive arguments she was not to be denied. Barely three months after her arrival in Seattle, her plan was viewed with favor, money was provided by the city, and by the issuance of bonds, and, after the usual delays, the hospital came into existence. An admiring health commissioner, who was also instrumental in the creation of the hospital, wrote in the *Health Bulletin of Seattle* (May, 1910): "Miss Adele M. Fielde has probably given the subject of sanitation and hospital construction as much attention as any other woman in the U.S.A. Since she has become a resident of Seattle she has taken a great deal of interest in such work, and her advice has often been sought by this department."[17] Fielde, an issue-oriented Reformist who was not partisan, talked to politicians of every persuasion.

Fielde was concerned with the possibility that the bubonic plague would become a serious problem in Seattle as it was in California. In October 1908 there were five fatal cases of the bubonic plague in Seattle, prompting Fielde, an entomologist, to concern herself with the flea, the insect vector that spreads the disease from infected rats to humans. In two articles in the *Seattle Post-Intelligencer*, Seattle's leading newspaper – "A Woman Scientist on Flea Extermination," and "Urge Fight on the Ubiquitous Flea" – based on her experience with the plague in China, Fielde informed the public about the flea's role as a plague carrier, and to prevent spread, she prescribed alum as an inexpensive insecticide for washing clothing and sheets. Stressing the danger of rats and the fleas they carry, she enlisted the public's support for the Board of Health's drive to destroy these rodents. As a professional entomologist her newspaper articles were filled with reliable information about insects, rats and their role as reservoirs of disease-causing bacteria.[18]

Tuberculosis was still prevalent in Washington State, relentlessly taking its toll of both the rich and the poor, even in the wide open spaces of the west. Fielde decided to form a branch of the Society for the Prevention and Relief of Tuberculosis in the Seattle area, wrote its constitution and by-laws, and formed a board made up of many wealthy and prominent citizens. Meetings were held on a regular basis to educate the public on this ancient scourge. Fielde, the driving force behind this effort, never missed a meeting. In response to the society's influence, the city floated a bond issue for $10,000, and a wealthy citizen whose son had died of tuberculosis contributed generously to build a sanitorium and to further the work against the disease.

Once this cause was seen to be successful, Fielde seemed to lose interest, and went on to other challenges, which were never in short supply. One of these was the recently founded Children's Orthopedic Hospital whose Association she joined in 1908, and again she advised the Board on the writing of by-laws, contributed money, attended meetings, and organized groups to support the hospital. Fielde would sometimes walk about the hospital, inspecting wards, the kitchen and surgery, and talk to the children, just to make sure all was running properly.

In Europe and New York, Fielde had been a dedicated devotee of the arts, had attended the theater, opera, and concerts, and had spent endless hours in museums and galleries. Seattle lacked these refinements, and so she suggested to some of her friends that this unsatisfactory situation should be remedied. Six months after Fielde arrived, and with her prodding, the Seattle Fine Arts Association was founded (March 1908), with several, separate departments – painting, plastic, ceramic, decorative art, applied design, art in attire, architecture, and landscape gardening. Fielde wrote the by-laws but did not become an officer of the Association. Each monthly meeting was highlighted by a lecture, three given by Fielde in the first year of its operation.

Seattle was the American gateway to Alaska, a land so remote and challenging that Fielde could not resist seeing it for herself. She had busied herself in Seattle for the past year and required a little adventure, and so she sailed for Alaska on an excursion steamer, the beginning of a strenuous two-month, 6000-mile tour. She was awed by the "grandeur of the snow-crowned mountains, beauty of the crystal bergs and glaciers, and the soul-inspiring throb of its restless waters," while most of her fellow passengers played bridge as they passed by the mighty spectacle. Scornfully, she dismissed the card players: "Perhaps they were overcome by the beauty of it and were driven to the frivolous for refuge."[19] Fielde did not spare herself, for having become familiar with wild country, she challenged it to show her its roughest nature. After a week in Sitka, she experienced a "pioneer life at the Hot Springs on Baranof Island." Returning to Sitka by Indian war canoe, she took off for Skagway and then crossed the White Pass, famous for the many lives it had taken a decade before. At White Horse, she coursed down the Yukon River, "a journey that I shall advise no one else to take," and from Dawson, returned to Seattle.

> I could not obtain a tumblerful of clean water to drink, and the few tub-baths I could get only added a layer of Yukon mud to my surface. Then the mosses are breeding grounds for swarms of mosquitoes and gnats. So fierce are these that prospectors for gold prefer to endure a temperature sixty degrees below zero rather than meet them, and they prospect in winter cold instead of among summer insects. The food is mostly tinned stuff, carried in from Seattle and nothing short of a mining appetite can long tolerate it. . . . It is not a health trip. Nevertheless, having returned alive and well, I am glad I went. It was fun to be carried ashore in the arms of a giant.

Perhaps the best thing about the ordeal was that "it took Alaska out of the system."

Fielde sailed back to Seattle through the Behring Sea, on a ship carrying over 300 passengers – a mixed group of "murderers and missionaries, Eastern society dames and dance-hall girls, fiends and saints. . . . But the thrilling hours have been those in which I had long talks with those who had spent many years in the solitudes near the Arctic Circle – heroes who have failed and heroes who have succeeded in the quest for 'pay-streak'." Fielde was a good listener, and just as she had gathered stories and legends in China, she learned about a legendary hero of Alaska. She related the story of Alexander MacDonald, King of the Klondike, a grizzled prospector who became rich with gold-mines and property, married a girl forty-two years his junior in London, lost his fortune and spent the rest of his life alone in a cabin near the Yukon River.

By the fall of 1911 Fielde was exhausted, with a chronic bronchial condition which had worsened, and she admitted that "she had become strangely weak."[20] She had been deeply involved in the suffrage movement, lecturing on politics and government, and had traveled across the state, giving one or two talks a day, attending meetings, and writing pamphlets and newspaper articles. A rest was needed in a dry southern climate, and so she chose to spend fall, winter and early spring in Arizona, which was just preparing for statehood. She arrived at Tucson in mid-November 1911, apparently not unknown, and incredibly, a new cycle of furious civic activities commenced. By December 5 she had written several articles for Tucson newspapers on prohibition, suffrage, and direct legislation, and had lectured to the State Federation of Women's Clubs. In the next three months she spoke over thirty times about women's suffrage. Passionate, dedicated crusader that she was, she could not resist taking up the frenetic activities in Arizona and Tucson that she was attempting to avoid in Seattle.

She did not give the impression of battle fatigue, although early in her stay in Tucson, uncharacteristically, she felt too poorly to visit and care for her dying friend, Mrs. E.M. Cauldwell in New York City. She wrote to Mrs. Cauldwell's daughter that in the warm dry climate of Arizona her bronchitis and general health were improving, and she was beginning to feel stronger, and perhaps after a few months in the south she would be able to make the arduous journey east. In her letter she spoke about the joys and sorrows of aging, and that despite the inevitable, one must not give up hope. As for herself: "I am aware that . . . my present tranquil and comfortable state lacks the glamour that has illumined preceding years. It is good to live many decades, because each decade brings knowledge that no earlier one has capacity to grasp."[21] Soon after her return to Seattle in April she was informed of Mrs. Cauldwell's death, and was moved to confide to her diary:

> My very soul is bereft by her departure. For forty years we were friends and no cloud ever came between our hearts. Without her, this world never can be so good a place for me to live in. She never once failed me in fidelity or affection.

For outdoor recreation, Fielde made a study of cacti indigenous to the area, and in one of several experiments demonstrated that she could extract enough water from a Mammilaria cactus to sustain a human. Her co-experimenter was a young woman from Portland, Oregon, Mrs. Rose McBride, whom she had met soon after her arrival in Tucson, and they had formed an instant friendship that lasted until Fielde's death. Their relationship casts some light on how Fielde was regarded by others. After Fielde's death in 1916, Helen Stevens, Fielde's biographer, wrote to Mrs. McBride asking for her remembrances of her friend. She replied:

> There was a mutual attraction from the start. A few days after we met in Tucson, Arizona, she said to me "I would like to have been your mother." The compliment, coming as it did from such a fine and wonderful source, could not otherwise than impress me highly. We spent two months in Tucson, meeting every day. We both loved the sunshine, the mystic haze of the desert and the grandeur of the canyons. Once we spent a whole day in one of these beautiful natural chambers, she seemed so carefree, enjoying making coffee on the campfire.

After helping Fielde with the cacti experiments, she states, "She loved to try things out." They wrote to each other regularly, and in 1915 they attended the Panama Exposition in San Francisco:

> She was indeed wonderful, her mentality simply astonishing. During our stay in San Francisco, my happiest experiences consisted in lying curled-up on the foot of her bed listening to her talk. There was no subject that she could not discuss learnedly and interestingly. We often sat up very late while she told me of her life in China.[22]

Despite all her activities, Fielde's health seems to have been restored in Arizona, and she returned to Seattle to find that several important events had taken place during the winter of her absence (1911–1912). The unsavory Mayor Gill had been recalled, and in the election that followed he ran again, only to be defeated by a Reform Mayor, George F. Cotterill. He promptly appointed Fielde a trustee of the Seattle Public Library, a great honor, for she was the first Seattle woman ever to be appointed to political office. She noted however that this was hardly more than a gesture, for at a dinner with city officials, she was the only woman among fifty men, despite the fact that the election of Mayor Cotterill was largely due to the efforts and the votes of women. She filled her days working to improve library services, continuing her lectures, her courses in civics, and her writing. Many of her articles appeared in a newly established journal *Western Woman's Outlook*, which became the official organ of the Washington State Federation of Women's Clubs, an organization that Fielde was instrumental in founding and financing as a united voice for the numerous women's organizations.

Having witnessed the ravages of alcohol in China and the U.S.A., Fielde was a confirmed advocate of temperance. With the backing of the Washington

Women's Legislative Committee, she took it upon herself to establish a committee of one to prepare pamphlets on prohibition, and to organize a petition to bring a prohibition law before the legislature, the first test of direct legislation in the State of Washington, now possible under the recently passed Initiative law. Pamphlets emphasized the social and domestic chaos produced by alcohol while the liquor interests profited were widely distributed. The tracts were not only written by Fielde; she also paid for the printing expenses, postage, and clerical help to address the circulars, costing her over $800. She also contributed $500 for the printing and distribution of 40,000 petitions throughout the state. While only 32,000 signatures were necessary, 112,000 signatures were obtained to place the issue before the voters, and in the election of November 1914 they favored temperance by a majority of 19,000. The religious community, the Anti-Saloon League, and women's groups could claim credit, but without question, Adele Fielde played a major role in initiating the drive, educating the public, and keeping the issue alive.

But the distillers and dispensers of liquor were not easily defeated; they formed a war chest estimated at $550,000 to $3 million, with which they bribed corrupt politicians and voters, bought space in newspapers, and bombarded the public with their literature to reverse or defuse the Prohibition law. They were able to get their man, Hiram C. Gill, elected Mayor of Seattle once again, and they persuaded the citizens of Seattle to vote against the law in the city, but they could not overcome the dry vote of the rest of the state. Although the Prohibition referendum was enacted, it was stipulated that if it was approved by voters it would come into effect after a period of two years (January 1916), giving the "wets" further opportunity to fight the measure in the courts, and do whatever was necessary to prevent final implementation of the law. Once again the liquor interests, with vast amounts of money at their disposal, mounted a challenge, spent money freely, and forced the temperance group with its modest financial budget to respond. Fielde contributed an astonishing amount of money, disproportionate to her income. She writes in her diary: "I put nine hundred dollars into the Prohibition campaign of the Washington Women's Legislative Committee; five hundred dollars into the work of the Anti-Saloon League; gave five hundred dollars to the expense of defending the court action; making a total of nineteen hundred dollars."[23] There were few as generous as Adele Fielde. She earned enough money lecturing not to feel any want, she lived modestly, spent relatively little, and felt secure enough to give away most of her savings to support worthy causes, and her cause proved victorious – the prohibition law stood.

One of Mayor Gill's first acts in office was to remove Fielde from the Seattle Library Commission, a move that was condemned by most of the women's groups of the city. The forces of corruption were now having their way, and they saw to it that the reformist, prohibitionist *Western Women's Outlook*, to which Fielde contributed regularly, was put out of business. The journal was owned by stockholders, and by devious means the Liquor Dealers Political Association and its allies acquired a controlling interest, and then stopped publication. While the struggle was in progress Fielde confided in her diary: "By the liberal use of their great corruption fund, by bribing women, lawyers and courts, the brave little paper may not be able to hold out against the machinations of the enemy."[24]

This reformer, although she appreciated the larger issues in the creation of a fair and equitable Republic, was especially incensed by the abuse of women and children, and the conditions that undermined the stability of the family. In the life of the country there were issues of broader importance than excessive drinking, yet this vice passionately aroused Fielde, not because of her Baptist past but because of its social consequences. At the very heart of her ideal of life on Earth for women was domesticity – making a home and raising children – which she believed was superior to intellectual or artistic achievements. In a letter to a sympathetic City Councilman, Mr. C. Allen Dale, she wrote:

> I have never worked harder for any public good than for state-wide prohibition in Washington. All along I have had a vision of two possible evenings for a Washington woman in the future. In the one, she waits and listens to see how badly her husband staggers as he approaches the home at a late hour; in the other, she watches joyously for his coming home at the end of the day's work, confident of sane companionship. If just one woman, ten years hence, awaits her husband with serenity rather than with anxiety as to his condition, that alone will pay me for all that I have done to further prohibition. And then there are the little children that will have more food and better clothing; and the mothers who will find it easier to rear their sons to right lives. Within ten years "we the people" of Washington, have gained equal suffrage; the initiative and referendum; the red light abatement, and the prohibition law, with several other good enactments – Hallelujah, Amen.[25]

Adele Fielde, a Victorian American woman, described the evil of drink in terms of high Victorian melodrama.

An entry in her diary provides a compelling affirmation of her devotion to the young, perhaps a yearning for the children she never had:

> Yesterday I walked on Capitol Hill. The sky was gloriously broad and blue; the mountains loomed resplendent in the azure; there were stretches of bloom in the Park where I lingered long. Then, on my way homeward, I passed a little go-cart holding a baby girl who smiled enchantingly at me, a stranger. Ever since I have not thought much of the broad sky, the mountains or the flowers, but of the smile of that baby. When one is about to plunge into the last quarter of a possible century of life, one thinks carefully of what one might do to make the State a better place for babies to grow up in. To me that is politics; and I am merged in politics.

Children's welfare was Fielde's major interest in the last two years of her life. Nothing on Earth was more important, for the future of the race depended on the rearing of healthy children. To Fielde, maternal instincts could be depended upon to nourish and protect the very young, far more so than the preaching of religion, or the arguments of science and philosophy. Indeed, Fielde stated that the women's movement was based on this notion – on the free expression of immutable, maternal instinct. But mothers had to be informed about how to rear children, and to provide them with information Fielde formed a Fielde Pamphlet Fund and a committee of volunteers under the auspices of the Seattle Congress of Mothers and of the Parent–Teacher Associations. After extensive study, she selected short publications on the care of babies by the American Public Health Service, the Russel Sage Foundation, and the American Medical Association, and sent at her own expense a package of pamphlets to thousands of mothers throughout the state with the hope that positive results might become evident in the future: "A stronger, handsomer, happier folk may live in the Northwest fifty years hence, if we do this work now," and we "hope to save an Edison, a Goethals, a Gorgas and maybe a Lincoln out from among the saved babies."[26] To target the literature, it was necessary to obtain the addresses of thousands of young mothers throughout the state, and to do so, Fielde and her volunteers virtually established a bureau of vital statistics.[27] Among her colleagues she became known as the mother of mothers. Convinced that all children should be given every assistance to fulfill their potential, she was active in organizations that provided scholarships for bright young women in need.

A devoted follower of Darwin, the author of *On the Origin of the Species by Means of Natural Selection or the Preservation of Favored Races in the Struggle for Life*, Fielde and many contemporary thinkers were believers in social Darwinism and eugenics – intervention to assist the evolutionary process. To white, Northern Europeans and their descendants, natural selection and the survival of the fittest were compelling ideas that in fact could be interpreted in more ways than one, but to some, they were the validations for racism, *laissez-faire* capitalism and imperialism.[28] Regardless of whether she drew the right or erroneous conclusions, Fielde's thinking about societal problems was rooted in principles of biology. Such issues as race and the survival of infants were considered in the light of "science" and its great authority. She was driven to do something about the care of infants because she felt that the death of a single baby meant the end of a future line of humans of unlimited potential. Harkening to past experience she wrote: "I have seen cities in China where all the people were of one surname, and could point to a tomb on a neighboring hill as the resting place of one pair of ancestors as the progenitors of all the inhabitants of the city. . . . When an infant dies, all its possible posterity dies with it." For the same reason, she condemned war in which the posterity of young men killed in battle is forever lost.[29]

Witnessing the influx of great numbers of poor, illiterate immigrants from Europe and Asia living under the most wretched conditions, she was concerned that, in the long run, they would outbreed the native stock with catastrophic deterioration in the quality of the American stock. Without question, she believed in the superiority of the old native population of North European origin (of which she was a member), and when she spoke of improvement of the race she was thinking of the white race. She truly loved the Chinese, but she had experienced the profound hopelessness of their culture, she did not trust their political instincts and could not accept them as equals, for surely she felt their sad state was a reflection of a deficiency in quality and ability. Fielde had no difficulty accepting, and fervently admiring *individuals* of every race and background. In 1915, Fielde was troubled because she felt that as Japan overran China, the Chinese would be forced to emigrate to North America, and "with the slaying of millions of white people [in the First World War] who might have come to strengthen their kind, there will be *lack* of immigration of white men, and yellow men will silt in" to occupy the vacant land.[30] Fielde's views of the Chinese, and her grand, "yellow peril" scenario, was believed by her and many others to be based on "scientific" principles – genetic and evolutionary theory. Racist notions had been codified into law by the Chinese Exclusion Act of 1882 (made permanent in 1902).[31] Although Fielde and her acquaintances held strong abolitionist sentiments, the desperate plight of black people was rarely discussed, and did not seem to exist in Fielde's writings on poverty or social injustice.

Fielde was adamantly against America's entry into the European conflict in the First World War. In the past, she had denounced the destruction of the Chinese by opium and alcohol, forced upon the Chinese by imperialist Britain, and she had little sympathy with the British establishment which was running the war with some American assistance. Having spent time in Germany studying its government, she was an unabashed admirer of that country:

> I consider the German people to have made the closest approach to civilization. The German government conserves the resources of nature more perfectly than does any other ruler . . . the waste and misery of unemployment is well forestalled. *Order* is preserved, and education is universal . . . I should like to see Germany win out in this war – that she might continue a scientific pursuit of truth – but war is murder, it "is hell."[32]

She had found President Wilson's assistance to the Allies in providing munitions "untenable." A neutral America was placing American lives at stake as it provoked Germany to respond, for Germany had the right to make war on those transporting munitions to its enemy.

> I am a tender hearted person – but I once stood with a loaded pistol, my back to a wall, intending to shoot just as many pirates as I could hit. . . . War does not consist of drawing-room amenities. . . . Are

> Americans *also* to go mad, and enter the world combat? Wilson is *wrong*. Yet he is involving us in *war*, inexcusable war.[33]

Seattle's cool weather was perfect for Fielde, and by 1915, when many of her friends had motorcars, outings and picnics in the countryside were frequent. Motoring about under blue skies, marveling at the flowers and the rich vegetation, gave her peace, and her aging body rest, although at least on one occasion she delivered "an hour's talk on Parliamentary Law" to a "group of fine women in a windless dell." This she did without fee, for she no longer lectured for dollars as she put it. Lecturing had been a lucrative activity, and she had amassed sufficient capital to live comfortably for the rest of her life, despite her incredible generosity to support worthy causes.

A dynamo, from her very first days in Seattle in September, 1907, she had accomplished wonders, and yet, reviewing her many successes over her first three years in Seattle, she was still not satisfied with what she had done:

> How small it is in comparison with what many other women have done in that same time! Probably many women have given birth to poets, artists, inventors, whose future outputs will bring unreckonable good to the world. Many women have bestowed money for the building of hospitals where frightful suffering will be abated. Many women have written books that will delight tens of thousands of readers through decades to come. Many have been "angels, unawares," and who knows how far or how deep into the universe the influence of any angel extends? Really, I who live so peacefully and at ease, am much ashamed.[34]

Given her strong ego, Fielde's belittlement of her efforts comes as a surprise. Her self-doubt was certainly concealed from her colleagues who regarded her as an unstoppable force of nature, tough, and often overbearing. A colleague from her missionary days commented on her energy, determination, and persistence in her younger days: "If there were obstacles they must be overcome. If houses, churches or schools were needed they had to be provided in some way. With her as with Napoleon, there must be no Alps. . . . Sight once gained of some end, it must be reached; by sheer weight of mind and fixity of purpose she pushed her way through until the goal was won." A member of a Seattle organization to which Fielde belonged described one of their meetings: "We talk, discuss and argue a proposition until the matter seems exhausted; and, in the end, Miss Fielde rises with her 'queen mother' air and reduces us all to silence. Her decisions are so absolutely final that often we have difficulty in becoming resigned." She was not a consensus seeker – as a natural leader, she listened to other voices and then decided what was best – she *knew* what was best, and was quite willing to override the opinion of others. In spite of this, Fielde commanded enormous respect and love because, in fact, she usually did know best, and her motives were so forthright, and her efforts so selfless.[35]

13 A model death

> Any world is good for me to live in and I approach the Great Silence with reverence and serenity.[1]

At age 76, Fielde was still a healthy and vigorous woman, widely known, revered, and dedicated to the social good. Quite simply, she could not stop working. Such a person, a woman of iron, who never discussed health, might go on forever, her friends thought. But in January 1916, Helen N. Stevens, Fielde's intimate friend and co-worker, who saw her almost every day, noticed that she did not look well, and that she had remained indoors in inclement weather, unusual behavior for Fielde.[2] She admitted that she felt poorly and was experiencing increasing bouts of weakness, which she ascribed to her age. At Steven's insistence, Fielde consulted a physician, and the news was catastrophic. After a confirmatory examination the conclusion was reached that she had only weeks, perhaps a month or two, to live, probably the victim of cancer that was relatively silent until it reached an advanced stage. On February 9, the day after Fielde's second physical examination, Stevens was summoned by Fielde's maid to come quickly, and upon her arrival found Fielde in bed. She informed Stevens that her life was nearing its end, and that what remained to be done was to arrange her earthly affairs. Stevens recorded the dying woman's remarks:

> My dear, Dr. C.W. Sharples has just told me that I am afflicted with a malady for which, at my age, there is no remedy or cure. As I wished to be fully informed I asked him to tell me how long approximately I would remain here. In reply he said "it might be several months, but more probably it would be only for a few weeks and perhaps but for a few days." I am perfectly satisfied to go into my next life and I hope the call will soon come; but we will talk of my journey to eternity later on. At present I have many things to do before I go. My financial affairs are already off my mind, as this morning I gave them into the hands of Mr. George H. Walker, my friend and lawyer. Now I must go to work to "set my house in order" while I have possession of my mental faculties

> and the necessary physical strength. I sent for you and Mrs. W.D. Perkins to help me do this.

What followed in the next two weeks was pure theater, directed and orchestrated by Fielde, who maintained her serenity as was called upon to calm her distraught friends. Fielde made every decision about her dying and her death, with explicit instructions about the disposal of her earthly goods and her remains, and details of the memorial services to be held. She approached the process of dying as she would an experimental study in physiology in which she would make whatever observations she could. Fully alert, and with an unwavering belief in God and the heavenly home she would inhabit, she enthusiastically planned to describe the transition from this life into the next, confident that dying was the beginning of a new adventure and a better life; she looked forward to a reunion with all her dear friends who had preceded her.

Fielde gathered about her a very small group of people to look after her – her maid, a nurse, a great admirer of Fielde who had attended her class on parliamentary procedures, and two friends (Helen Stevens and Mrs. W.D. Perkins). Her lawyer and her physician paid daily visits, but all others, so many of them cherished colleagues, were denied access, and she asked, as she felt herself sinking, that distant acquaintances not send letters. She would be gladdened to see her friends once again, but parting would be so unbearable, she would rather they not visit. She received letters, notes, and flowers from alarmed friends and colleagues who found it difficult to believe that such a vital powerhouse was a mere mortal, dying like everyone else. Two friends suggested that the doctors might have made an incorrect diagnosis, and that she should not accept her death sentence, but must obtain another opinion about her condition. This she refused to do – "my going is irrevocable." To many of her friends, her decline seemed sudden, almost a collapse, which some ascribed to a letdown after two years of ardent struggle followed by the great victory of the temperance movement in November 1915.

She *knew* she was dying – in fact she confided to Stevens that she had been aware that something was seriously wrong well before she had visited the doctor. It was understood that Stevens would continue with and complete various projects in which they were involved, but then she seemed to shed her accustomed sense of duty and responsibility: "I have reached the time when the 'grasshopper seems a burden'."[3]

She then directed that all of her clothing be packaged so that it might be distributed appropriately to friends and charitable organizations. Fifteen keepsakes and items of jewelry were to be given to friends according to directions – after her death. Her copies of the books she had written, eleven in all, were to be given to the Smithsonian Institution, and her scrap-books (her "literary remains") were to be sent to her dear friend Mrs. Samuel Millbank Cauldwell in New York. Her collection of books, some rare and valuable, were to go to the library of the University of Washington in

Seattle. All this was done to avoid the red tape involved in settling the estate of the deceased. Fielde dictated letters to four intimate friends in the East informing them of her condition. Movingly, in one message she says "How glad I am that you and I have had so profound a friendship and so much of true happiness in our converse. Any world is good enough for me to live in. Through all the centuries great throngs have been passing over into the 'Great Silence.' The universe could not stand the strain were there not something desirable and joyous in the progress of mankind from this life to the next." With the necessary tasks completed, her lodgings at the San Marco Apartments almost bare, she settled down seriously to the business of dying.

Stevens, who remained by her side almost the entire time, noted that Fielde's conversation was still humorous and sparkling. She brought Fielde news and messages from the outside, and read the newspaper to her, all of which interested her "intensely" at first, but in the last few days of her life she lost focus. Her interest in various subjects fell away one by one; the last to go, just a few days before her death, was the news of the war. As long as she was lucid, the Great War in Europe was still of deep concern to her, and she followed it closely. Her familiarity with the terrain on which the great, bloody battles were being fought imparted an immediacy to the daily news. Just before becoming bedridden she had written to a friend:

> I am very, very sorrowful under the daily news of the fiery maelstrom in Europe; sick at heart on account of the killing of men and all the evils that come of war. It is all so horrible that I cannot let myself think of it much less write of it. The situation with us is ominous and I can only say "Heaven help and keep America." In my heartsickness I have turned again to my beloved natural sciences for consolation and distraction, and am reading J. Henri Fabre, entomologist, and am fascinated.[4]

She was especially perturbed by the war because the best young men, the hope of the future, were being killed – for her a confounding of eugenic principles, and a violation of the law of the survival of the fittest.

The daily routine was conducted in as normal a fashion as possible, without tears or displays of grief. In the last few days, she refused food that might prolong the life in a "worn-out and useless body." Despite her pain, she ordered that she be given no opiates because she wanted to die with a clear mind: "I want to die intelligently. I have many friends who have gone over and I wish to be in a condition to speak to them at once if I should chance to meet them. As long as my brain is alive I will endure the pain that will come with my passing." Eastern influences are evident in her philosophy:

> I believe that in the world to which I am to go preparations are being made for me as my mother awaited my infant advent. If everything was ready I would automatically go hence. I was born into this life full time and I want to go into my next life at full time in order that my

> development may be complete. I do not want to enter a weakling as one does who goes prematurely.

She was well prepared for the inevitable. Her attitude toward death was always calm and accepting, a harmonizing of her religion, science, and concern for the human race. A few years previously she had written:

> When one who is in the seventies considers the future, that consideration must needs extend into another world than this. Having studied Buddhism, Confucianism, Zoroastrianism, as well as Christianity, among the people who profess to believe them, I became wise enough to know that I do not know. I hope and trust. Whatever bit of earth I chance to stand upon, it is a bit of the great world that I love as God's footstool. In any place, at any moment, still loving the world that I know so well, I can go serenely into my next life, hoping for an endless existence in which love and service will be an unmixed joy.[5]

Fearless, Fielde seemed able to view her dying with detachment, as an interesting phenomenon that was worth thinking about. She engaged those around her in discussions about the mystery of death, trying to grasp some insight into its meaning. No doubt her friends found the experience as remarkable as it was painful. Hours before she died, she was aroused from what Stevens called a coma, and said, "I am passing through a very peculiar phase of existence; I am not here, nor am I there. I am now on the brink." These were almost her last words, and she died just before light of the next day, February 23, 1916 – this unique experience came to an end.[6] The city had lost a champion, and Seattle publications praised her to the heavens: "probably no woman in America has done more to uplift humanity than this woman . . . she died full of years and honors."[7]

According to Fielde's instructions, funeral services were private and very simple. As a Christian who had maintained herself outside the Church, she wanted no clergymen to officiate, nor were there to be eulogies or flowers, but three of her favorite hymns were to be sung, and two poems were to be recited; 200 mourners were in attendance. Two weeks later a public memorial was organized by fifteen organizations to which Fielde belonged. It was held at the Moore theater in Seattle, attended by the present and former governor of the state, nine supreme court justices, judges, politicians, lawyers, physicians, friends, and colleagues – many hundreds in all. Heralded as the last of her illustrious family, she was eulogized by six close friends who reviewed the many facets of her life.[8] This "mother of mothers" had reached and affected the lives of so many. Charlotte Perkins Gilman, the renowned suffragist, wrote of Fielde:

> She was a woman to whom the word great deservedly applies; a great character, strong, wise, courageous, progressive. I have never known a

> woman more richly "human". . . . Her life of varied achievement has left her best monument in the hearts and minds of thousands whom she has taught and helped; and biological science is helped by her labors. Besides all this she was a "likable" person, with hosts of friends, and this popularity she retained to her latest years. Such a life is an inspiration and an example.[9]

From a small town in the hinterland, Adele Fielde had journeyed afar, and now her pilgrimage had run its course. But even in death she could not be confined, for her last wish was fulfilled:

> My ashes are to be cast on the waters of Puget Sound. I have loved this old earth, and I belong to it, the air, the sea and the sky, so I want my ashes to be washed and purified before returning to their natural elements.[10]

Notes

1 Beginnings

1 Much of the information of Adele M. Fielde's early life was found in Helen Norton Stevens' biography, published in 1918, two years after Miss Fielde's death. Stevens was a close friend of Fielde in her later years in Seattle, WA. Steven's papers, which must contain many of Fielde's records, have not been located.
2 Howe, 1976, pp. 3–28.
3 Stevens, 1918, pp. 36–37; Fielde lecture, "Reasons for a Coterie."
4 Pearson, 1959.
5 Stevens, 1918, pp. 31–32.
6 None of Fielde's early writing has been located, or seems to have survived.
7 Fielde to Adaline M. Payne, 1911; Stevens, 1918, p. 38.
8 Stevens, 1918, pp. 29–31.

2 Out of the nest

1 Stevens, 1918, pp. 56, 57, 60. Stevens received information from several of Fielde's friends and incorporated excerpts (verbatim) into her biography which I have used. Stevens' notes cannot be located.
2 They were all descended from Robert Field of Rhode Island and Flushing, Long Island, who died some time before 1672 (Field Family Notes, HSP Archives). Information also kindly supplied by Robert Singleton of the Greater Astoria Historical Society (Long Island).
3 Flexner, 1959, pp. 23–29. The Troy Female Seminary, founded in 1821 by a pioneer of women's education Emma Willard, still exists.
4 Fielde to Anna H. Shaw, cited in Stevens, 1918, p. 317.
5 Flexner, 1959, pp. 41–61.
6 Kraditor, 1973, pp. 254–278.
7 Flexner, 1959, pp. 73–77; DuBois, 1981, pp. 2–85.
8 There is no apparent reason why Fielde's three older sisters and an older brother were unable to provide for their parents.
9 Fielde, "A sea voyage of fifty years ago," *Spinning Wheel Magazine*, July 1915.
10 Stevens, 1918, pp. 80–81.

3 Bangkok

1 Fielde, *BMM*, November 1867, p. 43.
2 Stevens, 1918, p. 80.
3 William Dean, letter to *BMM* from Bangkok, July 27, 1866. Published December 1866, p. 465.

4 *BMM*, July 20, 1866. Published December 1866, p. 465.
5 Fielde to Warren, August 22, 1866.
6 Fielde, *Sketch of Missionary Work in China*, *BMM*, April 1876, pp. 105–107.
7 In 1870, a mob destroyed a Roman Catholic orphanage and church, and murdered several Frenchmen and women, including the French Consul, nuns, and a priest. Latourette, 1929, pp. 297–299; Mr. Knowlton to *BMM*, vol. 49, 1869, pp. 384–386; W. Ashmore to *BMM*, vol. 50, 1870, p. 409.
8 *Missionary Herald*, vol. 81, 1885, pp. 33–34.
9 Dean to Warren, August 18, 1867; August 10, 1866.
10 The discussion in this chapter, on the evangelical movement in the East, is largely based on the informative studies of Montgomery (1910), Hunter (1984), and Seabook (1993). Much of their marvelous knowledge is recycled in my pages. Surprisingly, no mention is made of Fielde in the books by Montgomery and Hunter.
11 Bowie, 1993, p. 8.
12 Property laws were changed in Pennsylvania and New York in 1848. In 1854, the State government of Massachusetts passed a Married Women's Property Bill, and in 1860 the New York State Legislature approved reform laws giving women full property, parental, and widow's rights, but they stopped at giving women the vote.
13 Jacobi, 1894, pp. 16–59.
14 Montgomery, 1910, pp. 21–39; King, 1969, p. 118.
15 For a moving account of the sufferings of a missionary wife see *The Exile*, a biography of Carie Sydenstricker by her daughter, Pearl Buck.
16 Beaver, 1968, pp. 59–115, 138; Merriam, 1900; Hunter, 1984, pp. 91–94.
17 Bridgman, 1853, p. viii; for women's struggle against male domination in the foreign missionary movement see Beaver, 1968, pp. 59–84, 85–113; Mild, 1993, pp. 194–209.
18 Fleming, 1989, pp. 1–10.
19 Ibid., *Preface*, p. xvi; ch. 6, "Imperial Evangelism", pp. 174–228.
20 Hunter, 1984, p. xvii; pp. 261–265.
21 Fielde, *BMM*, vol. 53, 1873, p. 391.
22 Bridgman, 1853, p. iv.
23 DuBois, 1978, pp. 183–188.
24 Fielde, 1884, p. 2.
25 The quote is from Fielde, vol. 57, 1877, p. 64; see also Hunter, 1984, p. 1.
26 Latourette, 1929, pp. 297–299.
27 Whitman, 1986, Introduction; pp. 230–235.
28 Swatow, now called Shantou, is a port city on the South China Sea, almost two hundred miles north-east of Hong Kong. The name "Swatow" will be retained in this story since all documents refer to it as such.
29 Fielde, *BMM*, vol. 48, 1868, pp. 12–13.
30 Ibid., vol. 47, 1867, pp. 431–432; letter to Warren dated April 22, 1867.
31 Fielde to Warren, December 1, 1869.
32 For a detailed discussion of Fielde's strategies, and styles of writing, see Seabrook, 1993, pp. 66–95.
33 Fielde, *BMM*, vol. 47, 1867, pp. 431–432.
34 Fielde to Miss Sands, October 19, 1868.
35 Barr, 1973, p. 92.
36 Seabrook, 1993, p. 12.
37 Dean to *BMM*, vol. 47, 1867, pp. 429–431.
38 Typical of this view is the writer of the following tract in *BMM*, vol. 72, 1872:

> A Chinaman's Idea of Blessedness. . . . The three especially desired are 1. Wealth, 2. Numerous Posterity, 3. Long life. These are all that a Chinaman

considers necessary to his happiness in this world, and with these he is willing to run the risk of the world to come. My teacher says that in all his life he never heard a heathen Chinaman express a wish for anything beyond this list. When two acquaintances meet even after years of separation, their first question is not "How are you?" but "making money?" They say to take life, to steal and to revile, are wrong; but to lie and cheat is nothing, if in this way one can make more money. This is heathenism, and there is no weapon but the sword of the Spirit, that will prove effective against it.

39 Ibid., pp. 407–408.
40 Dean to Missionary Board, May 6, 1867: "in this heathen country of pirates and pestilence, of robbery and rapine, it is more than we ought to ask of young ladies, accustomed to the protection and refinements of civilized life."
41 Fielde to Warren and *BMM* (written October 2, 1868), March 1869, pp. 80–81.
42 *Missionary Herald*, vol. 63, 1867, p. 28; vol. 66, 1870, p. 92.
43 Ibid. (written October 20, 1869) vol. 50, 1870, p. 105.
44 Buck, 1933, p. 149.
45 Fielde, Report to the Baptist Board of Missionaries, 1869.
46 Seabrook, 1993, p. 9.
47 Fielde to Warren, November 4, 1867.
48 Ibid., February 6, 1867.
49 Ibid., September 29, 1867.
50 Seabrook, 1993, pp. 22–24.
51 Fielde to Warren, October 18, 1867.
52 Hunter, 1984, p. 52.
53 Warren to William Ashmore, O-C January 16, 1869.
54 Julia Ward Howe, 1891, p. 1.
55 Dean and Partridge to B. Stowe, Chairman of the Executive Committee of the ABMU, December 5, 1869.
56 Partridge to Warren, December 19, 1869.
57 Warren to Fielde, February 16; March 19, 1870.
58 Fielde to Warren, May 20, 1870.
59 Fielde to Murdoch, July 21, 1871.
60 Murdock to Dean, April 24, 1871; Murdock to Partridge, May 10, 1871; Warren to Dean, November 19, 1870.
61 Fielde, *The Therapeutic Gazette*, vol. 4, 1888, pp. 449–451; Stevens, 1918, pp. 289–295.
62 Dean to Murdock, March 8, 1871.
63 Warren to Fielde, July 15, 1871.
64 Ashmore to Warren, November 8, 1871; December 1, 1871.
65 Murdock to Fielde, January 9, 1871.

4 Passage through America

1 DuBois, 1978, pp. 53–78, 162–202.
2 Ashmore to Warren, November 8, December 1, 1871.
3 Murdock to Ashmore, February 6, 1872.
4 Heilbrun, 1988, pp. 11–31.
5 Smith, Judson, *North American Review*, March 1901, p. 398. By 1901 there were 120 auxiliaries which raised $2.5 million each year.
6 Dean to Murdock, April 30, 1872.
7 Murdock to Dean, July 24, 1872; Murdock to Partridge, January 31, July 24, 1872.
8 Fielde to Murdock, October 21, 1872.

9 Murdock to Fielde, September 20, 1872.
10 Ibid., July 15, 1871.
11 Ibid., March 5, 1871.
12 Murdock to Partridge (Overseas Letters).
13 Sklar *et al.*, 1998.
14 See Middleton, 1965.
15 Fielde, *Private Diary*, Archives, University of Washington, Seattle, WA (microfilm). It is notable and peculiar in this handwritten work that the cross of the letter *t* is grossly misplaced to the right and down, as if it were a dash.

5 Swatow, China

1 Mr. Johnson, a missionary at Swatow, *BMM*, October 1867, p. 406.
2 Knowlton, *BMM*, vol. 49, 1869, pp. 384–386; Stanley, 1992, pp. 175–178; Latourette, 1968, pp. 273–304.
3 Smith, Judson, *BMM*, *Missionary Outlook*, 1891, p. 84.
4 Ashmore, *Missionary Magazine*, vol. 64, 1864, pp. 613–614.
5 Soper, 1948, pp. 178–189.
6 From The Boston Register, March 1894, reporting on a lecture by Fielde; see Stevens, 1918, pp. 186–188.
7 Ashmore, *BMM*, vol. 65, 1885, p. 116.
8 George L. Mason, *BMM*, vol. 65, 1885, pp. 418–420.
9 Reverend Y.K. Yen, *BMM*, *Missionary Outlook*, 1891, p. 84.
10 Ashmore, *MMM*, vol. 44, 1864, pp. 413–414.
11 Lottie Moon, from *The Foreign Mission Journal*, reprinted in *BMM*, vol. 67, 1867, pp. 128–130.
12 Ibid., vol. 49, 1869, pp. 145–149.
13 Ashmore, *BMM*, vol. 48, 1868, pp. 141–142.
14 *Missionary Herald*, vol. 74, 1878, pp. 243–245.
15 Ashmore, *BMM*, vol. 47, 1867, pp. 406–407.
16 Ibid., vol. 47, 1867, pp. 427–429.
17 Ibid., vol. 50, 1870, pp. 312–316; vol. 51, 1871, pp. 354–356.
18 Reverend George L. Mason, *Chinese Shams, BMM*, vol. 64, 1884, pp. 350–351.
19 Fielde, 1884, p. 2.
20 Selden, 1926–1927, p. 24.
21 "Morality among the Chinese," *Popular Science Monthly*, vol. 16, 1879, pp. 270–274.
22 Ashmore, *BMM*, vol. 50, 1870, pp. 354–356.
23 Ibid., vol. 45, 1865, pp. 301–303.
24 Selden, 1926–1927.
25 Ashmore to Murdock, September 25, 1883.
26 Ashmore to Lida Scott, 1920.
27 Ashmore, vol. 44, 1864, pp. 67–68; vol. 45, 1865, pp. 161–165.
28 S.B. Partridge *BMM*, vol. 53, 1873, p. 323.
29 Hunter, 1984, p. 129.
30 Fielde to Mrs. E.M. Cauldwell, 1886; Stevens, 1918, pp. 105–106.
31 Fielde, *BMM*, vol. 53, 1873, p. 391; vol. 55, 1875, pp. 152–153.
32 Wolf, in Wolfe and Witke, 1975, pp. 111–141.
33 Fielde, letter of November 5, 1877, published in *BMM*, vol. 58, 1878, pp. 48–50.
34 Ibid., *BMM*, vol. 58, 1878, pp. 348–349.
35 Mild, 1993, p. 202.
36 The tasks of two Bible-women in India were described in *The Foreign Missionary*, vol. 25, 1866–1867, pp. 293–294: "Their work is to go from house to house and from place to place, and read the Bible to their ignorant and benighted countrywomen."

37 Merriam, 1900, pp. 164–165.
38 Abbie G. Sanderson, "The Mother of Bible Schools," *Missions*, May 1925, p. 297.
39 Fielde, 1884, p. 145.
40 Fielde, *BMM*, vol. 53, 1873, pp. 324–325; Fielde, 1884, pp. 138–150.
41 Norwood, *BMM*, 1880, pp. 358–360.
42 Fielde, *BMM*, 1884, p. 144.
43 King, in Fleming, 1989, pp. 117–135.
44 Ibid., pp. 118–135.
45 Fielde, *BMM*, 1878, p. 315.
46 Ibid., 1873, pp. 324–325.
47 Ashmore, "Village preaching," *BMM*, vol. 44, 1864, pp. 381–383.
48 Fielde, *BMM*, vol. 50, 1870, pp. 13–15.
49 Ibid., 1882, pp. 8–9.
50 Fielde, "The Education of Chinese Biblewomen," *BMM*, vol. 58, 1878, pp. 399–401.
51 Fielde, *BMM*, vol. 61, 1881, pp. 70–71.
52 Fielde to Warren, February 25, 1868.
53 Stevens, 1918, p. 118.
54 Fielde, 1884, pp. 172–176.
55 Wolf and Witke, 1975, p. 113; 1981, p. 170; Wolf, 1985, pp. 2–4.
56 Ashmore to Murdock, May 23, 1873.
57 Partridge to Murdock, February 21, 1878.
58 Partridge to Murdock, June 26, 1877; Stevens, 1918, p. 136. Pearl Buck discusses the submission of women (including her mother) to male authority in the missionary movement (see Buck, 1936, pp. 187–193).
59 Fielde, *BMM*, vol. 56, 1876, pp. 7–8.
60 Fielde, letter of October 6, 1875 in *BMM*, vol. 56, 1876, p. 52.
61 Ibid., letter of October 6, 1875.
62 Ashmore to Murdock, August 7, 1872.
63 Fielde to Warren, February 28, 1868.
64 Fielde, "Missionary outlook," *BMM*, vol. 67, 1867, p. 410; *BMM*, 1887, p. 410.
65 *Missionary Herald*, vol. 80, 1884, p. 456.
66 Ibid., November 12, 1869; an editorial comment in the *BMM*, vol. 62, 1882, outlines the problem:

> Opium in China – So much feeling has been aroused among the missionaries in China on the use of opium among the Chinese, and the responsibility of the British Government for its introduction and increasing consumption, that a petition to the British House of Commons has been drawn up, and is being generally signed by the missionaries and ministers of the gospel in China praying that measures may be taken to remove from the British treaty with China the clause legalizing the opium-trade, and to restrict the growth of the poppy in India within the narrowest possible limits. The curse of opium in China is even greater than the curse of intemperance in America, and forms one of the greatest obstacles in the way of the success of missionary work. The Chinese hold the English responsible for the introduction of opium into their country, and the continued forced importation; and this feeling reflects upon all foreigners to their disadvantage, whether connected with government and the opium trade or not.

67 "Report on Committee on Chinese Missions," *BMM*, vol. 66, 1886, p. 187.
68 Fielde, "Missionary outlook," *BMM*, vol. 67, 1887, p. 465.
69 Mark Twain, "To the person sitting in darkness," *North American Review*, February 1901, pp. 161–176.
70 Latourette, 1929, pp. 315–319.

71 Stevens, 1918, pp. 124–129.
72 Partridge to Murdock, April 10, 1875.
73 Ashmore to Murdock, September 22, 1874.
74 Murdock to Fielde, January 14, 1873.
75 Murdock to Fielde, August 5, 1873.
76 *National Baptist*, September 28, 1875. Quote taken from a letter sent by Murdock to Fielde September 28, 1875. Discussed by Seabrook, 1993, pp. 66–68.
77 Murdock to Fielde, October 11, 1881; December 31, 1881.
78 Partridge to Murdock, November 2, and December 23, 1883; March 1, 1884.
79 Ashmore to Murdock, June 2, 1884, Ashmore file, ABC.
80 Stevens, 1918, pp. 132–136; Hoyt, 1977, pp. 18–19; Seabrook, 1993, p. 80.

6 Philadelphia, 1883–1885

1 For a superb account of the Philadelphia scene in the late nineteenth and early twentieth centuries, see Burt and Davies, 1982.
2 Fielde to Murdock, May 21, 1889.
3 Fielde's speech was so striking that it was reported in a daily newspaper, and in *The Medical News*, vol. 44, January 12, 1884, p. 55.
4 Fielde to Nolan, June 18, 1885, ANS.
5 The list of those in the photograph is in the Fielde papers of the ANS.
6 Ibid., Proceedings, ANS, 1885, pp. 20–22.
7 Ibid., December 18, 1883, p. 312.
8 Ibid., 1886, pp. 319–321.
9 Ibid., 1886, pp. 298–299.
10 Ibid., 1887, pp. 30–31.
11 Ibid., 1887, pp. 293–294; 1888, pp. 129–130; 1888, pp. 176–177.
12 Ibid., 1887, p. 115.
13 Fielde, "The Demand for Scientific Books in China," *Popular Science Monthly*, vol. 33, 1888, pp. 556–557.
14 Fielde, 1884, p. 191.
15 Ibid., pp. 279–281.
16 Stevens, 1918, pp. 255–257.
17 Fielde to Nolan, August 17, 1892.
18 Stevens, 1918, p. 170.
19 Fielde, "The Chinese Theory of Evolution," *Popular Science Monthly*, vol. 36, 1889, pp. 397–400.

7 Last years in the Far East

1 Fielde, *BMM*, October 30, 1885; January, 1886, p. 21.
2 Letter dated January 12, 1889: Stevens, 1918, pp. 175–177.
3 Article in a Philadelphia publication, April 8, 1886; Stevens, 1918, pp. 178–180.
4 Ashmore to Murdock, September 23, 1883.
5 Fielde to Nolan, May 3, 1888.
6 Ibid., February 2, 1888.
7 Ibid., January 20, 1889.
8 Ibid., May 3, 1888.
9 Fielde, "An Experience in Hasheesh Smoking," *Therapeutic Gazette*, vol. 4, 1888, pp. 449–451.
10 Fielde to Murdock, July 18, 1888; January 17, 1889.
11 Lyall to Murdock, June 13, 1888; Fielde to Nolan, June 11, 1889, *ANS*.
12 Beard, 1972.
13 See Feinstein, 1984, pp. 182–222; Strouse, 1980.

14 Ashmore to Murdock, September 25, 1873.
15 Murdock to Fielde, August 17, 1887.
16 Fielde to Murdock, May 21, 1889.
17 Fielde to Board of ABMU, May 20, 1889.
18 Stevens, 1918, pp. 164–166.
19 Heilbrun, 1988, pp. 11–31.
20 See Merriam, 1900; E. Ashmore, 1920; Mild, 1993; Bonta, 1991, pp. 147–149; Seabrook, 1993.
21 Fielde to Murdock, November 28, 1889.
22 Thomas, 1983, pp. 13–50.
23 Report in the *London and China Telegraph*, reprinted in *BMM*, "*Missionary Outlook*," 1891, p. 84.

8 The voyage home

1 Much of this chapter is taken from Stevens' biography. She was privy to numerous letters and writings of Fielde which she includes in her work without providing the provenance of materials; unfortunately, Stevens' papers cannot be found.
2 Fielde to Murdock, June 12, 1889.
3 The lives of her father and mother are movingly described in *Fighting Angel*, and *The Exile*, respectively.
4 Buck, 1933, pp. 147–148.
5 Fielde, *BMM*, April 9, 1891; Stevens, 1918, pp. 194–198.
6 Fielde to Nolan, December 25, 1890.
7 Osborn Henry, Fairfield, 1896, *Biological Lectures Delivered at the Marine Biological Laboratory, Woods Hole*, Athenaeum Press, Boston, 1896, pp. 29–30.
8 Communication dated May 1, 1891, probably to Nolan from Fielde; see Stevens, 1918, pp. 210–211.
9 The planned expulsion of four to five million Jews created the great wave of emigration of Russian Jews to America and other countries in the 1890s. Czarist abuse also gave rise to the Jewish nationalistic and Zionist movements. (*Encyclopaedia Judaica*, vol. 3, 1971, pp. 696–697).
10 *New York Times*, "By appeal to the Czar, thus would Baron Hirsch attempt to get justice," May 28, 1891, p. 1.
11 Ibid., "Russia's fierce assault, Europe amazed at her treatment of Jews," May 31, 1891, p. 1.
12 Ibid., "Russia's war on Jews, No longer any doubt of the sweeping intentions of Russia," June 14, 1891, p. 1.
13 Ibid., "Told by an eye witness, A narrative of the Czar's cruel treatment of Jews," June 16, 1891, p. 5.
14 Stevens, 1918, pp. 224–225.
15 Keen performed the first successful brain tumor operation, and is regarded as the father of American neurosurgery. He assisted at the secret operation on President William Howard Taft to remove a malignancy of the jaw. His textbook on surgery was widely used.
16 Stevens, 1918, p. 278.

9 New York

1 Fielde to Nolan, January 1, 1893.
2 See Dickens' *Martin Chuzzlewit*, and his *American Notes*; Mrs. Frances Trollope was relentless in her criticism of Americans in her *Domestic Manners of the Americans.*
3 Fielde's opinions were recorded by her biographer, Stevens (1918, pp. 14–16).

4 Bowler, 1993, pp. 75–86; Kevles, 1995.
5 Smith, 1985, pp. 5–36; see Darwin (1932) for an early general discussion of eugenics when still in favor.
6 Neering, 1912.
7 Bowler, 1993.
8 See David D. Hall, "The Victorian Connection," pp. 81–94, in Howe, 1976; quote is from Geoffrey Blodgett, "A New Look at the Gilded Age: Politics in a Cultural Context," in Howe, 1976, pp. 95 and 96.
9 Connable and Silberfarb, 1967, pp. 197–268.
10 DuBois, 1978.
11 Kraditor, 1973, pp. 254–278.
12 DuBois, 1981, pp. 14–16.
13 DuBois, 1978, pp. 53–78, 162–202; 1981, pp. 107–108.
14 Flexner, 1959, pp. 216–222.
15 Excellent overviews of the feminist movement can be found in DuBois 1981, pp. 2–26, 88–112, 172–200; DuBois, 1992, pp. 147–192; Flexner, 1959.
16 The scrap-books have not been located, nor have texts of her lectures been found. Stevens presents an incomplete list of lecture titles in her biography of Fielde, but she does not say where any of the reports of lectures were published (pp. 234–236). The titles listed are: The making of laws – legislatures; The administration of laws – officers; The interpretation of laws – courts; The labor Unions; Industrial revolutions; The coming revolution in Russia; Airships and the law of gravitation; The Russian peasantry; The greatest man in China; The Empress dowager; What Europeans are saying about American women; The spread of the white race in Africa; Curious facts about travel by railway; The new international language – Esperanto; The international conference concerning Morocco; The new theory of the origin of the species; Civilization in Siam; Porto Rico and the Isle of Pines; Our Island of Guam in its international relations; Our lesser possessions in the Pacific; Tutuila and Manua; Present opportunities for higher education without personal cost; What animals think; Natural evolution of the German government – from autocracy to socialism; The wonders of ant life; The memory of ants; Recent travels among the pygmies of Africa; Evidence that the planet Mars is inhabited; The farming operations of our national government; Arctic explorations by airship; Effect of the Panama canal and Pan-American railway on North and South America; The influence of sunlight upon the present and future distribution of the races of mankind; What restrictions should be placed on Japanese and Chinese immigration; What should be the status of Asiatics in this country; Affairs in the Congo Free State; The giving of free meals to underfed school children in the public schools; the new theory of matter; Poland in revolution; Canada and Canadians in their present relations to the United States; The world's battle with consumption; The old and new woman in Japan; The utilization of great deserts; Persia in the politics of Europe; The passage of a race – the Australian Aborigines; Present aspects of the negro question in the United States; Kingdom yoked with Empire – Austria-Hungary.
17 Stevens, 1918, pp. 285.
18 Fielde to Nolan, February 16, 1894.
19 *New York Times*, December 11, 1904, p. 23.
20 A. Gopnik, "Mary Cassat's baby world", *The New Yorker*, March 22, 1999, pp. 114–119.
21 Sanger, 1922.
22 Baker, 1912, pp. 86–100.
23 Fielde to Nolan, December 13, 1892.
24 Stevens, 1916, pp. 216–217.
25 Fielde to Nolan, February 16, 1894.

26 An incomprehensible judgment.
27 Fielde to Nolan, December 13, 1892.
28 Ibid., December 29, 1901.
29 Ibid., May 10, 1894.
30 See Van Voris, 1987; Stanton, 1971.
31 Ellis *et al.*, 1973, p. 391.
32 Fielde to Nolan, May 10, 1894.
33 Ibid., August 23, 1895.
34 Ibid., July 21, 1895.
35 *World*, New York, February 24, 1895.
36 Stevens, 1918, pp. 239–249.
37 *The New York Journal*, November 7, 1897.
38 Fielde to Nolan, October 8, 1893.
39 Fielde, 1894, pp. 111–119.
40 Latourette, 1968, pp. 307–313.

10 Religion, science, and the occult

1 Douglas, 1977, pp. 3–13.
2 Stevens, 1918, p. 284.
3 E.O. Wilson, personal communication.
4 Fielde's views of religion are taken from Stevens, 1918, pp. 168–180, 273–283.
5 Fielde to Nolan, December 20, 1893.
6 Ashforth, 1969, pp. 34–38.
7 Fielde to Nolan (from Chalons-sur-Marne, France), August 17, 1892.
8 Fielde, *The Therapeutic Gazette*, vol. 4, 1888, pp. 449–451.
9 Wright, 1928, pp. 218–252.
10 Fielde's account of the Gandhi lectures is in the archives of the University of Washington in Seattle. A microfilm of the work was kindly provided.

11 Ants

1 Leidy, 1879.
2 Fielde, *Proceedings*, vol. 40, 1888, pp. 129–130; 1888, pp. 176–177; 1885, vol. 37, pp. 298–299; vol. 39, 1887, p. 115; vol. 39; 1887, pp. 122–123.
3 Fielde, "Observations on Ants in their Relation to Temperature and to Submergence," *Biological Bulletin*, vol. 7, 1904, pp. 170–174. Errors of this sort should have been detected by the reviewers of the paper, or the editors.
4 Daniels, 1968.
5 Rossiter, 1982, p. 16.
6 Goode, 1991. The author refers to the Colders on pp. 65–66.
7 Rossiter, 1982; Bonta, Hinding and Bower, among others.
8 See Stevens, 1918, pp. 159–163; Cheyney, 1940, pp. 299–300.
9 Fielde to Nolan, undated, summer 1895.
10 A fine account of early women entomologists and naturalists can be found in Bonta, 1991, pp. 145–180.
11 Fielde to Nolan, July 8, 1901.
12 Stevens, 1918, p. 268.
13 See Morley, 1953, pp. 7–23 and 176–184: Lubbock, 1896, pp. 1–29.
14 See William Morton Wheeler, translation of Réamur's *The Natural History of Ants*, chapter on the life and work of Réamur, 1926. Quote is from L. Huxley, *Life and Letters of Thomas Henry Huxley*, vol. 1, 1902, p. 515.
15 Leidy was the foremost human and comparative anatomist of his time, and is regarded as the father of American vertebrate paleontology, as well as the father

of American protozoology and parasitology. For an account of Leidy's life and researches see Warren, 1998.

16 Morley, 1953, pp. 7–23. Wheeler, 1910, pp. 123–144.
17 Wheeler, 1910, pp. 1–2, 505–517.
18 Stevens, 1918, pp. 268–269; Fielde, *Proceedings*, vol. 53, 1901, p. 449.
19 Wilson, 1980.
20 Fielde, *Proceedings*, vol. 54, 1902, p. 600.
21 For a more complete general discussion see Wheeler, 1910, pp. 1–12; Hölldobler and Wilson (1990) is an excellent, definitive treatise on the ant; Hölldobler and Wilson (1990) is a shorter, more accessible description of the ant and its culture.
22 Hölldobler and Wilson, 1990, p. 1.
23 Fielde, *Biology Bulletin*, vol. 7, 1904, pp. 227–250.
24 Ibid., vol. 10, 1905, pp. 1–16.
25 Forel, 1928.
26 Lubbock, 1896.
27 Forel, 1904.
28 Schneirla, in Roeder, 1953, pp. 656–779.
29 Forel, 1928, p. 202.
30 Fielde, *Proceedings*, vol. 53, 1901, pp. 521–544; Schneirla, in Roeder, 1953, p. 732.
31 Fielde, *Proceedings*, vol. 54, 1902, pp. 614–625.
32 Other myrmecologists, including some of her contemporaries, observed starving ants eating their eggs and even their larvae (personal communication from Bert Hölldobler).
33 Fielde, *Proceedings*, 1901, vol. 53, pp. 425–449.
34 Forel, 1904.
35 Fielde, *Biology Bulletin*, vol. 10, 1905, pp. 1–16.
36 Ibid., *Biology Bulletin*, vol. 5, 1903, pp. 326–329.
37 Ibid., vol. 7, 1904, pp. 227–250; vol. 10, 1905, pp. 328–329.
38 Ibid., pp. 320–323.
39 Personal communication, Edward O. Wilson.
40 Albrecht Bethe, *Pflüger's Archives*, vol. 70, 1898.
41 E.G. MacGregor, *Behaviour*, vol. 1, 1948, pp. 267–296.
42 MacGregor, *Proceedings*, vol. 54, 1902, p. 599.
43 Ibid., 1901, vol. 53, pp. 521–544.
44 MacGregor, *Biology Bulletin*, vol. 5, 1903, pp. 320–325.
45 Ibid., *Proceedings*, vol. 67, 1915, pp. 36–40.
46 Fielde and G.H. Parker, *Proceedings*, vol. 56, 1904, pp. 642–650.
47 Fielde, *Proceedings*, vol. 55, 1903, pp. 617–624.
48 Ibid., vol. 56, 1904, pp. 639–641.
49 Fielde, *Biology Bulletin*, vol. 7, 1904, pp. 300–309.
50 Fielde to Nolan, July 30, 1901.
51 Culled from *Current Contents*, Institute for Scientific Information, Philadelphia.
52 Fielde, *Proceedings*, vol. 67, 1915, p. 42.
53 Ibid., pp. 93–95.

12 Seattle

1 Parts of this chapter are derived from Stevens's biography of Fielde. Stevens quotes Fielde's letters and her friends, but none of the original records can be found. The quote is from a letter to a friend quoted by Stevens (1918, p. 322).
2 Ibid., pp. 351–352.
3 Ibid., pp. 342–343.

4 Fielde, *Seattle Post Intelligencer*, September 28, 1907.
5 Fielde's diary, 1907, in Stevens, 1918, p. 299.
6 Fielde to Mrs. Wheeler, July 13, 1907.
7 Fielde to Dr. and Mrs. Wheeler, January 9, 1909 (HUA).
8 Ibid.
9 Stevens, 1918, pp. 311–312.
10 *Seattle Post-Intelligencer*, October 31, 1907.
11 The account of Fielde's suffragist activities, and Anna Howard Shaw's letter can be found in Stevens, 1918, pp. 313–328.
12 Hurwitz, 1970, p. 503.
13 A fictional account of such conflicts was written by Hamlin Garland in 1892. It is likely that Fielde read the book.
14 Sale, 1976, pp. 1–135; Berner, 1991, pp. 109–226; Stevens, 1918, p. 298.
15 *Seattle Post-Intelligencer*, January 19, 1908.
16 Fielde's letter to "a friend in New York" summarizing her activities during her first three years in Seattle cannot be found but is printed verbatim in Stevens, 1918, pp. 307–315.
17 Stevens, 1918, pp. 308–309.
18 *Seattle Post-Intelligencer*, October 31, 1907, and November 24, 1907.
19 Stevens, 1918, pp. 301–304; Fielde to Dr. and Mrs. Wheeler, January 9, 1909.
20 Ibid., p. 348.
21 Ibid., pp. 349–350.
22 Ibid., pp. 354–356.
23 Ibid., p. 338.
24 Ibid., p. 337; Diary entry of September 3, 1914.
25 Ibid., pp. 339–340.
26 Fielde to Nolan, September 28, 1915.
27 Stevens, 1918, pp. 361–364.
28 Himmelfarb, 1967, pp. 314–332.
29 Fielde to Nolan, September 28, 1915.
30 Ibid., June 6, 1915.
31 The law permitted 105 Chinese to enter America in 1943 (Hurwitz, 1970, p. 107).
32 Ibid., September 28, 1915.
33 Ibid., June 6, 1915.
34 Stevens, pp. 314–315.
35 Ibid., pp. 40–41. The latter statement was made by a missionary colleague of Fielde, William K. McKibben.

13 A model death

1 Fielde to Nolan, February 9, 1916. Letter dictated to Helen N. Stevens.
2 Stevens to Nolan, March 18, 1916; Stevens, 1918, pp. 365–377.
3 Stevens, 1918, p. 365.
4 Ibid., pp. 367–368.
5 Ibid., pp. 281–282; from a letter to Adaline M. Payne and published in the *Representative* of Nevada, Iowa.
6 Ibid., pp. 374–376.
7 *Seattle Saturday Night*, March 1916.
8 *Seattle Post-Intelligencer*, February 24, March 4, and March 6, 1916; *Seattle Daily Times*, February 23, 1916.
9 Stevens, 1918, pp. 48–49.
10 Ibid., p. 376.

Bibliography

Ashforth, Albert, *Thomas Henry Huxley*, Twayne Publishers Inc., New York, 1969.

Ashmore, Lida Scott, *Historical Sketch of the South China Mission of the American Baptist Foreign Mission Society, 1860–1920*, 1920.

Baker, La Reine Helen, *Race Improvement, or Eugenics*, Dodd, Mead, New York, 1912.

Barr, Pat, *To China With Love*, Doubleday & Co., New York, 1973.

Beard, George Miller, *American Nervousness, Its Cause and Consequences* (1881), reprinted in *Medicine and Society in America* (series), ed. Charles E. Rosenberg, Arno Press and the *New York Times*, New York, 1972.

Beaver, R. Pierce, *All Loves Excelling: American Protestant Women in World Mission*, William B. Eerdmans, Grand Rapids, MI, 1968.

Berner, Richard C., *Seattle, 1900–1920, From Boomtown, Urban Turbulance, to Restoration*, Charles Press, Seattle, WA, 1991.

Bonta, Marcia Myers, *Women in the Field, America's Pioneering Women Naturalists*, Texas A & M University Press, College Station, 1991.

Bowie, Fiona, in *Women and Missions: Past and Present. Anthropological and Historical Perceptions*, eds. F. Bowie, D. Kirkwood, and S. Ardener, Berg, Providence RI, 1993.

Bowler, Peter J., *Biology and Social Thought: 1850–1914*, University of California, Berkeley, CA, 1993.

Bridgman, Eliza J. Gillett, *Daughters of China, or Sketches of Domestic Life in the Celestial Empire*, Robert Carter and Brothers, New York, 1853.

Buck, Pearl S. "Is There a Case for Foreign Missions," *Harper's Monthly Magazine*, New York, pp. 143–155, January 1933.

—— *The Exile*, Methuen & Co., London, 1936a.

—— *Fighting Angel, Portrait of a Soul*, Reynal and Hitchcock, New York, 1936b.

Burt, N. and Davies, W.E., "The Iron Age, 1876–1905", in *Philadelphia, a 300-Year History*, ed. Russel F. Weigley, W.W. Norton, New York, 1982.

Cheyney, Edward Potts, *History of the University of Pennsylvania, 1740–1940*, University of Pennsylvania Press, Philadelphia, 1940.

Connable, A. and Silberfarb, E., *Tigers of Tammany, Nine Men Who Ran New York*, Holt, Rhinehart & Winston, New York, 1967.

Daniels, George H., *American Science in the Age of Jackson*, Columbia University Press, New York, 1968.

Darwin, Leonard, "What is Eugenics?", Third International Congress of Eugenics, 1932.

Douglas, Ann, *The Feminization of American Culture*, Knopf, New York, 1977.

DuBois, Ellen Carol, *Feminism and Suffrage, The Emergence of an Independent Women's Movement in America, 1848–1869*, Cornell University Press, Ithaca, NY, 1978.
—— *Elizabeth Cady Stanton, Susan B. Anthony, Correspondence, Writings, Speeches*, Schocken Books, New York, 1981.
—— "Working Women, Class Relations, and Suffrage Militance: Harriot Stanton Blatch and the New York Woman Suffrage Movement, 1894–1909," in *History of Women in the United States*, vol. 19, part 1, pp. 147–171, ed. Nancy F. Cott, K.G. Saur, Munich, New Providence, 1992.
Ellis, D.M., Frost, J.A., Syrett, H.C., and Carman, H.J. *A History of New York State*, Cornell University Press, Ithaca, NY, 1973.
Feinstein, Howard M., *Becoming William James*, Cornell University Press, Ithaca, NY, 1984.
Fielde, Adele M., *First Lessons in the Swatow Dialect*, Swatow Printing Office Company, Swatow, 1878.
—— *A Pronouncing and Defining Dictionary of the Swatow Dialect, Arranged According to Syllables and Tones*, American Presbyterian Mission Press, Shanghai, 1883.
—— *Pagoda Shadows, Studies from Life in China*, W.G. Corthell, Boston, MA, 1884.
—— *Chinese Nights' Entertainments*, G.P. Putnams Sons, New York and London, 1893.
—— *A Corner of Cathay, Studies from Life Among the Chinese*, Macmillan & Co., New York, 1894.
—— *A Political Primer of New York State and City*, Macmillan, New York, 1897.
Fleming, L.A., in *Women's Work for Women, Missionaries and Social Change in Asia*, ed. L.A. Fleming, Westview Press, Boulder, CO, 1989.
Flexner, Eleanor, *Century of Struggle, The Woman's Rights Movement in the United States*, Harvard University Press, Cambridge, MA, 1959.
Foner, Eric, "The Republicans and Nativism," in *Past Imperfect, Alternative Essays in American History*, ed. B.W. Cook, A.K. Harris, and R. Radosh, vol. 1, Alfred A. Knopf, New York, 1973.
Forel, August, *Ants and Some Other Insects, An Inquiry into the Psychic Powers of These Animals*, Open Court Publishing Company, Chicago, IL, 1904.
—— *The Social World of the Ants Compared With That of Man*, G.P. Putnam's Sons, London, 1928 (2 vols).
Garland, Hamlin, *A Spoil of Office*, Johnson Reprint Corporation, New York (1969), 1892.
Goode, George Brown, *The Origin of Natural Science in America*, ed. Sally Gregory, Kohlstedt, Smithsonian Institution Press, Washington, DC (1901), 1991.
Heilbrun, Carolyn G., *Writing a Woman's Life*, W.W. Norton, New York, 1988.
Himmelfarb, Gertrude, *Victorian Minds*, Alfred A. Knopf, New York, 1967.
Hofstadter, Richard, *Social Darwinism in American Thought*, Becon Press, Boston MA, 1955.
Höldobler, B. and Wilson, Edward O., *The Ants*, Belknap Press, Cambridge, MA, 1994.
Howe, Daniel Walker, ed., *Victorian America*, University of Pennsylvania Press, Philadelphin, 1976.
Howe, Julia Ward, "Introduction," in *Woman's Work in America*, ed. Annie Nathan Meyer, Henry Holt, New York, 1891.
Hoyt, F.B., "'When a Field was too Difficult for a Man, a Woman Should be Sent': Adele M. Fielde in Asia, 1865–1890". Lecture at the Southern Historical Convention in New Orleans, November 14, 1977. ANS.

Hunter, Jane, *The Gospel of Gentility, American Women Missionaries in Turn-of-the-Century China*, Yale University Press, New Haven, CT, 1984.

Hurwitz, Howard L., *An Encyclopedic Dictionary of American History*, Washington Square Press, New York, 1970.

Hutchison, William H., *Errand to the World*, University of Chicago Press, Chicago IL, 1987.

Jacobi, Mary Putnam, *"Common Sense" Applied to Woman Suffrage*, G.P. Putnam's Sons, New York, 1894.

Kevles, Daniel J., *In the Name of Eugenics: Genetics and the Uses of Human Heredity*, (Knopf, 1985), Harvard University Press, Cambridge, MA, 1995.

King, Marjorie, "Exporting Femininity, not Feminism," in *Women's Work for Women: Missionaries and Social Change in Asia*, ed. L.A. Flemming, Westview Press, Boulder, CO, 1969.

Kraditor, Aileen S., "The Woman Question," in *Past Imperfect, Alternative Essays in American History*, ed. B.W. Cook, A.K. Harris, and R. Radosh, vol. 1, Alfred A. Knopf, New York, 1973.

Latourette, Kenneth Scott, *A History of Christian Missions in China*, Macmillan, New York, 1929.

—— *The Chinese, Their History and Culture*, Macmillan, New York, 1968.

Lee, Bernice J., "Female Infanticide in China," in *Women in China*, ed. Richard W. Guisso and Stanley Johannesen, Philo Press, Youngstown, NY, 1981.

Leidy, Joseph, *Fresh-water Rhizopods of North America*, United States. Geological Survey of the Territories, Washington, DC, 1879.

Lubbock, John, *Ants, Bees and Wasps*, D. Appleton & Co, New York, 1896.

Merriam, Edward F., *American Baptist Missions*, American Baptist Publication Society, Philadelphia, 1900.

Middleton, Dorothy, *Victorian Lady Travellers*, Routledge & Kegan Paul, London, 1965.

Mild, Mary L., "'Whom Shall I Send?': An Overview of the American Baptist Women's Foreign Missionary Movement from 1873–1913," *American Baptist Quarterly*, vol. 12, 1993, pp. 194–209.

Montgomery, Helen Barrett, *Western Women in Eastern Lands*, Macmillan, New York, 1910.

Morley, Derek Wragge, *The Ant World*, Penguin Books, London, 1953.

National American Woman Suffrage Association, *Victory, How Women Won It, A Centennial Symposium, 1840–1940*, H.W. Wilson Company, New York, 1940.

Neering, Scott, *The Super Race, An American Problem*, Huebsch, New York, 1912.

Osborn, Henry, Fairfield, *Biological Lectures Delivered at the Marine Biological Laboratory, Woods Hole*, Athenaeum Press, Boston, 1896.

Pearson, George Wilson, *Toqueville in America* (abridged), Doubleday Anchor, New York, 1959.

de Réamur, René Antoine Ferchault, *The Natural History of Ants*, from an unpublished manuscript in the Archives of the Academy of Sciences of Paris, translated and annotated by Wiliam Morton Wheeler, Alfred A. Knopf, New York, 1926.

Roeder, Kenneth D., *Insect Physiology*, John Wiley & Sons Inc., New York, 1953.

Rossiter, Margaret, *Women Scientists in America*, Johns Hopkins University Press, Baltimore, MD, 1982.

Sale, Roger, *Seattle, Past to Present*, University of Washington Press, Seattle, WA, 1976.

Sanger, Margaret, *The Pivot of Civilization*, Brentano's, New York, 1922.
Seabrook, Ginny, *The Missionary Writing of Adele M. Fielde*, Thesis for the M.A. Degree, Northeastern University, Boston, MA, June 1993a.
—— "Pagoda Shadows: The Life of Adele Marion Fielde, Missionary to China 1865–1889," *American Baptist Quarterly*, vol. 12, 1993b, pp. 235–241.
Selden, Charles A., *Are Missions a Failure? A Correspondent's Survey of Foreign Missions*, Fleming H. Revell Co., London, 1926–1927.
Sklar, K.K., Schüler, A., Strasser, S. eds, *Social Justice Feminists in the United States and Germany*, Cornell University Press, New York, 1998.
Smith, J. David, *Minds Made Feeble, The Myth and Legacy of the Kallikaks*, Aspen, Rockville, MD, 1985.
Soper, Edmund Davison, *The Philosophy of the World Christian Mission*, Abingdon Press, New York, 1948.
Stanley, Brian, *The History of the Baptist Missionary Society, 1792–1992*, T. and T. Clark, Edinburgh, 1992.
Stanton, Elizabeth Cady, *Eighty Years and More, Reminiscences, 1815–1897*, Schocken Books, New York, 1971 (reprint of 1898 original).
Stevens, Helen Norton, *Memorial Biography of Adele M. Fielde, Humanitarian*, The Fielde Memorial Committee, New York, Philadelphia, Chicago, Seattle, 1918.
Strouse, Jeane, *Alice James, A Biography*, Houghton Mifflin Company, Boston, MA, 1980.
Thomas, Keith, *Man and the Natural World, A History of the Modern Sensibility*, Pantheon, New York, 1983.
Van Voris, Jacqueline, *Carrie Chapman Catt, A Public Life*, The Feminist Press, City University of New York, New York, 1987.
Warren, Leonard, *Joseph Leidy, the Last Man Who Knew Everything*, Yale University Press, New Haven, CT, 1998.
Warren, Mary Anne, *Gendercide, The Implications of Sex Selection*, Rowman & Allanheld, Totowa, NJ, 1985.
Wheeler, William Morton, *Ants, Their Structure, Development, and Behavior*, Columbia University Press, New York, 1910.
Whitman, Narcissa, *The Letters of Narcissa Whitman*, Ye Galleon Press, Fairfield, Washington, DC, 1986.
Wilson, Edward O., *Sociobiology, The Abridged Edition*, Belknap Press, Cambridge, MA, 1980.
Wolf, Margery, *Revolution Postponed, Women in Contemporary China*, Stanford University Press, Stanford, CA, 1985.
Wolf, Margery and Witke, Roxane, *Women in Chinese Society*, Stanford University Press, Stanford, CA, 1975
Wright, Richardson, *Forgotten Ladies, Nine Portraits From the American Family Album*, J.B. Lippincott Co., Philadelphia, PA, 1928.

Index

NOTE: Page numbers followed by *illus* indicate a full-page illustration; page numbers followed by *n* indicate that information appears in a note. The initials AMF are used for Adele Marion Fielde.